# FIVE RING CIRCUS

Also by Jack Ludwig

Confusions
Above Ground
A Woman of Her Age
Hockey Night in Moscow
The Great Hockey Thaw
Games of Fear and Winning
The Great American Spectaculars

# FIVE RING CIRCUS

*The Montreal Olympics*

## Jack Ludwig

**Doubleday Canada Limited**
Toronto, Canada

**Doubleday & Company, Inc.**
Garden City, New York

1976

ISBN: 0-385-11540-7

Library of Congress Catalog Card Number: 76-22855

First Edition


Printed and bound in Canada

Book design by Robert Garbutt


Portions of this book have appeared in another form
in *Canadian* Magazine.


The letter to the sports editor that appeared in the
Los Angeles *Times* on August 21, 1976, is reprinted
on pages 51-52 by permission of its author,
Mrs. Babashoff.

*To Reuben David Charles McLaughlin*

*But boy, when you look up in the stands and see 68,000 people . . . and they have the Olympic rings up there, you know it's just not any other track meet. It's the Olympic Games. Nobody's holding anything back.*

**Bruce Jenner,**
after winning
the decathlon

**CONTENTS**

# ▮ Drapeau's Law: Good News Will Drive Out the Bad

At 2:28 P.M. on July 17, 1976—32 minutes from the appointed hour for Canada's, Quebec's, and Montreal Mayor Jean Drapeau's Olympics to begin—a great festive transformation was already under way. At either end of the Olympic Stadium huge black electronic scoreboards were amberlit with Montreal's own Olympic logo, those three romanesque arches forming an M over the five interlocking Olympic rings. Up above, the Stadium's pressure ring that had—tough luck!—come six inches short of closing effectively, inscribed a perfect circle forktailed swallows skittered through. A massive yellow crane costing thousands of dollars a week to rent was, for the Games, converted into a money-earning television gondola for overhead camera shots.

The Olympics were on hand. The hour of bad raps was temporarily over. One could think of the unfinished Stadium tower with its exposed steel rods making vertical penmanship strokes in the sky as some imaginative sculpture breaking the monolithic façade of concrete. One could hold in abeyance the projected images of a completed tower on postcards, handbooks, magazines, and in scale models all around Montreal. *That* tower was full of restaurants and gyms and club facilities. More important, its cables operated the retractable roof so necessary to the Olympic Stadium's becoming Montreal's showpiece—eventually artificial turf would replace pastoral grass; eventually football and baseball would be the business of this Stadium.

And the Olympics were all set to begin. With an unfinished tower. With temporary ramps and walks and staircases; wooden flooring that boinged under bodyweight and, looked at closely, showed in spaces between boards an unbroken prospect of ground 30 or 40 or 50 feet below. A strong fresh smell of epoxy, the bonding material used to join the blocks in Roger Taillibert's building plan, charged the air with an effluvium of newness. A close examination of M. Taillibert's structure revealed a striking absence of wished-for symmetry. His grand geometric plan called for the Stadium to lock into place like a finely wrought puzzle. Thirty-four consoles would support this massive concrete structure.

Alas. Here two sections joined evenly, without sunshadow. There the sections were askew and ajut. Planes had bulges. Surfaces that should have been flat, rippled. Poorly met joints had been hurriedly filled and packed and sprayed or painted. Just below the pressure ring, where floodlights were banked and arrayed, damp stains memorialized the heavy rain of the night before which cascaded down on seats and aisles and refreshments stands in mini-waterfalls, gushing rivulets that formed instant wind-rippled pools and ponds.

Time ticked toward the great moment; children marched out on the track, neat, costumed—traditional vestal virgins waving flags and trailing ribbons. These kids were really transformed. During that yester rain which broke into their rehearsal, the children, wearing T-shirts and shorts and jeans, had responded to the sudden downpour with a magnificent spontaneous wet hysteria, running barefoot through murky puddles, skipping around in mock raindance rituals, arms upraised. Some just slid or skidded into the rain-spattered squashy turf. Their leaders blew whistles, called, threatened. The kids continued to cut up.

A sudden lightning flash and reverberating thunderblast sent the kids screaming back up into the high reaches of the Stadium. Sheltered from the rain, and the leaks in the roof, the kids shouted and waited for answering echoes. The public-address system came on and wiped them out.

The night before. Now, their hair in place, their dresses spotless, the children were transformed in Olympic magic to quiet gentle lambs. Warm July afternoon sun played on their costumes and otherwise cleansed human imperfections away. The stands were filling. The colored seats picked up reinforcement in the shirts and skirts and trousers of the festive spectators. The Olympic hostesses in their bold red dresses and hats, the ushers and usherettes in their cheery yellow, began daubing the core of the Stadium with colors the athletic delegations would soon add to and intensify.

Excitement soared with a blasting roar of RCAF jets passing over the Stadium roof in acrobatic formation. It was all coming together—the sight, the sound, even that epoxy smell. The Olympic festival was about to overcome—architectural faults, building omissions, and, temporarily, the politics and financial troubles that had attended the Montreal project from almost its beginning. In a power struggle, Mayor Jean Drapeau had seemingly been pushed aside. The provincial government, through its environmental minister and the Olympic Installations Board,

*3*

had turned scapegoat and allowed Jean Drapeau to dump his two big headaches, construction and financing, on a nice little kids' doctor, Victor Goldbloom. In battles with Drapeau it's easy to confuse defeat and victory. Drapeau knew something Prime Minister Pierre Elliott Trudeau might not have cared about; Premier Robert Bourassa was too little jock to get the point. What Drapeau knew was that the Olympic opening ceremonies allow for the presence of only one "head of state." His enthusiasm for Queen Elizabeth could be read, by the cynical, as *un*enthusiasm for Trudeau and Bourassa. With Queen Elizabeth in Montreal, there was no place for those other two guys. There was room for only the President of the International Olympic Committee, Lord Killanin; the President of the Canadian Olympic Organizing Committee, Drapeau's *un*charismatic and *un*ebullient irritant, Roger Rousseau; and, of course, the Mayor of the host city, His Worship himself, Jean Drapeau.

Goldbloom could sweat, Goldbloom could slave. There was no way for Goldbloom to make an official appearance during the Olympics. As Mayor of the host city, Drapeau was guaranteed a place at the most dramatic, spectacular, stirring, even sentimental rituals of the Olympics—the opening *and* closing ceremonies.

The Queen was almost ready to make her opening ceremony entrance. Dancers swirled out of the tunnels. The orchestra played at rock-concert pitch. Everything ordinary was being transmogrified. The scene was set, the mood established. In the high excitement there were no sour notes, no blunders, no wrong turns by a dancer: pageantry made wrong and right equal. Kids banging into each other were as harmoniously absorbed into the celebration as those counting off each step precisely.

Thousands of writers, television and radio commentators and technicians, photographers, sports experts, cultural observers, sob sisters and sob brothers, columnists, gossip-catchers, joined a mass of retired, active, or neo-jocks. In the line-up were:

para-jocks
meta-jocks
proto-jocks
pseudo-jocks
quasi-jocks
insta-jocks
hemi-jocks
demi-jocks
hemi-demi-semi jocks
somno-jocks (conscripted counter-sportsculture wri-
        ters so bored by the proceedings they yawned
        openly during every flash of the Olympic logo)

A sudden loud royal fanfare stunned the Stadium's talky buzz into silence. The Queen, dressed in her best garden-party pink, was arrived, her coming thunderously reverberated over the public-address system thus:

*"Mesdames, Messieurs, Sa Majesté la Reine!"*

"Ladies and Gentlemen, Her Majesty, the Queen!"

A huge welcoming the-FLQ-doesn't-live-here-any-more cheer rolled through the stands—one of the three or four loudest sounds to be heard during the afternoon. The band played "O Canada," which got its own roar of welcome. A second trumpet blast—not quite as loud as the Queen's welkin—ushered in the march of the athletes. The hour of glory of the day of glory had arrived! Montreal entered that charmed circle of great cities which had hosted the Olympics—Athens, Paris, London, Stockholm, Amsterdam, Berlin, Helsinki, Rome, Tokyo, among others.

"In keeping with tradition and the Olympic regulations," the loudspeaker voice called out, "the team from the country which gave the world the Olympic Games will have the honor of leading the parade." Out came the Greek sign, held by a French-Canadian lass in traditional Quebec dress and headcovering; out came the Greek flag; out marched the Greek contingent of athletes and officials dressed in the athletic issue tabbed as safe civvy: blue blazers and gray flannels. A great wave of tradition-observing applause sounded in the Stadium.

Then there was a slight pause.

After Greece the march of athletes was to follow in alphabetical order. That meant Algeria. But Algeria didn't show.

Those who came to the Games as spectators may have missed the significance. Or hardly noticed the Algerian absence. But in the media trades a threatened African boycott was that instant real. Every missing African delegation implied more to come. The rumors began. Not only African nations were dropping out. Cuba was leaving. And if Cuba left, what would Eastern European countries do? The hysteria, mostly self-generated among bored journalists, led to further speculations: black American athletes would surely follow the African lead.

In 1976? In this year of careers and safe-playing? The boycott of the Games by American blacks was only as absurd as the idea that the U.S.S.R. and East Germany, which since 1972 had been counting gold medals to be won in 1976, would cut out of this ready-made world-wide demonstration stage.

But in the absence of Algeria, and the other African boycotting countries that cut out of the opening ceremonies or, a day later, out of all competition, lay a sad story that could not but affect the 1976 Games. In protest against New Zealand's All-Black rugby team's tour of the all-white rugby enclaves of South Africa during the Soweto massacre, the African countries refused to participate in the Montreal Olympics unless New Zealand was expelled from the 1976 Games. The African countries found, in the boycott issue, the only area of agreement likely to unite Kenya and Uganda, Zambia and Zaire, etc. The tasteless good old boys rugger spirit that kept New Zealand playing during the hideous killing at Soweto was almost matched by the mindless response of the IOC: that rugby wasn't even an Olympic sport!

New Zealand was not expelled; the African boycott was no longer a mere threat. The missing Algerian flag pointed up the political reality. But absence can never compete with presence: for every missing flag there were two or more waving. In the spaces left by the walk-out, competing teams simply spread themselves thinner. At best the African boycott ran in counterpoint to the gala parade. The whole thing resembled a meeting of the Supreme Soviet: some folk were missing but the body proper was more or less intact.

Closing the gap between Greece and the missing Algerians came, in the French listing, *"Allemagne,"* West Germany, their flagbearer the famed horseman, Hans Winkler Guenther. From the spectator view here were the colors, the countries, the flags, a great variety of dress and style streaming into the Stadium. East European countries, stung by past middle-class put-downs of their couture and fabrics, turned out in dresses and suits supposed to put one in mind of Cardin, Chanel, and Saint-Laurent. Nothing drab about the U.S.S.R. women this time, in orange suits and bright green blouses. Nothing drab about the picture-hatted Rumanians all in mauve or the East Germans in white suits and multicolored shirts.

From a less generalized spectator angle, the march was not abstract pageantry. In among those delegations passing before the Queen and waving to the crowd were the faces that would soon be caught in slow time, Olympic history, the frieze of achievement. The Cubans made a spectacular entrance, wearing white suits and scarlet shirts, some of the athletes in 1917 Soviet-style sailor hats or berets reminiscent of Ché Guevara. The spectacle was much enhanced by the flagbearer, the great Cuban heavyweight, Teofilo Stevenson, who carried the flag in one hand as if it were a bullrush.

In that mauve Rumanian costume topped by a striped picture hat was Nadia Comaneci, whose appearance in Montreal was as eagerly awaited as the Queen's. Striding and waving in the casual East German costume was another teenage phenomenon, the magnificent Kornelia Ender, who would fulfill every anticipation—beginning early next morning on the first day of competition. There striding massively in his beige suit and green shirt and tie was the world's superheavyweight weightlifting superstar, Vasilyi Alexeev, taking in the marchpast as if every cheer were for him alone.

Montreal would not let cold-war politics get in the way of this grand party. Great cheers met the Soviet Union, Great

Britain, France, Italy, Australia. The loudest cheer of all was held back till the final delegation, Canada's, entered waving kerchiefs and hats. But before that, thunderous sounds greeted the United States team and, shortly after, that small heroic band of Israeli athletes, some of them actual survivors of the PLO attack on the Olympic Village in Munich, 1972. They carried two small black flag pompoms to commemorate the dead the IOC would not remember in any ceremony. They marched out in the midst of tremendous security precautions, gallantly doffing their hats and bowing as they passed the Queen. This uncoerced remnant was recognized for its valor. But as one press wag remarked, "I wonder how much of that applause is for Entebbe [the Uganda airport rescue of the hijacked passengers and crew by Israeli commandos]."

Athletes who had already established legends in Olympic and world-class competition were flagbearers in the procession. Finland chose Lasse Viren, its double medal winner in the 1972 Games (who would repeat the double in Montreal) to lead its parade; France's flagbearer was the world's most famous cyclist, Daniel Morelon (who would leave Montreal without a gold). Jamaica's bearer was Donald Quarrie, favored to win the 200-metre sprint (which he did); Trinidad and Tobago's choice was Hasely Crawford (who won the 100-metres). Among those who had been chosen to lead their national delegations were Africans such as Uganda's great hurdler, John Akii-Bua, and Ethiopia's gifted distance-runner, Mirruts Yifter. They were in Montreal—but not in the parade.

From the Canadian point of view the sentimental focus was on its own flagbearer, Abby Hoffman, limping as she struggled under the flag's weight. Past her peak as a middle-distance runner, Abby was still looked on as the Canadian team's spiritual leader, and spoke up for amateur athletics wherever she went. The American team, which had entered early, was made up of athletes who were considered almost automatic gold-medal winners—the men swimmers, Shirley Babashoff, the women divers, the men's basketball team, and individual performers like Mac Wilkins in the discus, Dave Roberts and Earl

Bell in the pole vault, Dwight Stones in the high jump, Frank Shorter in the marathon, Bruce Jenner in the decathlon, and that great band of boxers—the Spinks brothers (Leon and Michael), Leo Randolph, Howard Davis, Sugar Ray Leonard, gold medalists all.

There in the embattled New Zealand crew was one of the most publicized athletes in the Games, John Walker, whose momentous confrontation in the 1,500 metres with Filbert Bayi of Tanzania—styled as yet another "race of the century"—had inspired *Sports Illustrated* to prefigure in a dream article (destined to remain a dream). Tanzania was part of the African boycott. Bayi not only would not face John Walker at the Olympics: chances were that the boycott against New Zealand might continue in perpetuity. In any event, the most attractive one-on-one meeting of the Games was not to be. Not only Ethiopia's Yifter and Uganda's Akii-Bua but Kenya's Mike Boit would miss the Games.

The earlier political issue—as to whether Taiwan could march in the Olympic Games as the "Republic of China" and carry a Republic of China flag—had developed acrimony between the International Olympic Committee and Prime Minister Trudeau. Given the 1920's political awareness of the IOC in these 1970's, Prime Minister Trudeau, and the rest of us, were lucky the IOC didn't also insist on Herzegovina's participation, or a White Russian team of horsemen. Throughout the Games the IOC seemed to come up with lapse-Hapsburgs and distant relatives of robber barons for most of the medal ceremonies. These same anachronistic people served to populate the aristocratic soirées the Queen sometimes appeared at during the Games, and sometimes didn't. A Queen in the 1970's has a lot of out-of-work relatives living in exile all over the world.

In the circle of sunlight playing over the south side of the Stadium, and in the dark contrasting shadows of the rest of the field and track, a design pattern was being formed by the delegations settling into their marked positions. This would be the print of the 1976 Games, the recognizable tableau soon to be as familiar as a postage stamp or coin. Nations that had worked out their costumes and uniforms without concern for what would contrast or clash with their chosen color scheme now watched the pieces fit into the larger picture. Here was the bright yellow of Australia falling between the blue of Argentina and cream jackets of Austria. Here was the Bermudian delegation in light blue jackets, bright yellow shorts, black ties and knee socks. Here came France with the women in light blue redingotes, the men in cream jackets, teal turtlenecks, black trousers—a fashion show to remind everyone where the great designers lived. Hungary came out in magenta next to an Indian delegation in yellow turbans and blue suits. Venezuela made a sensational entrance in white, with brown leather plainsman hats, matching leather boots, and, for the women, matching leather bags. All that was missing was the name of the dealer who carried this stuff in Montreal.

Funny tricks of the alphabet occurred in the parade. The French listing put Czechoslovakia (as Tchécoslovaquie), perhaps the tallest over-all delegation, next to Thailand, one of the shortest. Some of the countries ranged their athletes according to size. Some, like the British and Canadian and American teams, ignored the marching cadence and strolled most unmilitaristically to the pounding beat of the accompanying music.

At 4:17 the Canadian team filled the last empty space in the infield design; the Queen had been standing for well over an hour, the usual Queen fate. The music that had been dinning and repeating the same themes and beat for the entire march of the athletes miraculously ceased. It was a liberation devoutly to be wished. Everything was still. There appeared to be nothing left to applaud.

But the show was just beginning. The virgins stopped dancing, ending up in five interlocking Olympic rings. A few minutes later, like performers in some kind of halftime show, they made a huge "80" on the field—to indicate this was the 80th anniversary of the first, 1896, Athens Olympics. Step followed formal step in the totally prescribed ritual. The chief of protocol led to Roger Rousseau, who led to Lord Killanin, who introduced the Queen so she could say the head-of-state thing that officially opened the Olympics:

*"Je proclame l'ouverture des Jeux olympiques de Montréal célébrant la XXIe Olympiade de l'ère moderne."*

"I declare open the Olympic Games of Montreal celebrating the XXI Olympiad of the modern era."

The official opening scenario estimated it would take the Queen exactly 24 seconds to fulfill her formal duty. The figure was almost accurate.

On the electronic scoreboard the hugely enlarged face and figure of the Queen undulated a black and amber data display message broken slightly as if received from a distant satellite station. Under cover of her short speech, stretcher-bearers and a nurse rushed to minister to a sign carrier who had simply fainted. Using disaster printouts, computerized inputs from other gala occasions such as the opening ceremonies of Expo '67 and similar extravaganzas, the COJO people responsible for safety had predicted 200 people would be injured or otherwise affected during the opening ceremonies; 60 to 70 of them would require hospitalization.

The actual figures?

One.

A single person—a diabetic—required medical aid.

On the field the athletes, many of whom had been standing for over an hour, began jumping up and down, doing backbends, flexing their fingers, arms, rotating their heads, furtively falling into calisthenic and warm-up poses. Some bumped against each other like football linemen clashing shoulderpads in readiness for a bangbang game.

The International Olympic Committee had not wanted to mark the murdered Israeli athletes of 1972, but COJO did mention the 11 workers who lost their lives during construction of the Olympic complex. (The families of the dead men were rewarded with some free tickets to Olympic events!)

Proscribed in the official scenario were cameras for the competing athletes. For a long time cameras remained hidden. But

*11*

the appearance of the Olympic flag being carried in solemn ritual made the athletes break national ranks. The solid blocks of national color were dissolved. At the east end of the Stadium 50 or 60 costumes switched in and out of the best photographing slots. When the Bavarian dancers came in for the Munich ritual (when the 1920 Olympic flag is transferred from the last to the new host city), the athletes left the east end of the Stadium and scrambled to the edges of the northside tartan track to kneel and stand tiptoe and shoot pictures like the thousands in the stands who popped their useless bulbs in vain attempt to illuminate a subject 200 or 300 yards away.

Television, particularly the coverage of the Winter Olympics at Innsbruck, had prepared the crowd for a participatory phase —handclapping to some bouncy music sure to come. The Bavarian march ushering in the dancers served that purpose. Unfortunately the combination of public-address-system time lag and assorted tin ears made the clapping off-target, if fun.

It was in this happy context that Mayor Jean Drapeau's bit part in the Olympic ceremony came up. As he was handed the 1920 Olympic flag by the Mayor of Munich a tremendous cheer went up, an ovation almost as long and as loud as the Queen herself got. Drapeau's small ceremonial role called for him to hand that flag over to a costumed Quebec dancer; this exchange also got a huge cheer and wave of handclapping. The party atmosphere picked up as the Canadians and Bavarians joined in a series of dances climaxed by the singing of "*Vive la compagnie,*" which many in the stands sang and stomped to.

The ritual gun salute sounded. The virgins rushed to release the traditional pigeons, which somehow found their way up through Taillibert's circle into the blue sky—only partially deflected by the swallows and starlings game-playing in the concrete "eaves."

The great symbolic moment had arrived. Just shy of 5:00 P.M. the Olympic torchbearers appeared in the Stadium and, on the data display board, a young man and a young woman sharing the single torch. To the called-for standing ovation they ran one victory lap, then mounted the platform at midfield where the temporary Olympic flame would burn. They saluted the west, saluted the south, saluted the east, saving their final salute for the Queen's side, the north, then touched the torch to the flaring Olympic standard. The young "Greek" boys and girls—over 1,600 of them—were thrown into a frenzy of dancing, twisting, running, leaping, ribbons flowing, flag pennants whirling, hoops and veils and scarves moving. A corny gymnastic choreography followed, with green, yellow, red, blue veils shimmering in the sunless shadow.

At 5:09 the music, again, mercifully stopped. The signbearers raised their banners. The flagcarriers lofted their flags. The broken color patterns re-formed, for the last time, into that indelible 1976 Olympic imprint. Abby Hoffman climbed up on the platform to take the Olympic athletes' oath; Maurice Forget followed with the Olympic oath for officials.

The ritual was all but over. Already the VIP's—who lose points on the beautiful-people scale if they are in their seats early or stay in them late—had vacated the Stadium. The west end of the field showed empty seats. But the people in the east-end "temporary" seat section did not move. This was, after all, their party. Their big day. The VIP's and the athletes and the journalists had designated places to settle in. For the temporaries the Stadium was it. This was their time capsule, their nostalgia package, their second-by-second, instamatic-frame-by-instamatic-frame record of being there and seeing Her and choking back tears when this flag appeared, or this anthem was sung, or Canada's, Quebec's, Montreal's first ever Olympic flame was carried in.

This was the once-in-a-lifetime promise. This was the thing unlikely ever to happen again. This was the moment of moments a grandchild was supposed to hear about, and marvel at.

The teams hurried out, waving, but anxious to get to where the food and drink and restrooms and action were. Finally all the teams were gone. For the last time the music stopped. Only the TV consoles at the media tables played a cacophony of French and English, CBC and ABC explainers and recapitulators. The swallows and starlings, no longer frightened by loudspeakers, jets, bands, actually flew down on the well-tramped turf.

It was almost six o'clock.

The temporary stands had not emptied yet. Perhaps something grand—unexpected, unplanned—would happen next. One last flash cube remained to pop that fabulous final picture. The sun made a slanted broken oval on the south-side stands. The Stadium was whipped by a chill wind.

Finally the people had to face it. The last act of this great memory festival was indeed over. Tomorrow the Olympics proper would begin.

# 2 The Great Leap~Year Review of How We're Doing

Early Sunday morning, July 18, 1976, Olympic competition began—with no national flags, no banners, no buntings, no official rhetoric, no speeches of any kind. The march that had brought the athletes into the Stadium the previous afternoon and had gone on and on and on, now, foreshortened (and thus foresweetened), led eight young women to their starting blocks for the 100-metre freestyle competition at the Swimming Pool. Every swimmer came out in a terry or velour bathrobe, peeled down to a swimsuit, and stood on the starting block waiting for the gun.

This was the archetype. An event. Competitors. Referees. It could have been any year, except for the electronic scoreboard, timing, and starter's gun. In past Olympics dozens of officials would swarm around the pool, many given the task of catching time with a stopwatch. Now an official at each end for each swimmer sufficed.

Each of these women would try to do what athletes attempted in all previous Olympic Games: excel, using what coaches, trainers, science, and nutrition had made available for this day. The individual will and the individual imagination would try to put it all together. The best athlete would win a gold medal.

At the same moment the swimmers entered the pool, the women gymnasts marched into the Forum, home of the Montreal Canadiens halfway across the city. They threw off their warm-up suits and began, instantly, to use the full three minutes allowed for working out prior to the beginning of the compulsory exercises. About an hour later the men gymnasts entered the Forum and began their warm-ups.

Over at the Olympic Basin, the rowing preliminaries began; at St. Michel Arena, weightlifters in the 52-kilogram class started the competition that would reach its climax, days later, with the superheavyweights. Cycling was the business of the Velodrome; basketball eliminations took over the Étienne Desmarteau Centre. Football (soccer) occupied four cities: Toronto, Ottawa, Sherbrooke (Quebec), and Montreal. Football would, in fact, inaugurate competition for the year 1976 in the Olympic Stadium.

Boxing began at the Maurice Richard Arena; the equestrian event of the modern pentathlon was taking place at Bromont. Volleyball got under way, and pistol shooting and water polo and field hockey and team handball. In a few days, all the other Olympic events would come into play. The archetypes here would be simple, too. Women and men were engaged in contests with space, time, gravity, and—almost secondarily—with each other.

Not the silly Taiwan intrusion, not the serious African boycott could deter athletes from the primary contest. Who could run faster would, in the days that followed, run faster. Some would jump higher or farther than any previous personal best. Records would crumble. At the end of the swimming competition, for instance, almost every previous record would have been broken, some by six or seven or 10 seconds, some by a precious few hundredths. Breakthroughs would be numerous; seemingly impenetrable barriers would be smashed.

Reduced to their essence, the Olympic Games, each and every time they are held, tell the same heroic story: humankind, a mere microdot in galactic space, a piddling minisecond in cosmic time, a poor slave and fool of G-forces, every leap year ignores its low speed rating in the animal kingdom Book-of-Records, its slam-splash ways of making it in water, and tries, once again, to beat time, reduce space, and trick gravity into momentary release from its harsh laws.

The simplicity *is* all. Small children, for example, almost always know who among them can run fastest or throw farthest or most accurately, who can lift the heaviest object, who's the best scrapper or wrestler, who can kick a ball hardest. We can assume, without too much romanticizing, that in a primitive world without flags and uniforms the relative achievements of women and men were similarly recognized. Before there were clocks there was light. One could run from *here* to *there* and get back to *here* before the sun went down. Someone else could go a greater distance and still make it back before dark.

So must it have been with something as basic as the budging of boulders. One person could lift what others could not. And what everyone could lift easily, one person could throw past all other dents in the dust.

No matter how organized, political, economic, sophisticated, and complex the Olympics become, they never lose touch with what's childlike, almost primitive. That connection with the elemental and the elementary establishes the Games as a significant demonstration of humankind's physical continuity.

The confrontation of barriers such as space and time and gravity touches a significant area of human definition. Science, from one point of view, may be read as humankind's attempt not only to discover, to understand, but to break through, limits. Science fiction, science fantasy, fairy tales, and even dreams anticipate such breakthroughs. Our familiar legends are about wing-footed messengers and winged horses, seven-league boots that reduce space to a few footsteps. Heroic younger sons have no trouble running up sheer walls; imaginative fathers can fashion flying equipment for slogfooted sons (by using nothing harder to get than feathers and wax). Time in fairy legends is knocked off in the twinkling of an eye. A wellplaced wish in the ear of the right kind of wizard makes even beggars ride horses— or brooms or moonbeams.

Our dreams and fairy tales anticipated even our cosmonauts and astronauts. The barriers were the same. Buck Rogers, *Star Trek*, the Soviet and United States space labs are on a wavelength with Daedalus and Icarus and those brainy polevaulters who knew it was time to switch to a flexible pole. When a limit is reached it may—just may—be overcome. Or circumvented (through craft and guile). Or, in those cases when an absolute limit has been reached, accepted, with reluctance.

Take the men's high jump as a model of how science and athletics treat barriers. In the nineteenth century it was inconceivable that a human being would ever be able to leap as high as six feet. Jumpers tried to hurdle the bar, and that approach could carry one only so high. Technique, then, was developed—to take the body up at a different angle. Just by trying out new approaches, one could see that hurdling was inferior to a headlong dive, or a horizontal fly-over, or a scissors kick. Soon the run from the side and the roll had upped the high-jump record over not six but seven feet. In recent years the backward flip-flop has raised the world record to over 7 feet 7 inches.

Bio-mechanics, that combination of science, engineering, and systems analysis, has addressed itself not only to jumping but to running, lifting, throwing, leaping. Coaches have been aided in their work. Science prescribes optimums: the best method of warming up the body's muscles for a particular task; the best way to bring those muscles along in a training regimen covering many years; the best diet needed for the expenditure of energy in spurts or over long demanding races; the best way to expend oxygen and built-up acids in the system so that the ultimate in oxygen economy would be reached; i.e., zero reserves would be left at the exact moment an event ended.

Science and athletics thrive on nice, neat onward-and-upward tales, mini-epics illustrating the modern doctrine of progress. But all is not Eden. These Olympics, like most others in the recent past, have been troubled by rumors and realities about illegal drugs, hormones, and miracle muscle-builders like steroids. A month after they stood on the highest level reserved for gold-medal winners at the St. Michel Arena, Poland's Zbigniew Kaczmarek and wonder-boy Valentin Khristov of Bulgaria—Olympic champions in the lightweight and heavyweight classes respectively—were told by the International Weightlifting Association that they had failed the doping tests (for steroids) and would have to return their Olympic medals. Bulgaria's Blagoi Blagoev, silver medalist in the lightweight division, had to kick back his medal for the same reasons (and also face the scientific indignity of recognizing that Kaczmarek's steroids were more powerful than his own!).

Science, that is, works as a witting, and unwitting, tool of athletics. Any connection established, or even rumored, between male sex hormones and enlarged muscle mass will lead to hormone or artificial hormone (steroids) intake. It will lead, further, to ways of escaping detection by Olympic or other sport-federation testing: by stopping the use of the drugs anywhere from 23 to 33 days before testing; by utilizing other, legal, drugs that supposedly have a masking effect on the intake of illegal drugs.

The space program and, at the other extreme, deep-sea exploration, have pointed up ways for human beings to endure unnatural strains and stresses. Each discovery in science may lead to special adaptations in sports. Whatever affects endurance affects crosscountry running, the marathon, other distance races, and road cycling, rowing, etc. Any disinterested scientific findings about pulse rate, the care and maintenance of the heart as a fuel pump, the expansion and contraction of blood vessels, the conversion of food into energy or slow-down enzyme-depletion substances, have obvious meaning for most sports.

In 1972, while in Moscow with Team Canada for the great hockey inaugural series against the Soviet Union, I observed the close connection between science, medicine, training, coaching, and sports teaching that had obviously allowed the U.S.S.R., and other East European countries, to explode on the sports scene of post-World War II Olympic competition. Instead of whining about "professionalism" and "state support," Western countries, I suggested, should look at the intelligent methods being used by East European countries to nurture, train, and coach athletes in particular sports. Yapping about "auto-matons" was vulgar cold-war-ese as out of date as the "Republic" of China.

Athletes have a public and a private attitude toward substances such as steroids. On the record, athletes are either mum or oblique; off the record, they frequently boast about their hormone intake. Medical observers and coaches frequently deplore steroid-gobbling—by athletes from some other country than their own.

Weightlifters, according to one close observer of the sport, were able to add as much as 16 percent more muscle mass through the intake of steroids. When I passed that figure on to Dr. Ted Percy of the Canadian Olympic Association, he countered by saying that no double-blind experiment (in which neither the administering agent nor the participant knew which was steroid, which was placebo) had ever demonstrated the effectiveness of steroids. The weightlifter-monitor's response was a loud "I don't believe those guys [medical men]!" He claimed that a California medical calibration of steroid effects was available to everyone—including the medical volunteers working with the COA—and that the standard response to steroids and natural male hormones by medical men was an eyes-shut gritted-teeth "they don't exist, they don't exist, they don't exist," usually at the moment a discus-thrower or a weightlifter was popping a steroid or two.

Other Olympic observers were amazed by the massive quantities of steroids being openly absorbed by competitors. The random tests for steroids were a great enough "edge" for users to think they could go through the Games undetected. According, again, to the California study (I did not see it first hand), athletes—depending on various variables—could stop taking the steroids 33 days before testing and be sure of a negative reading; others could stop only 21 days before testing and still get a negative reading. Rumors, to repeat, persisted that other drugs—legal ones—when taken in conjunction with steroids, gave a negative steroid reading. I must again point out that I, personally, saw no raw scores or primary research findings to make what I am saying more than hearsay, or gossip.

But the big story of the Olympics wasn't the usual painkiller or hormone and steroid rumors. Depending on who was making the "charge" or "allegation," the subject was called:

Blood *washing*
Blood *supplement*
Blood *altering*
Blood *buffering*
Blood *reinforcement*
Blood *doping*.

I first heard these terms in a whisper from officials of the Canadian swim team, then, again, identified as rumors by officials of the American swim team. I picked the subject up again from some of the American swimming competition writers. In each case the "accusation" was directed against the East German athletes generally, and the East German swimmers specifically.

Blood "washing" or "doping" (or whatever else it may be termed) refers to a specific practice: of taking an athlete's blood out of her or his veins, keeping it refrigerated while the body replaces the missing blood, and then, just before an important sporting event, injecting the blood back into the system so that the athlete then has a reserve of strength and oxygen to draw on for a spurt of extra effort. That rumor of blood washing persisted throughout the Games and reached its climax in stories about Lasse Viren, the gold-medal winner of the 5,000-metre and 10,000-metre races, who also placed fifth—one day after the 5,000 final—in the 26-mile marathon.

I attended Viren's press conference after his 5,000-metre win, and he claimed never to have heard about this blood routine. Nevertheless, most journalists not only associated his double-medal performances with the blood-oxygen miracle but were willing to apply it to Waldemar Cierpinski, East Germany's victorious gold medalist in the marathon, and all of the brilliant young women on the East German swim team.

When I asked why the East German *men* swimmers, with the magic blood potion available to them, performed so dreadfully at the Games, nobody was able to explain the discrepancy. For myself, I had to mark blood washing as an unconfirmable rumor, less capable of substantiation than steroid intake but, most important on a mythic level, the kind of story that develops *whenever humankind confronts a barrier and, one way or another, overcomes.* The blood-wash explanation was never linked to the spectacular performance by the American men swimmers, probably because North American middle-class children were assumed to have such a head start over socialist country boys that miraculous blood infusions simply weren't needed. (Again, why the American women performed in the runner-up—or worse—role throughout all competition except one relay race seemed beyond rational explanation.)

Just as I cannot say that blood washing was common, so I am unable to testify that blood washing was not used at all. The Olympics release a race of village explainers and inside-scoop witnesses. Interpretation is in the air. Ways of modifying and improving the way the body behaves in certain sports are an ongoing question.

Just recently a team of Cincinnati doctors and scientists has come up with the startling suggestion that human beings are far from the absolute limits in all footraces. When Roger Bannister was interviewed after New Zealand's John Walker had broken the 3:50 barrier in the mile (by doing a 3:49.4), he reacted with little surprise and suggested that by the end of this century one might indeed see a three-and-a-half minute mile. The Cincinnati team's conclusion is more amazing still: they argue that almost all barriers (or records) in footraces up to this point are *psychological*, and that there seems to be no physical reason for a man *not* to run a three-minute mile. They spell out the problem of footracing in an almost simple-minded way: *the runner should have exhausted all of his available energy just as the race ends.* Anybody watching the crosscountry event of the modern pentathlon couldn't doubt that the collapsed athletes who fell into soldiers' arms at the finish line (and were set down on yellow plastic sheets while a nurse administered oxygen) were anything but totally exhausted.

Sports in various countries have used science to improve athletic performance for years now. Vladimir Kuts of the U.S.S.R. adapted scientific theory to construct his gold-medal-winning performances in past Olympics: these race techniques would force competing runners to do things that only Kuts had trained up for, like beginning a race with a sprint and keeping it going just that much longer than ordinary training could handle. Kuts would force other runners to run off their enzyme system (which would be "degraded" and could not be replenished) while he was still running on his oxygen supply. As soon as his opponent had been exhausted, Kuts would slow down almost to a walk, replenish his system and, when any runner drew near, pull the same sprint-and-slow-down trick again. Kuts' fabulous Olympic performances were a scientific triumph. The slow-down interfered with the setting of records, but in the Olympics, where, for the most part, the medal is the thing, Kuts' strategy worked perfectly.

In the field events, far more significant than steroids have been the contributions of systems analysis and instant replay television, to name but two coaching aids. Systems analysis can break down, for performance and for adaptation to teaching and coaching, the linked steps in any athletic task. Science has established the relevance of *maximum initial speed*, or *ideal trajectory*, or *angle above the horizontal*, to, say, the javelin and hammer throws, to the discus, to the shot put. What muscles should be developed for *the best techniques of release*, the connection between longterm training and those muscular developments—are other contributions of theoretical and practical science.

The javelin throw, like the high jump, is a fascinating focus for study. In 1906, 70 years before the Montreal Games, the record for the men's javelin throw was just over 175 feet. On July 26, 1976, in the Olympic Stadium, on his very first try, Miklos Nemeth of Hungary unleashed an incredible throw of 94.58 metres—310 feet, 3½ inches—to break the existing *recognized* world and Olympic records by 4.50 metres (14 feet, 9¼ inches). In countries all over the world, coaches adapting bioengineering concepts were able to add 50 or 60 feet to many an athlete's previous best javelin throw.

These same techniques, combined with others, raised the 16-pound shot put record from around 36 feet in the first modern Olympic year, 1896, to close to 72 feet in 1976—almost double. The 16-pound hammer throw record went from just under 100 feet in 1900 to just over 260 feet in 1976.

But because barriers fell throughout the 1976 Games does not mean that records will continue to fall forever. To put the proposition absurdly: will the human creature ever be able to throw a javelin *1,000* feet? The answer must be *no*. It follows, then, that somewhere between the present 310 feet, 3½ inches and considerably short of 1,000 feet is *the absolute limit* for the javelin throw.

Again, will a human creature ever be able to beat a horse in a 1,500-metre or mile race? The answer, again, must be *no*. The worst broken-down claimer on a country fair circuit is still able to do the mile in under *two* minutes. John Walker's "miracle mile" of 3:49.4 is light years away from a hobbled horse's worst time. Even if the Cincinnati team I referred to earlier is right—and the barrier to man's breaking the *three-minute* standard in the mile is all psychological—attaining that incredible record would still leave humankind far short of a mediocre horse's achievement at that distance.

Yet, even when the absolute limit is near—as one suspects it is in the high jump, the pole vault, the long jump, and the triple jump—men and women will continue to confront the real barriers, space, time, and gravity, with the heroic folly of a Don Quixote trying to overcome giant windmills.

Athletes who pay attention to science and adapt its findings will, in competition even after absolute limits have been reached, hold an edge over athletes ignorant of certain facts. Observers of the modern biathlon in the 1976 Winter Olympics saw competitors recognize the scientific fact that someone who skied fastest and thus speeded up his pulse rate would have to wait for that rate to drop before attempting to shoot. Accuracy, it had been determined, could not be guaranteed a target shooter with greatly elevated heartbeat. Roger Bannister, a doctor, considered the reduced pulse rate a significant factor in further assaults on the record for the mile—equal in importance, say, to the condition of a runner's legs.

Training techniques and scientific aids may help one athlete to defeat another, or give one country an edge over all others. But the secrets of biology and biochemistry, like the secrets of fission and fusion, eventually enter the world's public domain. Law is the category to cancel out drug and steroid advantages. Adaptation and intelligence will end the exclusive edge of a single athlete or a single country.

Before the Games and, indeed, after, the East German women swimmers seemed possessed of some great secret Marxian-Merlin potion, a breakfast *kuchen* perhaps, that had overcome Jack Armstrong's breakfast of champions. The performance of the American men swimmers, however, suggested that, among other things, it would help a competitive swimmer to belong to a suburban swim club, have a daddy and mummy earning 150,000 dollars plus per annum, or be enrolled in some California or Indiana university's support-the-jock scholarship plan.

The Olympic boxers and wrestlers who prepped psychologically by muttering—in English—"smash," "murder," "destroy," "crush," and similar instinct-for-the-jugular enhancers, discovered too frequently that the word was *not* master of the deed. KO'd or pinned, they could, on their backs, contemplate the possibility that the Cuban or Russian or Rumanian words for the killer aggressions possibly fill antagonist minds fuller and/or quicker. And those athletes who fed on kelp or garlic or molasses or massive doses of Vitamin C were only reliving the pleasant fairy-tale anticipations of characters able to overcome all obstacles, with only a little help from their magical mystical friends.

The Olympic fact is this: for every gold medalist who stands, every four years, at the top of a particular athletic pyramid, hundreds upon hundreds of other competitors have fallen, before as well as during, the Games. Some athletes encounter the Olympics as participants in team sports little affected by time or space or gravity. The same tiny ratio of winners to losers exists here too.

It is this isolation of the best athletes *eligible by Olympic standards and definitions* that makes the Olympics the most significant athletic contest the world currently knows.

When those women gymnasts and women swimmers began their serious work the day after the opening ceremonies, they performed in Olympic history and out of it. For what each athlete in these and the other Olympic sports was trying to accomplish, there was no past—only the here-and-now of existential challenge and definition. For the magical Olympic fortnight, time seemed to be buffeted, space seemed to shrink, and bodies seemed to be free, if only momentarily, of gravity's chains.

Everest was climbed *because it was there*. The moon was reached *because it was there*. Kornelia Ender's fantastic assault on world swimming records—matched by the U.S.A.'s John Naber and Jim Montgomery and Brian Goodell and John Hencken and Mike Bruner and Rod Strachan and Great Britain's David Wilkie, and by her own teammates, Petra Thumer and

Ulrike Tauber, the U.S.S.R.'s Marina Koshevaia, the U.S.A.'s 4 x 100 metre freestyle relay team—occurred, in effect, *because they were there*. Kornelia Ender's and all other record-breaking performances were the culmination of humankind's confrontation of the records Olympic events celebrate. On a vase, on urns, on the walls of caves, in the poems of an oral tradition, swimmers and wrestlers and runners are exalted. On that epic scale, in a real world setting, the Montreal Games of 1976 took place. For 15 days reality was surrounded by a golden nimbus. But the facts of Montreal—and all other spectaculars and extravaganzas—needed looking into.

# 3 Politics and the Money Game

Montreal's Olympics, in many ways unique, serve as a model for other Olympic cities and for any city wanting some kind of new permanent architectural establishment—sport or otherwise. *The good news that drives out the bad* is spectacle, worldwide attention, an architecturally interesting building complex, a sudden surge in employment or tourist spending, a place in the roll call of great cities, a place in the history of exhibitions, expositions, world fairs, world games, greatest of which are the Olympics. Cities and politicians—beset by bad news, flagging political support, high unemployment, inflation, charges of corruption or stagnation or lackluster leadership—have turned to the worldwide spectacular to sharpen a dull image. Opponents who can beat up on poor urban services like sewer systems, trash collection, hospital care, the teaching of children, the care of the elderly, etc., can't usually cope with an imminent world spectacular.

Before the Olympics, the city of Montreal—our modern model—was in bad financial shape; after the Olympics, the city is clearly in worse financial shape. So is the province of Quebec. So is the rest of Canada. But to match the achievement of the Olympics against the agony of a modern city is to put apples against oranges, or so some say. Yet everything that happens to one particular city is of a piece.

The Olympics as a sports spectacular was almost matched by its site as an urban spectacular—a place much modified by the pressures of worldwide attention. I was interested in the competition among modern cities to land the Olympics; in the power structure of the International Olympics Committee that granted the right to hold the Games; in the architectural, construction, labor, and financial problems that followed the awarding to a city of the great Olympic prize. Every huge sports complex wins acceptance through its promoters' presenting a fairly low initial estimate of total costs which, once the go-ahead is given, escalate rapidly—doubling and, in some cases, tripling. The remodeling of Yankee Stadium by the city of New York was a case in point: it was estimated, first, to cost 24 million dollars. Current figures are three times that high and still mounting. New Orleans was another city afflicted by the sports complex blitz—yet the ultimate 200-million-dollar-plus cost of the Superdome turned out to be peanuts when compared to Montreal Mayor Jean Drapeau's *modest, no-deficit* Games.

The reasons for escalation were obvious. First, in order to get a project accepted, politicos came in with Cloud Nine figures.

Next, once a project was begun it had to have a target date for its completion: that was a natural blackmail situation for contractors and labor unions. With *urgency* a given, "adjustments" would have to be made: overtime, say; or bonuses; or cost-plus gimmicks; or adaptations to the rate of inflation. A law one can observe in spectacular projects is: *when time is the problem, only money is the solution.* The results: massive deficits—even in Montreal, where the self-financing Olympics of Mayor Drapeau's imagining were supposed to be as immune from deficits as a man is from pregnancy. Money people, contractors, workers, finaglers weren't afraid of killing the goose that laid the golden egg. They knew it was destined to go out of the golden egg business on a set date—July 17, 1976—the day the Olympic Games would officially open. The scramble resembled a California gold rush. Almost everyone assumed that the amount of money available was limitless. It was also assumed that "if you don't grab yours, somebody else will."

Since the Olympics, like expositions and trade fairs, have traditionally been located in cities, the mayor of an aspiring host city is obviously a key figure. If he lands the Games, his power and influence expand a hundredfold, instantly. He is a dealer in *largesse*, a money conduit, a contractor's or construction worker's dream come true. He is, in an instant, the center of a complex universe. Ask any significant question and the print-out answer will be "The Mayor."

So it was in Montreal. No matter what the question, the answer came out "Mayor Jean Drapeau." Among the obvious questions were the following:

> **Q.** Who decided to bring the Olympics to the city of Montreal?
> **A.** Mayor Jean Drapeau.
> **Q.** Who brought Expo '67 to Montreal?
> **A.** Mayor Jean Drapeau.
> **Q.** Who, after Expo and the Expos, needed something big in the way of an encore?
> **A.** Mayor Jean Drapeau.

**Q.** Who convinced the Canadian Olympic Association that Montreal was a better Olympic site than Toronto?

**A.** Mayor Jean Drapeau.

**Q.** Who convinced the International Olympic Committee that Montreal was a better Olympic site than either Los Angeles or Moscow?

**A.** Mayor Jean Drapeau.

**Q.** Who dreamed up the essential sales pitch that the Olympics would be totally self-financing?

**A.** Mayor Jean Drapeau.

**Q.** Who forced the federal government to allow a special Olympic lottery as part of the self-financing strategy?

**A.** Mayor Jean Drapeau.

**Q.** Who got the federal government involved in philatelic programs and coin programs?

**A.** Mayor Jean Drapeau.

**Q.** Who chose the designer and builder of the Olympic Stadium, Velodrome and Swimming Pool, Paris architect Roger Taillibert?

**A.** Mayor Jean Drapeau.

**Q.** Who directly or indirectly negotiated the deals with builders, contractors, suppliers, workers?

**A.** Mayor Jean Drapeau.

A hundred other questions yield the same answer. And so does the final overwhelming question:

**Q.** Who was pushed aside by Dr. Victor Goldbloom and the Quebec government's Olympic Installations Board in order to ensure that the minimum facilities would be available to athletes, the media, and the public on July 17, 1976?

**A & Q.** Mayor Jean Drapeau?

It became clear to me, quite some time ago, that any questions I might have about the Olympics had to be addressed to one man—that same Mayor Jean Drapeau. His political opponents obviously read the Olympics differently from the Mayor's reading. They saw his Expo '67-Montreal Expos-skyscrapers-hotel complexes-six-lane highways-the Olympics as a continuing grandstand display of the objectively superfluous. Humankind's *circuses* were locked in a life-and-death struggle with Montreal's need for *bread*—food, shelter, clothing, safety.

Mayor Jean Drapeau was only the most spotlighted practitioner of the modern dictum, "never throw good money after bad"; i.e., anything that can be translated as "welfare." Mayor Drapeau knew that a financially disastrous showpiece is as upbeat *while it is going on* as one that is financially successful. Showpieces, again according to the modern dictum, "sell a city," make people want to hold conventions there, spend vacations there, be photographed in the middle of its instantly recognized architecture. Mayor Drapeau knew from his experience with Expo '67 that an opponent trying to attack the mayor while a showpiece was in progress always found himself tilting with the showpiece, which had few real enemies. The Mayor wanted his political enemies to struggle with:

*amateurism*
*competition*
*character-building*
*physical fitness*
*Olympic history*
*glamour*
*excitement*
*Montreal as a major-league city.*

There was no way to argue against the contention of the Mayor's opponents that if all the money spent on Expo '67 and the Olympics had been put into housing and education and reclamation and public transportation, the lot of Montrealers who live near or below the poverty level would be enormously improved. Mayor Drapeau knew what other Olympic mayors knew: that money which becomes available for showpiece projects is never—never—available for the upgrading of the poor's lives.

A mayor who sells his city's "image" knows you can't invite tourists in to inspect an improved, and needed, sewer system. Nobody can make a prime tourist attraction out of day care centers or the raised nutritional intake of a city's children. Conventions don't ask if cities do well by their infirm. Jean Drapeau and his fellow mayors know that in the 1970's a city must send out beautiful-people messages. Every metropolis must have its panoramic bar and restaurant at least 50 stories above its streets. From that height even slums look picturesque.

But when Jean Drapeau tried to get Montreal the Olympics, even the poor and the ailing were, for the most part, on his side. Not only in Montreal but elsewhere in the world people love circuses, even if the price is bread. Existentially, circuses are primary. They don't, and can't, displace bread. But a sufficiency of bread never eliminates humankind's demonstrated love and need for circuses. That need explains why women and men work at arduous and oftentimes hateful jobs not for bread alone but for a week or two at a Drapeau Disneyland.

Realistically, the Olympics, like all other extravaganzas, are for most people mere secondhand joys (far too costly to be experienced first hand). Misery, as the poor know it, is first hand, constant, and seemingly inescapable. Second-hand joy in the context of first-hand suffering is a mark of the downtrodden that causes reformists to despair. The enemy of the Olympics, say, might suddenly find himself regarded as the enemy of the poor.

I first met Mayor Jean Drapeau on May Day, 1975, in the Salon de la Mairie, Room 109, of the Hôtel de Ville, after I had been out to the Olympic site to study his great work-in-progress. The Mayor was dressed in a vested, neatly striped dark blue suit, his shirt light blue, his tie dark blue and Countess Mara-like in its small figures, his shoes slipper style and highly shined. I would be remiss were I not to report that all the women on the Mayor's staff—and there were a lot—were rather handsome and full blown, what used to be called Junoesque. As they passed in and out of the Mayor's oak-paneled hand-carved chamber of loveseats and comfy armchairs, I was reminded a little of the more modest bowers in the Palace of Versailles. What saved me from drowning in historical analogy was the Mayor's lapel pin—that gold M logo over the Olympic rings, his spirit of 1976.

Once we began to converse, and once the subject settled on the Olympics, I realized how that Olympic logo had taken hold of the Mayor's brain. His cerebrum and cerebellum were clearly shaped into interlocking Olympic rings. The Mayor was possessed by Baron-de-Coubertin-ism. His mouth was permanently pursed to suggest the letter O. If I had been an octogenarian on the International Olympic Committee I, too, would have been overwhelmed by such committed singlemindedness. Instead, I asked the Mayor if it was true that his first estimate of the total Olympic cost had been 125 million dollars.

"That was not an estimate," said the Mayor; "in 1970 we had no specific plans for any type of installation. One hundred and twenty-five million dollars was—how shall I put it?—a budgetary envelope."

*Budgetary envelope.*

I sat up. The Mayor was obviously putting me on. But no. He didn't seem to realize that a phrase like *budgetary envelope* was invaluable as an instant emetic—if fed to the English-language press in Canada, the Mayor's most constant critics.

I studied the fox closely. The Mayor was better looking than that mean pinch-mouthed mortgage-forecloser pictured in newspapers or drawn in cartoons. His mustache was almost white, his sideburns white with a touch of gray. His darkrimmed glasses made him look more innocent than ominous. His hands were pinkish, young for his face, the kind of hands you might find in a commercial for Ivory Snow. When we began our conversation the Mayor felt obliged to spiel a little. Once or twice he fell back into a set response that resembled operatic recitative. "Inflation" could trigger a tuneless aria. I learned to avoid other trigger words like "amateurism," "youth," "opportunity."

The obvious question I framed next—how did that 125-million-dollar budgetary envelope grow to almost two billion dollars (in late August of 1976 the Quebec government, looking for a loan of 800 million dollars estimated the Olympic *deficit* to be around 975 million dollars—or a billion)? I had obviously asked the Mayor's favorite question. How? Simple.

"The inflation," he said in the voice of someone discussing earthquakes, tidal waves, towering infernos. "The oil embargo, strikes, slowdowns. Concrete producers, and steel—steel went from 200 dollars a ton to 1,000 dollars—and was still hard to get. Our Olympic coins got caught in the silver market. At one point a five-dollar silver piece was worth—as silver—six dollars!"

The Olympics, Montreal, and, ultimately, Quebec, were trapped trying to resist inflation's centripetal suck: to avoid everything going down the drain, expensive—extravagant—countermeasures were applied. The one thing to be avoided: a decision by the International Olympic Committee that Montreal be scrubbed for the 1976 Games. So there it was, that catastrophic time-money double bind. Once the Quebec government began voicing the doubts already expressed by the Canadian and international media people, the scramble for money was on. A little shortage here, a little slowdown there, a little lag in delivery, a little hesitation to let something go at an earlier agreed-on price: whatever the ploy, it worked. Money, and more money, went into the project.

My question to the Mayor was: *how* did Montreal get itself tied into such an expensive project? And *why*? The Mayor began to explain. He told me that from the very beginning the usual method of handling a large construction project—advertising for open bids, requiring sealed tenders—was not "suitable" because of the "specialized nature of the materials used" and the "method of construction."

But who had chosen those "materials" and settled on that "method of construction"?

Mayor Jean Drapeau.

To the question of whether the materials and method had been deliberately chosen so that the "usual . . . handling of a construction project" could be avoided, the Mayor merely pursed his lips and looked hurt. The crux of this overwhelming question was the Mayor's decision to select Parisian Roger Taillibert to design the Olympic complex. Was the "specialized nature of the materials used" brought to Mayor Drapeau's attention by Schokbeton, the only firm able to provide "the materials" necessary for Roger Taillibert's "method of construction"?

Months later, when I finally met Roger Taillibert—first in the Mayor's office, and then in the Schokbeton plant in St. Eustache—I discovered that his Parc des Princes soccer stadium in Paris, which had so impressed Mayor Jean Drapeau, had, indeed, used *the specialized materials and method of construction* built into the Olympic project. But I found out something else quite astounding: M. Taillibert told me that his was not an Olympics mandate but a request:

> *To build a lasting sports installation for Montreal that would accommodate both baseball and football in a city much larger than the present one—using population estimates for the year 1990.*

The Olympics were, clearly, a means, not an end. Mayor Jean Drapeau's real goal was a huge sports complex which, even in its *unfinished* state, still was able to stage the Olympic Games on schedule. More than that, the Mayor's method of procurement and purchase ensured that though the tower, for instance, might be unfinished on July 17, opening day, the materials for its completion were already purchased (no returns on 20-ton custom-cast chunks of concrete) and stored ready for a more leisurely construction schedule after the Games were over. Thus though governments—federal and provincial—might protest, journalists howl, the Mayor's opponents cry "foul," M. Drapeau, once again, ended up doing exactly what he had planned to when he chose Roger Taillibert-Schokbeton to build the complex.

The modern model stands revealed: if a mayor in the 1960's or 1970's asked a council or a metropolitan authority, a province or state, the relevant federal power, either to grant money or to authorize a special lottery for the construction of a multimillion-dollar sports complex, he would hear a chorus of no's. But let that same mayor go the exposition, World Fair, Olympic route and he scores.

Once the bust-out has been achieved, and the Mayor has landed his pet project, why be a piker about anything? *A tower, a retractable roof*—both unnecessary, even prohibited, under the Olympic rule that says contests must be held in the open air—hell, if you're going to build yourself a sports complex, shoot the works, get the biggest pile of concrete other people's money can buy! A modern city shouldn't run up huge deficits for piddly shlock operations.

Okay, I say to the Mayor, so you weren't going to use the sealed-tender and open-bid methods to guarantee fairness and lowest possible cost. What were you going to do instead?

"A closed group was invited *by telephone* [my italics]," the Mayor told me, "to file a bid with an estimate."

How closed?

Pretty closed.

Like, say, a "closed group" of *one*?

Like.

The Mayor told me, further, that of course anybody anywhere in the country could bid for "certain parts of the over-all plan." How those people not telephoned could be in on the over-all plan, the Mayor didn't specify. All "other things being equal," he added, "we favored the firms based in the province of Quebec." This explains, of course, why it took the Quebec government so long to react to the Mayor's methods and the escalating costs—the Olympics boosted employment not only in Montreal but in the rest of the province. The Olympic sports complex upped the "gross provincial product."

The rest of Canada was not amused. In a bitterly captioned editorial in Toronto's *Globe and Mail*, Norman Webster accepted the Quebec separatist position:

*Canadians left out in cold*

Mr. Webster complained about the "great willingness to accept money from the national coin program," and Mayor Drapeau's "talks about our posterity's posterity buying Olympic Lottery tickets." Mr. Webster wanted to show how phony the calls for supposed public tenders were. He quoted from tender call RMS Number 5841 by COJO that invited

bids on "the manufacture of residential furniture and furnishings for the athletes' Olympic Village"—a separate project
from the main Olympics complex of Drapeau and Taillibert.
On the list were "beds, linen hampers, clothes closets, mobile
partitions, writing desks and chairs, lamps and lamp supports,
arm-rests, step-ladders for upper bunks, wastebaskets and ash-
trays."

What Mr. Webster objected to were the conditions imposed
by the tender call: "Only those individuals, associations, companies and corporations who are recognized specialists in the
manufacture of residential furniture *having their principal place
of business in the Province of Quebec and able to manufacture
the furniture and furnishings in Quebec* are invited to tender."

In other words, this was merely another version of the
Drapeau telephone call: the province clearly didn't object to
Olympic business being restricted to locally based manufac-
turers and suppliers.

The Mayor, in May, 1975, and, again, on Hallowe'en—
October 31—of that year, mere days away from the take-over of
the Olympic construction project by that same provincial
government, held fast to his contention that the Games would
be self-financing and would not produce a deficit.

"You understand," he told me without blinking an eye, "that
if Montreal can't do that [avoid a deficit], the Olympics would
be finished. *Nobody is going into debt and destroy his city
because of the Olympics* [my italics]."

The Mayor's main opposition, the Montreal Citizens Movement, had, from the very beginning, accused the Mayor of des-
troying his city. What the MCM didn't quite understand was the
Mayor's ability to present the Olympics project as an effort to
"save" his city: Montrealers might be hypnotized by Olympic
glamour and, even more significantly, fall for the Mayor's
implied line that if Montrealers were getting screwed, they at
least would have this huge permanent sports complex to show
for it. What would the rest of Quebec have—or the rest of
Canada, or the real gulls in the Olympic fast shuffle: the
suckers, the tourists, the strangers?

When I met with several members of the Montreal Citizens Movement on July 15, two days before the Olympic opening ceremonies, most of them, except for Nick Auf der Maur (who, by this time, had developed a wariness toward signs of Drapeau's demise) were gleeful about Drapeau's getting slapped down by the Quebec government. They finally had him, right?

Maybe.

Throughout the Games I spoke to people in various parts of Montreal and uncovered a complex, even contradictory response to the Olympics that the MCM might well ponder. Someone would say:

"Look what is happening in Montreal—look what I pay for the gasoline. Look what I pay for the cigarettes. More and more taxes. And the business we were supposed to get from the Olympics, where is it?"

The political translation of that lament seemed obvious: the villain who had foisted the Olympics off on Montreal was clearly Jean Drapeau. Yet when I asked people, "Are you sorry the Olympics were held in Montreal?" they looked at me as if I were on some alien wavelength.

"We are known in the whole world now," a cab driver who had just been bewailing the failure of the Olympics to increase his take-home pay told me, "I only am sorry the Mayor could not make the Olympics last long like Expo—six month, maybe more. Anybody see the Stade on television or right here ain't going to forget it. He shrewd, the Mayor. He always do what best for Montreal."

Even more baroque was an attitude I kept encountering among Montreal's young and old, its poor, and its French-speaking, which went something like this: "Jean Drapeau may be doing something to us, but he's doing something far worse to *them.*" "Them" were outsiders, tourists, the dummies in the International Olympic Organization, the patsies in the federal government (including Prime Minister Trudeau), the pretend winners in the provincial government (including Premier Robert Bourassa and the temporary minder-of-the-Olympic-store, Victor Goldbloom), and "the English."

What was Mayor Jean Drapeau?

The scourge of God, a vengeance on the rest of Canada, a genius who undoubtedly would dump all the grief on others while Montreal ended up with the gravy and pleasures of the greatest of all athletic festivals.

"He too smart for *them*," a nurse at the Royal Victoria Hospital said glowingly.

Proof?

What did Mayor Jean Drapeau want most?

*To get the Olympics for Montreal.*

What did he want almost as much?

*To make sure that a batch of somebody elses ended up holding Montreal's bag.*

Opponents who exulted in Drapeau's humiliation and inevitable demise couldn't believe Drapeau would emerge as the cheered hero of the opening ceremonies (and the recipient of a standing ovation at the closing). They might have contemplated the seeming defeat of Jean Drapeau in the context of the financial collapse of New York City. What wouldn't Mayor Abraham Beame of New York have given to be humbled the way Drapeau was humbled—dump all his financial woes on New York State or the United States federal government?

There was still another perspective to the Olympic complex: it was, when looked at from the right angle, the closest thing to a massive public-works project any municipality could manage. The first time I visited the site I understood the Olympic project as Mayor Drapeau's alleviation of Montreal's unemployment problem, particularly among those entering the work force for the first time.

In May of 1975 and on through the winter, right up to opening day, that site was the scene of tremendous activity (sometimes, of course, stilled by strikes). I was overwhelmed by the scope of what was going on: a continuous grinding pitch of cement mixers, unmuffled trucks with blinking lights, yellow beacons revolving, like ambulances lined up outside a disaster zone. Long loaded trailer beds roared in neutral, stuck in a long queue of similar carriers of Schokbeton's precast concrete

*41*

blocks, those units of Roger Taillibert's post-tension geometric design that, alas, would fail to fall into place as effortlessly as blueprints suggested they must.

In its earliest form, the Stadium was a scatter of concrete tubes and ovals, cisternlike masses, molded modules Henry Moore might have created. Parkland was being ripped up by earthmovers as relentlessly destructive as stripmining equipment. Bulldozers, cranes, scoopshovels crossed over, reversed, crisscrossed, David Smith metal animals seemingly choreographed by the new technology's master computer. Against the drone of those motored earthmonsters, steel beams clanging together raised the noise ante an octave, and steel pipe, shivered and vibrating, sent rods and wires into a yet higher screech.

In stages I watched the site floor go from a few scattered Towers of Babel—the Stadium called for 34 such consoles to support the huge structure—to, first, 16, then twenty-some, and, finally, to the requisite 34 Samsonian pillars from which Taillibert-Schokbeton abstract concrete dinosaur shapes shot up to form that not quite harmoniously met roof.

On July 17, to untutored eyes, the Stadium, except for the tower and the roof, looked not only finished but grand. The guided tours that had been going on for several weeks had sent back reports to the precincts of not an unfinished but of a terribly impressive structure. Quite unconsciously, those who were interested in athletics, in progress, in Montreal's future and the future of Quebec and the rest of Canada became aggressively committed to the Stadium and the whole Olympics project.

The Olympics became the symbol of middle-class wellbeing *vs* the unlucky, the poor, the lame, the halt. The Olympics were the Establishment, property, order. Killjoys alone were anti-Drapeau. That Killjoy category covered radicals, people favoring abortion, decent housing, health care, women's rights, concern for landmarks, concern for the aged. On Drapeau's side were the construction industry, trade unions, the board-of-trade chamber-of-commerce people, all those who live off tourists—hotel- and saloon-keepers, retailers generally, souvenir hawkers particularly, itinerant pimps, resident hookers, local and international pickpockets, drunk-rollers, cardsharps, shell-game operators, after-hours and key clubs, assorted rubbers, strokers, and more abstruse porn-pushers, the local dealers in cocaine, hash, and pot, but, most of all, scalpers. The formula was simple: no Olympics, no scalping.

Nothing is more bourgeois than scalping. It works over the middleclass fears of missing out, not being *there*, and not having hard facts to be sentimental and nostalgic about. The *nouveau riche* are the prime targets of scalping, those showy big spenders who in their heart of hearts *demand* to be scalped big.

*Scalping*, on another level, was a category that applied to Mayor Jean Drapeau's superspectacular expansionist strategy. Scalping, sentimentally, operates on a phony Robin Hood premise. The locals—so goes a naïve assumption—are the ones able to stand in line for tickets. The big spenders are paying out what used to be called economic rent—money not needed to keep them in business. Therefore scalping takes unneeded money and turns it over to the needy. The scalped are *always* from somewhere else, which makes scalping just another way of getting the tourist's buck.

When I went out to St. Eustache in May of 1975, Mayor Jean Drapeau radiated power. Everyone, even his Montreal Citizens Movement opponents, conceded that he was, at least for the moment, in control. The people at the key Schokbeton plant told me then that *they had no plans for the use of any of the special machinery and equipment* constructed to handle the massive units for the Stadium, Swimming Pool, and Velodrome. So uncritical was the climate at that time, the Mayor, Taillibert, and Schokbeton thought nothing of scrapping millions upon millions of dollars of construction molds, elevators, drying equipment, etc. In the "what the hell!" mood of that time, with nobody to account to, and power totally in Drapeau's hands, alternatives that saved money were irrelevant. The Bibeault brothers (of Schokbeton) didn't say whether the factory equipment would be destroyed; or whether ownership reverted to Schokbeton. They did tell me, in May of 1975, that ultimately only the walls would be left of the St. Eustache factories.

Six months later, when critics in Montreal, Quebec City, Ottawa, Toronto, Berlin, London, Paris, were shrieking about the unfinished state of the project and the escalated costs (called "obscene," "indecent," "flamboyant," "garish," etc.), the Bibault brothers told another story. Yes, in May there had been no plan to utilize the St. Eustache facilities; but in November, with Schokbeton's part of the production almost completed, thoughts had turned to what to do with the custom-designed equipment. With some adjustments the plant could turn out small bridges economically. Other adaptations were being planned.

No mention was made of the significant factor: the short distance between St. Eustache and the main Olympic site. Everything needed for the construction of the complex was manufactured within 17 miles of the Stadium. That was almost like building a factory on the site.

Ultimately, the total cost of the Olympic project will be little affected by plans to "adapt." Posterity's posterity may still have to buy Olympic Lottery tickets in perpetuity, or gather cobwebs in the temporary seats of the Stadium, permanently fixed in the role of Drapeau's ideal paying spectator.

The take-over by the Quebec government did put a crimp in the stylistics of Jean Drapeau. If, for instance, one were to ask the Mayor, as I did, how much Expo '67 "cost," the Mayor would reply, "We have not closed the books on Expo yet." By keeping Man and His World going, the Mayor was in effect making Expo a symbol of eternity. Had Drapeau continued to hold all the Olympic cards, he would not have fixed a deficit figure of a billion dollars on the Olympics. He would have considered the Olympics to be, even now, "modest" though blimped up by "the inflation." He would never have "closed the books" on the Olympics, and thus avoided ever answering any hard questions about its final cost. Reality would have successfully squeezed through the Olympic needle's eye. No matter what happens to Montreal (or to the Mayor) as a result of the

Olympic deficit, Drapeau will always believe that he was, after all, right.

During the high of the Games Jean Drapeau was the General Montcalm who finally made it. His good news circus kept his own personal five-ring logo up in the air for two unforgettable weeks. A Montreal voter, remembering those days, and facing the question "Are you for Jean Drapeau or against him? will probably prove that the Mayor really was right.

# 4 The Best, the Brightest, the Most Dazzling

The days, months, years of uncertainty were swallowed up by those five rings of Jean Drapeau's own personal Olympic circus. In one, the swimming ring, a tall young woman stood on the starting block, shivering. She leaned forward, dangled her long arms, let her muscles quiver and ripple, a rhythm soon to be passed into her legs. Head alertly forward, she windmilled her arms three or four times, then stopped all motion, alert, waiting for the starter's gun. Six other women's 100-metre freestyle heats had been swum before this young woman, Kornelia Ender, marched out for the seventh.

It was Kornelia Ender that almost everyone in the Swimming Pool was waiting to see. At 17 she was fabled, without doubt the greatest woman swimmer of all time. At the gun she drove herself flatly forward, hit the water ahead of all other swimmers, her arms cutting the accommodating lane's space into even foaming segments. Here was athletic elegance, churning power. Ordinarily, to see Kornelia Ender swim, one would have had to travel to Halle, Johann Sebastian Bach's and Kornelia Ender's home town. Or try to catch her swimming at some world meet. But this morning Halle's "mountain" was brought to Montreal. It would have been enough, for many, to see only Kornelia Ender swim. Yet here was Kornelia Ender in the company of the entire East German women's swim team. And swimming was only one of over 20 Olympic Sports Montreal and the other Canadian Olympic sites would feature in the days to come.

And who had brought Kornelia Ender, and her starry cast of thousands, to Montreal for Canada's very first Olympic Games *ever?*

The much maligned, castigated, abused, tossed-aside hustling impresario, the not-down and certainly not-out still-reigning Mayor of Montreal, His Worship Jean Drapeau. Drapeau's stock rose with every medal Kornelia Ender, and the other Olympic champions, won.

It was in the ahistorical human category—a woman swimming—that Kornelia Ender began to register an image. In the march-on of competitors she was just a tall, pretty, smiling, waving teenager, looking over to the East German swimmers seated at the turn-end of the pool. She came out swaddled in the long hooded burnt-orange-and-wine East German women's velour robe she would discard reluctantly. Under it she wore her light blue East German sweatsuit, under that a T-shirt and the East German women's swim suit of two shades of blue and white. She would peel off heavy wool socks and shoes, tuck her hair into her swim cap, crisscross her arms before stepping up on the block. Her shoulders were very broad, so were her swimmer's back and chest. Her arms were long, with long wrists, long hands. Her legs were long and smooth-muscled.

In time, Kornelia Ender's every motion became part of a unique signature on Montreal space. The pulling off of her bathing cap, her hair shaking free, her wonderful wide smile as she looked back at the Pool's electronic board to see her time. Almost always, Kornelia Ender equaled or bettered a world record. Her over-all achievement at the 1976 Games—four gold medals and a silver (in the 4 x 100 metre freestyle relay, which she led off, handing her number-two swimmer, Petra Priemer, a 1.16 second lead!)—was of course shy of Mark Spitz's remarkable seven gold medals in the 1972 Munich Olympics.

But the story of Kornelia Ender emerged more from how she won than from what she won. In the pool her speed was devastating: Shirley Babashoff, who had swept most events in the United States Olympic swim trials, seemed to feel the Ender triumph more sharply than most other contenders. In the 100-metre freestyle, in which Ender broke her own world record, Babashoff was not only out of the medals completely, she finished fifth behind her teammate, Kim Peyton. In the 200-metre freestyle, supposedly Babashoff's stronger event, Ender's world-record time of 1:59.26 (which, again, broke her own world record) was almost two seconds better than Babashoff's silver-medal performance. In Babashoff's best events, the 400-metre and 800-metre freestyle, she had to settle for silver behind two more world-record swimming performances, this time by East Germany's Petra Thumer.

Perhaps Shirley Babashoff's roughest experience was coming out to swim the 200-metre freestyle final only 20 minutes after Kornelia Ender had equaled Ender's own world record of 1:00.13 in winning the 100-metre butterfly. There was Ender, changed into a dry swimsuit, breathing in that relaxed Lamaze rhythm many of the East European athletes used to calm themselves and conserve energy. Babashoff was in an ideal position.

The 100-metre butterfly is an exacting race. The 200-metre freestyle was all sprint.

Less than 26 minutes had passed between the butterfly and the 200-metre freestyle when the gun went and Babashoff made the first turn—.07 seconds ahead of Ender. After 100 metres she was in better shape still—.09 seconds in front. Babashoff was supposed to have the superior last 25 metres kick—and her lead seemed a definite sign that Kornelia Ender had worn herself out in the 100-metre butterfly. But Ender suddenly picked up speed, made the touch at the 150-metre mark .07 seconds *in front*, executed a magnificent turn, and won "going away." Everything that had been said and written about Kornelia Ender was prelude to this world-record feat.

This was the stuff of legends. This was a race between Kornelia Ender and time. But Shirley Babashoff didn't read it that way. Her comments after that race—and, in fact, throughout the Olympics—were not only in poor taste but much like a gymnasium fighter's "we wuz robb'd" loser reaction. The Babashoff line, supposedly a winner in suburban dressing rooms on the North American continent, was, unbelievably:

"At least *we* [the American swimmers] look like women." Which prompted an American journalist to say: "Shirley's eyes are worse than I thought." And, later: "If Roland Matthes [Kornelia Ender's fiancé] would okay it, and I had to choose between Babashoff and Ender, in the pool or out . . ."—an indication of the level to which Babashoff had brought her event. Babashoff's other comments were not much classier, such as: "I don't really think they [the East German women] enjoy swimming—it's more like a job to them."

I watched not only Kornelia Ender and Petra Thurmer but the other East German gold medalists—Ulrike Richter, Hannelore Anke, Andrea Pollack, Ulrike Tauber—throughout the Games, and, for the life of me, could not differentiate their delight and playfulness before and during and after swimming from that of the American girls, the Canadian girls, the British girls, etc. I attended an East German workout at the University of Old Montreal Friday night, July 16, on the eve of the

Olympic opening ceremonies, and, had I not been aware of the colors of their sweatsuits—and their far-out space-age rainwear (boots and hooded jackets of a silver-blue plastic)—I would not have been able to locate them on a world map. The women, without eyeshadow and juliette nails, were women. They seemed to be enjoying themselves hugely. Those who spoke English were chatting away with the rifle-slung-on-shoulder teenage Canadian soldiers assigned to protect them. Those who didn't speak English used their teammates as interpreters to get into the exchange.

Some sat around drying their hair and brushing it out. The men swimmers and women swimmers seemed interested in the soldiers' walkie-talkies. They faked broadcast interviews, calls for help. There was a lot of horsing around, a lot of ribbing, a lot of interest in rock music, country western, newspaper and magazine special editions for the Olympics.

Looking at the East Germans, I recalled that after Team Canada's first-game loss to the U.S.S.R. in this same Montreal (September, 1972) one of the foolish raps put on the Soviet players was that they didn't enjoy themselves, that hockey to them was a fulltime job and that they weren't human but automatons. Shirley Babashoff was only voicing what was by now a standardized cold war lament. Writers and media people in Montreal picked her off for her lack of style. The displeasure with her grudging-cum-jealous response to the spectacular performance of Kornelia Ender was the subject of articles, columns, commentary, prompting—a month after the swimming events—this letter to the sports editor of the Los Angeles *Times* (Saturday, August 21, 1976):

"I would like to show you a different side of Shirley Babashoff. The girl I know has gotten up at 4:45 A.M. for the last four years. She has to drive for 30 minutes to work out and 30 minutes home twice a day. She has given up many of the social affairs that come with being a teenager in our country.... At 19, not many girls would be willing to come home at 12 from a party because of a training program. . . . She has been criticized by the press as being a snob, but the press is not all roses either. These kids are not trained for the tricky questions presented to them by many reporters. . . . Then you read an article that said Kornelia Ender said she was happy with a silver and someone said, 'That's class.' Yet when Shirley used those same words she was criticized.

"Today we went to Disneyland and I saw at least 30 people stop her for pictures or autographs, which she posed for and signed always with a smile. This is just a part of the story of Shirley Babashoff, who won four silver and one gold and did badly at the Olympics.

"Mrs. Babashoff
*Mother*
*Fountain Valley* [*California*]"

But the fact that Shirley Babashoff did not congratulate Kornelia Ender after the 200-metre final, and turned her back on the East German girls after the American women won the 4 x 100 metre relay, stood as not only bad form but perhaps the only real display of bad losing or bad winning during the Games.

[The *crowd* that was so down on Dwight Stones for his supposed anti-Quebec attitudes, and booed him when he received the bronze medal in the high jump, behaved badly. Stones congratulated Poland's Jacek Wszola and Canada's Greg Joy, the respective gold- and silver-medal winners. He turned up for a press conference. He sat outside the press conference room signing autographs for Boy Scouts and Girl Guides long after all other athletes had left the press area.]

Kornelia Ender was a bad target for Shirley Babashoff or anybody else, either as an athlete or as a representative of the unwomanly, no-joy East German socialist republic ideology pose. Her manners, for instance, were middle class, that politeness one finds throughout East Europe among people with a certain level of education. When Kornelia Ender bent her head forward to accept a gold medal on a gold chain she was the essence of high bourgeois courtesy. She shook hands like a nineteenth-century young woman out of finishing school, dipping her knee slightly, inclining her head a little.

She was, in that bourgeois tradition, betrothed and appeared in the Olympic Village and out of it in the company of her young man. He, Roland Matthes (who came to the Games as heralded as Shirley Babashoff, and met his Ender in John Naber) accompanied Kornelia in one of the gentler moments of the Games: her first meeting since she was two with her paternal grandmother, Mrs. Rosalie Lehmann, who now lives in the U.S.A. She had been brought to Montreal from the American Midwest by a Canadian television network to have a reunion with her world-famous granddaughter.

In the European bourgeois tradition, too, grandmother gave granddaughter a silver bracelet and a necklace, one an engagement present, the other to serve as memento of their meeting. Mrs. Lehmann said she decided to come to Montreal (though she had suffered three heart attacks in the preceding couple of years) because press reports of Kornelia's achievements told her nothing about what kind of *person* her granddaughter was. Through Kornelia she found out that she was to become a great-grandmother (Kornelia's older sister gave birth last August). Grandmother cried. Kornelia's eyes filled with tears. Grandmother knew what everyone else who had met Kornelia Ender knew: that this young girl, one of the great athletes of the 1976 Summer Olympics, was a very special person indeed. Barring injury, the first woman to break through the two-minute barrier in the 200-metre freestyle might well soon break through the one-minute barrier in the 100-metre butterfly.

Such was the nature of Olympic competition that on the very day Kornelia Ender flashed the image of her achievement, Nadia Comaneci of Rumania—destined to become The Face of the 1976 Olympics—put on an equally magnificent display in the Montreal Forum. Cheering spectators stood to acclaim her, shrieking bravos, demanding curtain calls as if Nadia were a ballet star exploding on the artistic scene with the force of a 14-year-old Maya Plisetskaya.

The second Olympic ring has to be filled with that face and that gesture everyone came to recognize—not from television alone: it became the cover photograph of publications around the world. There was the shy spunky smile, those bangs, that headband, those sparkling dark eyes. Nadia with her arms back above her head, her body arched, created an almost-pixie-image that blotted out 1972's pixie, Olga Korbut, who, more than any other single individual, had made women's gymnastics the glamour event of the Summer Olympics.

Olga was to suffer the fate of anybody who hangs around too long. She was applauded and appreciated, but only as a member of the chorus line. Women's gymnastics in Montreal needed only two people: Nadia and the U.S.S.R.'s *1976* star, Nelli Kim.

Nadia Comaneci dominated the Olympics because she was a revolutionary athlete. Her routines did not accept the limitations and strictures that went with being female. Many of the things she attempted, and performed, on the uneven bars moved her into the men's gymnastic area. Nadia Comaneci recorded seven perfect scores—10 out of a possible 10—during the gymnastic competition. The reason for those scores was clear. She did not do a 10 but an 11 or 12 routine. Nadia was fearless on the balance beam, spectacular on the uneven bars, never playing it safe. Olga Korbut suffered in 1976 not because Nadia Comaneci made people forget her. Worse, Nadia made everyone remember. And compare.

Both Nadia and Nelli Kim came on tough. Once Nelli, attempting something difficult she hadn't ever mastered, fell hard off the uneven bars, picked herself up quickly, swung right back into her routines. Nelli Kim, too, came up with perfect scores—one in the horse vault and one in the floor exercises—to put up against Nadia Comaneci's accomplishment. Once Nadia had scored one 10, the crowds at the Forum became hysterically committed to seeing her, or Nelli, do it again. And again. The cheers *demanded* perfect scores, not just from Nadia and/or Nelli, but from the gymnastic judges. With that kind of excitement in the Forum, what band of judges could resist unleashing the roars and cheers and standing ovations with another 10?

It was a deal only the "new" stars—Nadia and Nelli—were in on. Olga Korbut and her other talented teammate, the beautiful Ludmila Tourischeva, once considered the greatest gymnast in the world, came in, though only in their early 20's, as "old." They could score in the higher reaches—9.90, even 9.95 (recorded by Tourischeva twice)—but the 10's belonged to the new Olympic faces and styles. On the platform, above the number 2 that marked the silver-medal position, Tourischeva, glancing up at her teammate, Nelli Kim, the gold medalist in the floor exercises once regarded as Tourischeva's very own event, was the Olympics' mask of sorrow.

Nadia and Nelli told a realistic Olympic tale: competitors get younger and younger, better and better. Someone like Ludmila Tourischeva, born in 1952, by 1976 was an "older woman." In the earlier years of Tourischeva's career, a 9.90 would have won a gold medal. But no more. As she stood on the medal platform with Nelli Kim and Nadia Comaneci, the bronze-medal winner in the floor exercises (who would only be 18 when the 1980 Olympic Games were held on Tourischeva's turf, the Soviet Union), Ludmila wept. The difference between her silver and Nelli's gold was .025. The difference was concentrated in one score: Nelli Kim's single 10 in the final routine, for which Ludmila had been able to come up with only a 9.90. The judges had spoken. The spectators had made their preferences quite clear. Charisma, in Nadia and in Nelli, had to be garlanded with 10's.

The Rumanian gymnastic coach, Bela Caroly, pointed up the element he believed essential to Nadia Comaneci's competitive success. He had scouted children's playgrounds, looking for some tiny girl who showed "exceptional aggression." On one of those playgrounds, Caroly said, he spotted Nadia Comaneci, a scrapper. According to Caroly, Nadia loved mixing it up, and would force a fight—even with bigger kids. Again, in his own version of a Rumanian happy-ending tale, Caroly realized that all he had to do with Nadia's aggression and pugnacity was channel it. The small girl was naturally fearless and would try anything.

Fat is an enemy of good gymnasts, according to Caroly, and Nadia was lean, lithe, with an elegant grace. Caroly, to cap his

Pygmalion story, decided she would be his great champion. He took full credit for what her aggressiveness had accomplished.

Nadia's aggressiveness did not impress the equally aggressive Nelli Kim who, when asked to comment on Nadia's scores and medals, said: "Nadia Comaneci has good strength, she has good spring, but she cannot smile."

Nelli should have looked more closely at the cover photos of the world's leading magazines. On every one of them, a victorious Nadia Comaneci was exceptionally smiling.

In men's gymnastics, where no perfect scores were recorded, Nikolai Andrianov of the U.S.S.R. was, if anything, more impressive than Comaneci. Andrianov won four gold medals—in the all-around competition, the floor exercises, the rings, the horse vault—a silver in the team competition the U.S.S.R. lost to Japan by .40 points; a bronze in the side horse. More than that, Andrianov broke into areas the Japanese had dominated in past Olympic competition. He defeated Sawao Kato and Mitsuo Tsukahara, not only famed Olympic gold medalists in the past but innovators and perfectionists who had given their names to routines Andrianov carried close to perfection.

Andrianov worked deftly, with no charismatic flair. The cheers he received contrasted with the screams and shouting that greeted Nadia and Nelli. An even greater contrast lay in comparing the fates of Ludmila Tourischeva and Andrianov. They were roughly the same age (Andrianov was the younger) and had achieved great things in international competition before these Olympics. Tourischeva was totally surrounded by wonder-children; Andrianov had none to contend with. Because of the slow development of the muscular frame and skill required in men's gymnastics, the children's invasion had not yet begun. Chances are it would not; or, if young male Comaneci figures appeared, it would take them a long long time to develop the control Andrianov showed at his best on the rings.

Again, at 23, Andrianov would most certainly appear in world competition between 1976 and 1980, when he would doubtlessly be the defending champion in the major gymnastic

A view of the Olympic Stadium during the opening-day ceremonies, July 17, 1976. *(Ken Elliott)*

Mayor Jean Drapeau underneath the roof of the Olympic Velodrome. *(Canadian Press)*

Kornelia Ender, East Germany,
gold medalist in women's swimming.
(*Canadian Press*)

Graham Smith, Canada, won a
silver medal swimming in the
4 x 100 metre medley relay.
(*The Toronto Star*)

Shannon Smith, Canada, won a bronze medal swimming in the women's 400-metre freestyle. *(Canadian Press)*

Nikolai Andrianov, U.S.S.R., winner of four gold medals in men's gymnastics. *(Canadian Press)*

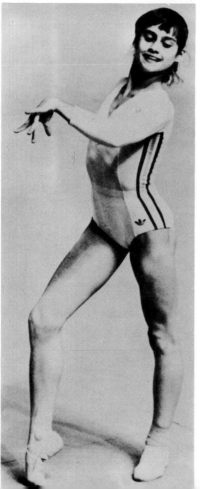

Nadia Comaneci, Rumania, won three gold medals and one bronze in women's gymnastics. *(Canadian Press)*

events. Tourischeva, on the other hand, was through. If she appeared in Moscow it would be as a noncompeting captain, say, or as a coach. She could contemplate 1976 as the year a 14-year-old outperformed and outcharisma-ed her, while no male equivalent turned up to haunt Andrianov. She could contemplate 1980 as a year some as-yet-unknown wonderchild—13, 12, or even 10 might turn up in women's gymnastics, while nobody in that age group would appear to sneak gold medals away from Andrianov, who might even be competing in 1984.

Andrianov, no matter how sensationally he had performed in 1976, was destined to be "Andrianov who?" to almost everyone but gymnastics aficionados: gymnastics in the Montreal Olympics meant Nadia and Nelli and, reduced even further, Nadia Comaneci alone.

If Nadia Comaneci had to share top billings with anyone at the Summer Games, her co-star in the third ring would be the U.S.S.R.'s greatest Olympic actor, wit, magician, camera subject, autograph target, quote source, perhaps the best-known athlete in the Montreal competition before competition began, the superheavyweight weightlifting champion of the world, Vasilyi Alexeev. Alexeev's arms measured the same as Kornelia Ender's waist. Standing next to him, Nadia Comaneci would have looked like one of the many dolls she herself took home as gifts from Montreal.

Alexeev's unchallenged superiority in his field, his scorn for those weightlifters who gobbled anabolic steroids and looked as if their badly bulged bodies had been outfitted at Rent-a-Muscle, gave his every move a wonderfully ironic tone. He was massive, yet pixie, a beetlebrowed basso profundo whose every blink and intake of breath inspired his worldwide audience to oooh and to aaah. During the early days of the Olympics, before the superheavyweight competition began, Alexeev was like a fishing vessel flocked after by hungry gulls. Thousands of people wanted to see him and only him, snap a picture (as a bonus), and leave Montreal. If women's gymnastics and both women's and men's swimming and the boxing program and track and field and men's and women's basketball held the very special places in the 1976 Games, only Kornelia Ender and Nadia Comaneci, from that cluster of glamour sports, emerged as individuals who could vie with the Alexeev image.

Ender and Comaneci appeared as soon as their events began; the nature of the weightlifting competition was orchestrated to make everyone wait for the star of stars to appear. Weightlifting started on the same day as swimming and gymnastics, but only one class of lifters could compete at St. Michel's Arena at one time. Slowly, then, and inevitably, the competition moved up from the lightest, 52 kilogram, class, through 56 kg, 60 kg, 67.5 kg, 75 kg, 82.5 kg, 90 kg, 110 kg, to the ultimate—Alexeev's class, 110+ kg, the realm of the 300-pounders.

The Arena was tiny, its seating capacity a mere fraction of the Forum's—Nadia Comaneci's existential theater—or Kornelia Ender's Swimming Pool. Stories of people being scalped to see Nadia competed with stories of those begging to be taken for 300 dollars, 500 dollars, or more, to see Alexeev in action. The night he appeared at the Arena was like a Hollywood première. The "beautiful people" had to be *there*. The Arena was charged with the excitement that met the first North American appearance of the great Kirov ballet star, Baryshnikov, or a one-time-only one-man show by Laurence Olivier.

Hundreds of photographers turned up to fight for the 60 positions the Arena people had prepared for them—one of the worst scrambles of the entire Olympics. Many of the camera people were shooting for magazine covers or page spreads or illustrations for feature articles. In many cases a photographer's professional life depended on what kind of pictures of Alexeev he would come up with. At one point four policemen tried to budge some French photographers who had ignored the seat assignments and simply asserted squatter's rights on the best front-row chairs in the house. The photographers would not move. The police gave up.

More photographers arrived, more pressures developed. Two back rows in the press section suddenly were lined with cameras. Outside, the shortage of tickets was so acute, the scalpers were scalping each other. A mass of Alexeev's people stood in the parking lot behind the Arena. Some sailed frisbees in the brilliant sunlight glancing off standing rainpools left from an early afternoon downpour. Inside, there was that nightclub listlessness of fans waiting for the headliner to come on. The Alexeev freaks didn't believe there would be any challenge to the champion of champions. They only wanted "those other people" to fail their lifts and get the hell off Alexeev's platform.

The night had its own orchestration. Nothing would hurry matters through to the appearance of Alexeev. Every competitor wanted his appointed camera time: the wringing of the hands in powder, the powdering of shoulders and thighs, the slow shuffling foot-drag through the resin. Some did a tiger-in-the-cage-pacing-back-and-forth act before turning to face the bar and its barbells. Others simulated painless childbirth with a series of set breathing exercises and contorted grimaces. Still others managed a Frankenstein confront with the bar and the audience, moving stifflegged and clumsy as if up on stilts. Gerardo Fernandez of Cuba, the only darkskinned man in the competition, didn't have brown powder to spread over his hands and body, and puffed up so much white stuff during his presentation that he came on like a mime. Fernandez also introduced a new thing into weightlifting: the *silent* primal scream. Lifting, he opened his mouth wide, his face distorted—but no sound came. The technique worked well enough for him to snatch 165 kilograms. But when the weight went up to 167.5, Fernandez did his giraffe call—and still lost his lift.

Jan Nagy of Czechoslovakia tried another tack, reciting, perhaps, an inspirational poem or sneaking in a nonsocialist prayer. He could have been mumbling a rollcall of all the East European lifters who had goofed and lost their athletes' special privileges. Nagy overprepped, maybe, or psyched his right side more than his left: the right side hup-hupped, the left side dragged behind. Nagy was out.

The parade of "others" continued. The room grew quieter. From time to time weights dropped to the platform in the invisible practice room thundered reverberatingly, like distant cannon. The writers, who usually had their television monitors on full blast, turned the sound off or on so low it couldn't be heard by the lifters. A light would glow on the Electroimpex Budapest scoreboard, showing who was up. Inevitably the light would go on for "Alexeev," Number 178, whose bodyweight on the program was listed as 156.80 kilograms—over 345 pounds.

With the snatch weights set at 175 kilograms, the door to the left of the platform opened and Alexeev finally emerged in a red lift suit (centered with his medal of the order of Lenin), wearing frayed pale pink elastic knee supporters, two-tone shoes (that emphasized the small feet of the huge man). The Arena was totally silent. Alexeev mounted the steps to the platform slowly, like a priest approaching the secret sanctum. He breathed through his mouth, blowing in, blowing out. He closed his eyes, backed against the platform's rear wall, faced the crowd, then blinked his eyes wide open as if closing them had been a mistake. He stepped forward, careful as a springboard diver, reached down with his right hand, wrapped his taped thumb around the bar, straightened up, went into a second trance, blinked his eyes open once more. Swiftly he reached down his left hand, then his right, and with a sudden explosion of speed, did his snatch, got the needed white lights from the judges, let go his weights, executed a deep nod and bow. His audience went wild, cheering, shouting, stomping, applauding. Flashbulbs strobed through the crowd.

Then those irrelevant others tried to get into Alexeev's act: Petr Pavlasek of Czechoslovakia, heavier than Alexeev, bearded, theatrical—and doomed to end tragic—staggered out after a failed lift like some olio villain pursued by hounds; cheery Gerd Bonk of East Germany seemed happy just to be on the same card as Alexeev; Sam Walker and Bruce Wilhelm of the U.S.A. gave the impression with every lift that serious injury was imminent; Jouko Leppa of Finland, if he partook of the blessings of blood wash, still couldn't get 160 kilograms up higher than his eyes, alas.

Finally the boys had retired, and the man, Alexeev, came on, programmed like a superstar. He waved aside mere victory and escalated Bonk's 235 kilograms not by 2½, 5, or even 10 kilograms. An Alexeev gold-medal lift had to set a world record. The electronic scoreboard sweepingly erased the amber "235," went dark, then flashed up "255." It took the crowd a second to realize the change. There was a loud collective gasp, then a cheer that didn't subside till Alexeev stepped rockingly out of the inner sanctum, his coaches and wellwishers gathered behind him like small unfurry toys.

Deliberate, unhurried by the time clock ticking down, Alexeev went through the trances and blinks and sags and sighs and sets. Then he bent over, his hands widely separated, brought the bar up swiftly, paused for a second, jerked the weights over his head, his elbows straight, his feet but momentarily staggered, then quickly aligned to get the white light from all three judges. "Down!" came the signal and Alexeev correctly let the weightman's burden go.

The arena reverberated. Shouts, olés, bravos. Alexeev, suddenly humble, bowed. Bowed again. Gave the judges a courteous nod, saluted his coaches and trainers with a courtly bow. The cheering increased. Alexeev, like Chaliapin stuck with a *Boris* of curtain calls, acknowledged the accolade with a low sweeping hands-crossed bow.

Later, for his press conference, Alexeev appeared on that same platform, muttering one-word answers to lengthy rambling questions. Or responding with fine wit:

"Now that you've won yet another Olympic gold medal, what would you like to do next?" someone asked.

"Now," said Alexeev, "I would like to win the weightlifting championship of my small village."

The fourth Olympic ring has to be filled with the face of Bruce Jenner, whose victory in the decathlon was perhaps the greatest individual accomplishment of the Games. Jenner and his wife, Chrystie, furthermore, introduced a new element into the Games—what victory means to a nice clean-cut American whose moves are being watched by Hollywood. Perhaps Shirley Babashoff's wretchedness toward Kornelia Ender's easy triumphs was related to Shirley's knowing that Mark Spitz, loaded down with gold medals after the 1972 Games, could have written his own ticket in Hollywood or New York. A triumphant 19-year-old California outdoor girl could have done almost as well. But Shirley didn't win, and Bruce Jenner did—spectacularly.

Bruce and Chrystie Jenner were what Hollywood fans and readers of Frank Merriwell dreamed of. They represented the All-American image of the good California life.

Both Bruce and Chrystie knew what could be gained by a smashing decathlon triumph. The toughest Olympic event was the means to their end: the world spotlight, movie contracts, testimonials, husband-and-wife commercials, any deal that needed "a name" up front. In track and field Jenner came on with a pre-Games build-up second only to John Walker (and the no-show Filbert Bayi). Feature articles, film clips, capsule interviews on radio and television, various sports profiles predicting winners preceded Jenner to Montreal. Half the world knew that Bruce and Chrystie Jenner lived with a hurdle right in the middle of their living room (Mac Wilkins, the discus champion-to-be for these Games, would have settled for a waterbed). Bruce was the Andy Hardy taller than Mickey Rooney; the James Dean who wasn't a rebel but had a great cause; the Wasp Portnoy without a single complaint.

Nine of the 10 decathlon events established Jenner as king. Running second in his 1,500-metre heat—the last decathlon event—Jenner came across the finish line, arms upraised, to a crowd that had been standing and cheering since he began his bell lap. As Jenner reached the line a happy young man waving a small American flag broke out of the stands with three Montreal policemen and a soldier in pursuit. The soldier had his gun out. They grabbed the man and took him away. Later Jenner said that when he looked up and saw the man coming toward him, he thought to himself, "I'm going to be killed." The man was only trying to get into the greatest Olympic victory act.

Jenner, a little shaken, took his winner's lap to an unstilled standing ovation, first walking, then running, finally waving to the crowd, throwing kisses at the stands. Near the end of his jog he saw Chrystie, tried to get her down from the stands, but the still-upset police wouldn't allow it. As Chrystie leaned out to kiss him, Jenner said he told her: "It's all over."

His words were more fitting for the end of an agony, a terrible illness, a long prison sentence.

More than any other Olympic event, the decathlon involves one individual in a contest with time, space, and gravity. He is faced with *10* stern tests, three of *how fast can you run?*, three more of *how far can you throw?*, two of *how high can you jump?*, one of *how far can you jump?*, and one more of *how fast can you run while jumping hurdles?*. The decathlon is a mini-track meet: in less than 36 hours, a single human body must be subjected to the varying demands of speed, endurance, and faultless technique (in seven different throwing or jumping events). The athlete training for the decathlon must develop his aerobic system, his anaerobic system, must condition his body to use up its energies economically, an erg at a time.

In Jenner's case, for example, an injury to a finger required a conscious effort to switch his delivery technique in the shot put, without throwing a new strain on an untrained muscle area which, in reaction, might produce further, yet more serious, injury. Ten events require 10 training programs harmonized to fit the field of combat, the decathlon athlete's body. For the Olympics, participants ordinarily train up in a single event. Sometimes two. Rarely three or more. Practice and preparation lead to the ultimate test on the Olympic field of grace: one event, one shot.

To win a gold medal, the decathlon athlete must score in all 10 events, and, indeed, finish in the top 10 of even his worst event (Jenner was never worse than seventh). He should, as Jenner was, be first, second, or third in his best events. The decathlon athlete is a medley track-and-fielder. Yet compare him with the medley swimmer (who combines freestyle and backstroke and breaststroke and butterfly) and the decathlon's extraordinary demands stand clear: a swimmer, even a medley swimmer, simply swims. A decathlon athlete does the whole track and field thing.

The combined decathlon body actions may not only not go together but may even work against each other. The leg muscles needed for the pole vault are not the same as those needed for the 1,500-metres or the 400-metres. The discus engages legs and arms differently from what is demanded in the shot put or the javelin throw. The legs that run the 100-metres are not the legs one develops for the high-jump approach, the 110-metre hurdles, or the long jump.

At his press conference after his medal ceremony, Jenner was asked one question: *"How did you do it?"* to which he responded in minute detail, uninterrupted (somebody did throw him a red snuff handkerchief with which to wipe his face) for well over 20 minutes. That recital revealed the decathlon athlete's fix: each knows precisely how well he must do to get the points assigned to each time, each distance, each height. In the course of his own preparation he learns about each of his main competitors. Out of statistical scraps that grow into a computer printout, he constructs his own grid of expectation. Here his best will do; here his personal best must be bettered.

"This is the last time I'll ever run in a meet," Jenner said in explanation of his driving performance in his final event, the 1,500-metre heat, "and I wanted to go out a winner."

He settled for second, but his total points for all events, 8,618, were a new Olympic and a new world record.

"I wanted to get 8,600," Jenner said. "The day I ran my first decathlon I decided this is what I wanted to do."

If other athletes are dedicated, the decathlon competitor is monomaniacal. Not only Jenner's day was circumscribed. His entire year was too. He would run at least 10 miles a day at first, then shorten his distance but pick up his speed as a meet approached.

"I only peak once a year. This [the Olympics] was the only meet I tried to peak for this year. I was very pleased I did all the work."

Chrystie entered the interview room, seemed concerned with what Jenner was saying.

"I'm very very sad to see it [the decathlon] go. It's been my whole life. . . . It's very difficult to keep going."

Jenner made clear the meaning of the Olympics for the decathlon:

"The only real challenge I had was the Olympics. There's nothing left for me. I set up goals for myself. I achieved every single one of them. . . . [it was] my destiny to win this thing."

Jenner spotted Chrystie, smiled.

"She's been working full time. So in a sense it's all over for the both of us."

It was also all over, one suspected, for New York Mets' All-American Boy pitcher, another Californian, Tom Seaver, and his All-American Girl wife, Nancy, who, for about seven or eight years had been the Mr. and Mrs. All-American Sport Homebodies. Bruce and Chrystie were coming. The music of the *cérémonie protocolaire* had barely finished before an agent was pushing Jenner as someone with "the looks of Robert Redford, the body of Tarzan."

The value of an Olympic gold medal to an East European athlete was estimated to be something in excess of 2,500 dollars: the reward for breaking a world record. The reward for double-wins, or triple, or quadruple, can't be guessed. Somebody from the West, like Lasse Viren, who took his shoes off after his victory in the 10,000-metres (and, in the company of two Finnish flag-wavers, did a victory lap for his sponsors, holding those shoes aloft), perhaps made 10,000 or 20,000 dollars out of that act. What was in it for decathlon bronze medalist Nikolay Avilov—1972's better buy as a gold—I can't say. He wore one orange shoe and one blue—either the most explicit superstition of the Games or the finest display of Adidas wares.

Yet put all the money spent by all the hustling athletic shoe and equipment companies together, and it might not equal the value of Jenner's decathlon gold medal. Bruce Jenner was the Mark Spitz of the 1976 Games.

To fill the fifth Olympic ring I turn to Canada, of whose negative accomplishment—the first host country not to win a gold medal—almost all Canadians, most Americans, and, indeed, most Olympic observers, were sharply aware. This ring is filled by Greg Joy, winner of a silver, not a gold. His achievement stood dramatically and emotionally as, perhaps, the high spot of the Games. The event it took place in—the high jump—wasn't usually that much more exciting than the pole vault or even the triple jump. It couldn't match the decathlon or the race programmed to produce the single most moving moment of the Olympics, the marathon (with its dramatic climax, the return to the Stadium of the runner leading).

*Time* was a factor in Greg Joy's emergence. The countdown had begun on the last day of track and field competition, July 31, 1976 (apart from the equestrian events in the Olympic Stadium on August 1, almost everything else was over).

*Expectations* were a factor in Greg Joy's performance: Canada, the host nation, had few anticipated winners in track and field. While the high-jump final was in progress, Canada's highest hope for a track and field gold, marathoner Jerome Drayton, fell back from the leaders. The massively magnified images on the electronic scoreboard above Greg Joy's head did not contain Drayton's image.

*Competition* was another factor. It seemed almost foolish to hold the high-jump event. The person chosen, all but unanimously, to win the gold, was the United States' great Dwight Stones, who had recently taken the world high-jump record up to 7 feet 7 inches (after the Olympics, Stones added a ¼ inch to his world record). Stones came into the Games as heralded as Lasse Viren, or U.S. marathoner Frank Shorter, or Cuban heavyweight Teofilo Stevenson, or U.S. pole-vaulter Dave Roberts—or Bruce Jenner.

In the New York *Times* special Olympic section of July 11, 1976, the high jump had the following predicted finish:

| | | |
|---|---|---|
| *First (gold):* | Dwight Stones (U.S.A.) | [*best jump, 7' 7"*] |
| *Second (silver):* | Jacek Wszola (Poland) | [*best jump, 7' 4 5/8"*] |

| | | |
|---|---|---|
| *Third (bronze):* | Bill Jankunis (U.S.A.) | [*best jump, 7' 3 3/4"*] |
| *Fourth:* | Sergey Senyukov (U.S.S.R.) | [*best jump, 7' 5"*] |
| *Fifth:* | Robert Forget (Canada) | [*best jump, 7' 4 5/8"*] |
| *Sixth:* | Rolf Beilschmidt (E. Germ.) | [*best jump, 7' 4 1/4"*] |

Greg Joy, whose best jump was, like Wszola's and Forget's, 7 feet 4⅝ inches, wasn't listed.

*Dwight Stones* was the main factor in Greg Joy's silver turning gold. In a Montreal indoor meet Stones had injured himself seriously because, he claimed, the landing mattress was placed in a wrong position. How that two-or-three-person mistake escalated into a war between Stones and the people of the province of Quebec wasn't clear. Diplomacy didn't engage Dwight Stones. Ask him a straight question, you get a long blunt answer. He had unnice things to say about the unfinished Montreal Stadium, the Quebec athletic facilities, and the manners of French Canadians. When he turned up in (a) the Stadium to use (b) the athletic facilities he soon felt (c) the manners of French Canadians in a new way. The audience at the west end of the Stadium—where the high jump was set—seemed overwhelmingly French Canadian. It booed Stones' name. It booed Stones getting ready to jump. It booed Stones jumping. And, when he missed, cheered.

It was as bad as booing a trapeze artist or a tightrope walker. Or greeting with loud boos the last putt of a contender on the seventy-second hole of the Master's Golf Tournament. One boos roller derby muggers, wrestler Barrymores, amateur comedians, but never Olympic athletes.

Montreal, the day before the high-jump finals, was in a lousy mood. First Stones was booed. Then the huge American contingent (over 3,000 alone brought on a *Track and Field News* junket) decided they weren't going to let the French Canadians get away with such breach of track meet etiquette. They saw a French Canadian name, Claude Ferragne, saw Ferragne suited up in the red and white colors of Canada, and had their hostage. French Canadians boo an American, Americans boo a French Canadian.

International and Canadian Olympic officials couldn't believe what was happening. Booing filled the Stadium. Ignored by all the shouting and howling was Greg Joy, whose name wasn't spelled "Joie." Stones did the qualifying height, 2.16 metres—7 feet 1 inch—despite the booing (I calculated his jump to have cleared the bar by at least four inches). He bounced up off the mattress, executed a grinning skip and dance while a few Canadian drunks rushed to the front row of a top deck, red-faced, screaming, shaking their fists at him. Several people who had been giving Stones their very best evil eye suddenly lost faith in the power of whammy. Stones finished off his little performance with a two-handed kiss thrown to the crowd—pure overkill. A few minutes later Ferragne sailed over the bar. The cheers were the day's second loudest (later, Jenner's roar meter would record perhaps the longest, loudest cheer of the entire competition).

By this time the unbooed athletes who failed the qualifying height might have thought there was magic in booing. In with the pack, Greg Joy made the qualifying height. All was ready for the morrow's final.

For that final, Stones turned up wearing a sweat shirt with *I Love French Canadians* on its back. The officials made him take it off (before the crowd recognized this was his kind of apology). A Japanese Canadian, holding a Canadian flag in his right hand, a Japanese flag in his left, and blowing hard on a referee's whistle, tried to get a little spunk into the Canadian cheering or booing. The drunks who had been hollering at Stones still managed a few scattered boos. Stones put his hand to his ear, trying to attract booing, it seemed. If he could tire the enemy now, he wouldn't have to cope with booing when heights reached the crucial medal stage.

It was his show completely. The Polish jumper, Wszola, cleared his first height. The action swung back to Stones. Now it wasn't his sweatshirt the officials wanted removed: Stones was jumping in a 1972 U.S.A. uniform—white gym shirt, black pants. The officials insisted he wear the red shirt of 1976's Olympic team. He protested, but complied.

On the electronic display board the marathoners showed up from time to time. It was raining where they were, and in the Stadium too.

Stones, instead of passing the lower heights, jumped, either for the psychological reason I've already mentioned (to psych out his "enemies" in the stands) or to get used to the rain and the slippery footing. The sky over Montreal was dark, the lights in the Stadium roof glowed strangely, spotlighting a cone of rain slanting in on the high-jump action.

That exciting Olympic counterpoint was in progress—the men's and women's relay finals taking place on the track, the marathon race getting closer and closer to the Stadium, the high jump slowly but inevitably reaching the heights that first-day qualifiers at the 2.16-metre mark might find impossible to leap.

To make things more exciting, the dream race that never was, the men's 1,500-metre final, was run shortly after 6:00 P.M., when the high jump had entered its first higher-than-qualifying phase, the bar set at 2.18 metres (7 feet 1⅞ inches). There was victorious John Walker in the familiar black New Zealand track suit, the almost-afro hair, the beads; somewhere on that wet track was the number-one ghost of the Olympics, the absent Filbert Bayi (whose world record for the 1,500-metres was almost *seven* seconds faster than John Walker's gold-medal winning 3:39.17).

While John Walker was taking his victory lap, Greg Joy made his third attempt at 2.18 metres, and cleared. At this precise moment, 6:11 P.M., the electronic board showed Frank Shorter running first in the marathon, Canada's Jerome Drayton running about fourth, with someone called Waldemar Cierpinski (East Germany) right behind him.

The bar in the high jump went up to 2.21 (7 feet 3 inches). Dwight Stones made the height easily and, without pausing, dashed off the landing mattress to get in out of the rain. In only a few minutes Greg Joy made 2:21. Canada seemed for the first time to be a participant in the track and field competition: up on that huge board who was in the marathon lead but Jerome Drayton?

A few seconds later, the U.S.A.'s Bill Rodgers (serving, it seemed, as Frank Shorter's pace setter), Shorter, and Lasse Viren passed Drayton, who remained in contention. Rodgers seemed to be working as Shorter's blocker, not letting Cierpinski or anyone else pass to take over the lead. On the monitors, the streets of Montreal were gleaming wet, reflecting car lights, street lights, the distorted blips and flashes of police and ambulance beacons striking the rain-pierced puddles. In the Stadium, rainwater gathered everywhere, but the important spot was the west end, where pools such as those the children had sloshed through on July 16 were beginning to gather. Attendants started sweeping the water to the side—fruitlessly. And absurdly. If they cleared the approach for one jumper they only succeeded in watering the run of another.

There were no dry spots anywhere. A jumper contemplating his approach for his allotted three minutes would be soaked, soggy of hair, soggy of shoe. Out on the streets, spectators watching the marathon were huddling four or five under some-one's tiny umbrella.

At 6:43, Canada's Jerome Drayton decided it was now or never, and took over the marathon lead again. The United States men's relay team a minute or two later won the 4 x 100 metre race (in a rain-ridden run just .14 seconds shy of the world record). A minute after that, Jerome Drayton discovered it was not to be "now." Frank Shorter, just as everyone expected, swept into the lead. The East German, Cierpinski, an uninvited guest, came right along with him. On the track, Cierpinski's teammates, the women's 4 x 400 metre relay runners, ignored the falling rain to set a smashing new record of 3:19.23—Olympic *and* world.

By 7:00 P.M. the high-jump competition had reached 2.23 metres (7 feet 3¾ inches). Dwight Stones was up. He examined the approach—an obstacle course of randomly located rain-fed pools. On his first try, Stones—who was given a great hand by the Americans and other spectators as he emerged from shelter —missed. He backed away from the bar, examining every inch of the approach. Track attendants in plastic rainhoods were sloshing away busily. Stones was not amused by their redistribution of water.

On our desk monitors in the Stadium we could see close-ups of those pools at a jumper's feet. They were obviously dangerous. Just as obvious was the uselessness of the new clean-up brigade applying vacuum water-sucks to the artificial clay. When we switched closed-circuit channels we discovered what the Stadium spectators had not yet been shown on the electronic board: that Frank Shorter, though the marathon leader at 30 kilometres, was swinging his head from side to side, laboring, "breaking up," as the descriptions of the race might have it. Past him, and running easily, was Cierpinski.

Stones by this time, 7:15 P.M., had grown exasperated at the job the squeegee-ers and vacuum-ers were doing. He took hold of the squeegee and began shunting streams of water off his own approach. The water could go only over into other jumper's approaches. Several more jumpers got into the water-slopping act.

Out on the marathon course kids on bikes were following the leading runners, spraying water in the wake of their wheels. Cierpinski's face was dripping wet. Runners looked like uniformed basketball players just pitched into a shower in celebration of some title won.

With eyes on the board (that announced again and again the coming of Cierpinski), with eyes on the high jump fixed almost exclusively on Dwight Stones, the spectators suddenly realized that Canada's Greg Joy was up. The cheering picked up slowly, then rose to an encouraging rumble. The Japanese Canadian cheerleader roused himself to blast out the parade marshal's whistle beat, some kids hollered a rehearsed "Go, go, Canada!"

And Greg Joy, on his first try, sailed over the bar, but somehow struck it on his way down. In a few seconds Stones rushed out again and began squeegeeing and pit-bossing the ineffectual clean-up crews. By 7:30 P.M. he was involved in some procedural hassle with track officials, and the victorious U.S.A. men's 4 x 400 metre relay team—finally having beaten Cuba's anchorman, Alberto Juantorena at something—was taking its bows in an easy lope around the track. The East German women's 4 x 400 metre relay team entered for their gold-medal ceremonies. The East German anthem was just fading when East Germany's Cierpinski made that dramatic entrance into the Stadium—all alone.

Stones kept up his colloquy with the officials, but, in out of the rain Greg Joy, wearing his warm dry sweatsuit, and Poland's Jacek Wszola, similarly muffled, merely watched. At 7:44 P.M. Dwight Stones, who on a warm day might have passed all heights before this one, made his final try at 7 feet 3¾ inches— and missed. Only a few dyspeptics in the crowd booed. But those were the people Stones heard: as he came off the landing pad he said, "Now they'll be happy."

As soon as Stones missed, Greg Joy was up, out of his sweat-suit, walking off his approach—step step, then the imagined soar as he brought his hands up in front of him. Following Stones' lead, Joy took the water rake out of the attendant's hands. Everything was confusion. Up in the stands, people—mostly Americans, it seemed—started to leave. In less than an hour their two cinch gold medalists had come up trailing. Dwight Stones' loss could be blamed on the French Canadian boos—but rain did not account for what had happened to Frank Shorter.

Suddenly Greg Joy stopped swabbing. Again he measured his approach, then moved back as encouraging cheers died down. The Stadium was quiet. It was his last try at the height that had stumped the world record holder. It was almost 8:00 P.M.. The Olympic football (soccer) final was scheduled to go on in the Stadium. Every other track and field event was over. The Olympics were almost over.

Loping, bounding, Joy went toward the bar, his hands rising just as they had in his shadow jump. Up up he rose, his head up, then arched back, his body following in a flowing line, his legs thrown up to avoid the bar. Over!

He had done it. Joy threw his arms up as though he were indeed the gold medalist. The crowd cheered and chanted as, up to that time, nothing short of a gold inspired. All over the

Stadium ushers and guides screamed and hollered. The officiating Canadians cheered.

This *was* a gold. Not, as logic choppers might have it, a *gold* gold. This was, instead, the gold of fruition, of just deserts, of good reward. It was almost irrelevant when Jacek Wszola made 2.25 (7 feet 4½ inches) on his second try, landing on his knees as if praying, jumping up, pounding the take-off spot just as Grey Joy ran up to congratulate him. Joy missed his try at that height and then two more at 7 feet 5¼ inches, which Wszola missed too. Arm in arm Wszola and Joy left the competition area, cheered by a crowd growing wet as wind blew rain into the seats. Dwight Stones, a magnificent athlete, was much more to be pitied than censured. He had knocked the Olympics from the very beginning. His reward for three and a half hours' work in the rain was anti-climactic: a bronze medal.

Wszola of Poland won the gold. But as Greg Joy stood receiving his silver, waving back at the deliriously happy crowd, he could consider himself the grand Canadian champion of the 1976 Summer Olympics. It was long past 8:00 P.M., the rain was still beating down on those spots the jumpers had but recently considered private turf. Puddles spread to meet puddles in wide, pelted pools. Joy's sweatsuit was no longer dry. He and Wszola left the medal platform together, after all three medalists had shaken hands warmly. Greg Joy's win was the finest Canadian moment of these Olympics.

# **5** *Tinker, Tailor, Promoter, Pusher, Rock Star, Pop Star, Film Star, Deb...*

In the Jet Setter's Calendar of Big Happenings the Olympics appear once every four years, the time scheme for the United States Democratic and Republican presidential nominating conventions. In the middle of July the phasing out of the Democratic Convention in New York City coincided with the phasing in of the Montreal Games. The Beautiful People could flit from one town to the other and not miss a Hustle beat.

Both New York and Montreal were suffering from the battered-city syndrome; New York's was the divine unction stage, Montreal's that still manic what's-another-billion-bucks-more-or-less blast which precedes total financial breakdown. The cities vied for top billing as prime pleasure centers. One could start just about anything in New York and expect to finish it in Montreal. Many of the planes rising in New York converged on Montreal. Montreal was the destination of hundreds of jets taking off in London, Paris, Berlin, Rome, Moscow, Tokyo, Rio—and Los Angeles, Chicago, Toronto, Calgary, Vancouver, too.

New York and Montreal were so close a high-rating prime-time TV star like Telly "Kojak" Savalas could flash his topless brow in the VIP section of the Democratic Convention, grin that familiar barcar-joke smirk, then pop up a night or two later in the not-quite-VIP section of the Olympic Swimming Pool. For a P.R. agent to stage something like the Olympics specially for his star would be expensive; yet here was a ready-made "scene," full of souvenir snatchers, autograph wanters—most of them more aware of a Telly Savalas than of even a Nadia Comaneci. Someone like Mick Jagger, a crypto-jock interested in and quite knowing about the Olympic events, could get the same 60 percent of the North American viewing audience watching Savalas on Olympic television.

The Olympics are great publicity theater. Among its 6,000 to 8,000 media people, at least 1,000 normally are not much concerned with athletics. Their usual interests—politics, economics, cultural events, society settings, business, entertainment—could be nudged by any knowing operator from the world of international happenings.

Montreal, then, was a model of how a great event is *used* (by people from a hundred different seemingly unrelated milieus). All over the city—in hotels, motels, condominiums rented out for the two weeks (or, more usually, an entire month), and houses (vacated by owners or tenants because a decent-size

place might bring from 3,000 to 7,000 dollars for July)—
"hospitality rooms," "hospitality centers," "hospitality suites"
were set up by commercial enterprises ranging from those with
an intimate connection to the Olympics to those with no
connection at all. Any organization could use hospitality to
reward its sales people or executives; to "romance" (a big word
in the business lexicon these days) its customers or clients. With
the media already in Montreal, it was a great place to introduce
a new product, a special offer, a tie-in deal.

I've already mentioned the shoe-display victory lap of
barefoot Lasse Viren after he won the 10,000-metres (after the
5,000-metres, Viren, perhaps because he had paid his dues once
or perhaps because the Montreal papers had derided his
commercialism, kept his shoes on his feet): his was but a grain
in the vast desert of sporting-goods involvement with Baron de
Coubertin's amateur special. Even before the Games began,
competition between Adidas and all other shoe manufacturers
was heavy. Moves would be followed by countermoves: few
European photographers or sportswriters appeared without a
black multizippered "Pony" gadget-bag or "Puma" shoulder-
tote. The "Nike" people entered the competition. I was told of
one East European journalist who had received (in actuality and
in promises of what would be delivered to him at home) *nine*
pairs of shoes.

Halfway through the Games, Puma suddenly discovered it
was surfeited with puma logo shoulder bags it subsequently
distributed to the "written press." A bagman for a sporting-
goods concern was sent to Montreal to distribute a fixed
amount of money to "sponsored" medalists (but the story
broke on CBS television). Whether this was a unique or typical
situation depends on how you register on the naïveté scale. The
amounts to be distributed were tied into the high-medium-low
profile factor of medal winners: a "high gold," for instance,
could expect about 10,000 dollars if her or his product-
identification factor was in working order.

Throughout the Games those who had the time or the
inclination to do a Woodward and Bernstein investigative job on

payoffs could have simply found out what athletes were *not* living in the Olympic Village; where they *were* living; who was paying the rent. They would also have discovered something else: that the sporting-goods outfits were no better at predicting Olympic gold-medal winners than most journalists. Oftentimes the investment—which ran into thousands of dollars—was lavished by a firm on someone who did not even qualify for finals.

Next to the sporting-goods firms were the photographic-equipment outfits, who kept some contact with the photographers from the day each arrived to the day each departed. Nikon was the most active partygiver and equipment-lender, its education-cum-sales-pitch presentations relentless. Cannon and Kodak ran a close second, with Kodak setting up a developing and printing service that catered to the photographers' needs. Swiss Timing was another conspicuous commercial presence throughout the Games.

On television and off, Coca-Cola, an approved supplier *and* sponsor, was ubiquitous. One could hardly touch a button or a lever in the Olympic Village, International or Press centers, without getting a gush of Coke. Xerox was the commercial outfit the written press encountered most frequently: all line-ups, all start lists, all result sheets, all statistics résumés bore the Xerox logo. During a full day one might receive as many as a hundred sheets from Xerox copiers. RCA television consoles were everywhere: writers sitting at assigned tables in the various sports centers could watch, in addition to the French and English networks of the Canadian Broadcasting Company and ABC, nine other closed circuits doing remote transmission from all the sites of action.

Almost every hour of the evening, sometimes at breakfast, less frequently at lunch, some Olympic sponsor would give a party (much booze, little food) featuring slide shows, Dale Carnegie chats, demonstrations by technical experts, and friendly greetings acted out by 10 or 12 Dorothy Hamils and about the same number of Mark Spitzes. The Cannon camera reception, for instance, used all the approved techniques in the selling syndrome but left room for a short speech by its top executive which stressed offers of assistance (an accredited photographer could borrow several thousand dollars' worth of motor-drive equipment and the latest innovations in telescopic lenses) while calling everyone's attention to:

    (a) the location of the bar

    (b) the location of the slide show busy alternating shots of the Cannon camera with shots of the camera's indoors and outdoors work.

Electronic alternatives to pain-killers were demonstrated for the press, both *in vacuo* and *in vivo*. A young woman journalist who had wandered into the Complexe Desjardins looking for free food (almost always available somewhere) found instead instant relief from pain in her recently sprained ankle. As far as I was able to discover, no manufacturer of anabolic steroids put a mesomorph on display. Nor did any pharmaceutical house hand out (publicly) samples of its latest in amphetamines.

Aramis, that powerful pungent lasting "male" cologne, won the Ubiquitous Award in Montreal. Tons of the stuff must have been handed out to Olympic athletes and journalists. One entered an elevator at one's peril: brushing against an Aramis wearer was a civet disorder. That odor of macho sanctity sat over Montreal for two weeks, like a heat inversion. Brut tried to get its man-scent into the dousing joust but wafted in a distant second.

Hundreds upon hundreds of other enterprises used the Olympics: in most hotel lobbies tables were set up to register guests, point to a hospitality suite, handle things like tickets to the Games, tickets to some of the cultural events, sightseeing, trips to the home office, local factory, or local display room. The hospitality package might include lodgings, food, transportation to and from the different Olympic sites, and a number of nights out on the town. Any executive or sales person would know how she or he stood if invited to partake of all the grand goings-on at the Olympics. Income tax regulations in most countries encouraged the use of hospitality suites to pep up productivity.

Untutored participants would settle for anything: a pre-liminary game, a heat, an elimination round. But prestige was directly proportionate to exclusivity: the power play a firm could come up with had to feature the glamour events and the glamour stars everyone knew about. Industries, commercial outfits, university organizations, fraternities, sororities, health clubs, jogging societies got points from scoring high in the hierarchy of events. That, of course, created pressure on track and field, women's gymnastics, swimming, weightlifting, boxing, basketball, which, combined with the opening and closing ceremonies, set up the ideal business climate for the promoter kings, the scalpers.

Big business—often the victim of scalping—should have been the enterprise's greatest admirers. Here was free enterprise at its best. Unregulated. Responding to the icons of Supply and Demand. Operating on the admired nineteenth-century law of "all the traffic will bear," plus the trick of "corner the market." It was one-shot—all or nothing (and always *all*).

One not only had to be at the Olympics; one had to be at the right places at the right times. [If all the people who have *seen* Nadia Comaneci and Kornelia Ender and Vasilyi Alexeev are toted up, they triple the capacity of the Forum, the Swimming Pool, and St. Michel Arena respectively.]

The magnificent performance of Bruce Jenner had been anticipated. Any number of people had come to Montreal with the decathlon as the number-one event they wanted to see. Anyone who could come up with tickets for July 29-30, the decathlon days, was demonstrating both power and influence. In track and field anyone with a chance at a world record stood as a glamour figure. Everyone world-famous and discussed in the pre-Olympic profiles had a following. Among the Americans, Dave Roberts and Earl Bell and Dwight Stones and Mac Wilkins could have popped new world records. People wanted to see if Alberto Juantorena of Cuba was real. Irene Szewinska, who had a fabled career as an Olympic sprinter, created all kinds of interest in her new event, the 400-metres.

John Walker, even without Filbert Bayi, was a runner everyone wanted to see. And on a par with Walker were young Nadia Comaneci in gymnastics and 1972's sentimental favorite, the U.S.S.R.'s Olga Korbut. The two of them created a huge demand for Forum tickets; gymnastics was a scalper's dream. Equally pressured was weightlifting on the night Vasilyi Alexeev would go for a world superheavyweight record at St. Michel Arena. In the Swimming Pool the top attractions were Kornelia Ender and the entire American men's swimming team. The demand for seats here was huge too: any firm or organization that could produce seats for the evening finals had it made.

By 1976 business firms, organizations, and scalpers realized long before the Games began that boxing would be a fan focus, and basketball; one could score well with Europeans, say, by delivering tickets to the football finals. Or to either the women's or the men's volleyball finals. A knowing scalper understood not only demand in general but realized the connection between certain social classes and certain sports, and, as sharply, the connection between certain nations and certain sports.

Canada, the host nation, and the United States (which, because of its huge contingent of spectators present at the track and field events, the boxing matches, swimming and diving, basketball, almost seemed to be co-host) were novices and—I must say it—amateurs in many of the sports. The modern pentathlon, for instance, found Canada occupying three of the last four positions in the individual competition. The combined American and Canadian accomplishment in cycling was negligible. In fencing, nonexistent. In handball and field hockey, token.

The Soviet Union, "winner" in both the medal category and in the various schemes of awarding points, had the largest number of athletes at the Olympics—526 marched in the opening day parade. It was able to field a participant in almost every Olympic event. Yet certain sports were quite clearly "Russian," while others were not: gymnastics, weightlifting, volleyball, football-soccer, basketball (for only the second time a significant Soviet Olympic sport), handball, women's track and field, shooting, modern pentathlon, were obviously U.S.S.R., "Russian." Others, like the equestrian events and yachting, were in the initial stages of redevelopment. Still others, like swimming and diving, were events the Russians will probably excel in during the 1980 Moscow Games, and after. Field hockey was no more a Russian than it was an American thing.

When Soviet fans arrived in Montreal in the Aeroflot specials put on for the Games, they clustered around gymnastics and weightlifting, volleyball and soccer. French fans, however, were more concerned with the equestrian events, and with cycling and fencing. West German interest was centered on the equestrian events too, which brought together the upper classes of Europe and North and South America (as well as Australia and Japan). The West Germans were much in evidence at the Olympic Stadium during the track and field competition, but in football, the national sport—in which the country has been at or near World Cup championship top ranking for years now—the West Germans found (like the Dutch or the British or the Brazilians in football, the Americans in basketball, the Canadians in Olympic hockey) most of their best players classified as professional and thus ineligible for the amateur Olympics.

True national aficionados, therefore, wouldn't attend the Olympic events of their select "professional" sport because the brand of competition was far inferior to what could be seen in regular league play at home among contending national and international teams. More frequently, however, national identification with a sport was explicit: the Bulgarians, for instance, clustered around the field events of track and field competition and, again, around weightlifting. The Rumanians also went for the field events and weightlifting, but gymnastics was the Rumanian thing.

The people at the different sites for the different sports could, on the whole, have been picked out of a police line-up and identified as this sport's or that sport's fan. Class, as I've already suggested, and style proved to be extranational. One could not have dragged an equestrian writer or broadcaster into the sweaty stews of freestyle wrestling. The Bromont crowd expected, wanted, and got not only the Queen but the entire Royal Family. Horses and yachts attracted horsy and yachty people. Some of the European writers sent by papers and magazines to do the equestrian events and/or yachting entered the Olympic Stadium only when the Queen made an appearance (some stretched their involvement and came to the closing ceremonies, even when the Queen didn't). Otherwise they avoided the plebeian places.

Nor did one find, say, judo enthusiasts at Bromont, though the jumping events were staggeringly simple for the judo mind accustomed to its immaculate differentiations between a *yuko* and a *koka* and a *waza-ari* and an *ippon*. In those equestrian jumping events either the horse knocked over a barrier or it didn't; either it splashed up water or it didn't; either it did its stint in the time allotted or it didn't. Every horse and every rider knew the difference between a did and a didn't.

Many of the judo participants and, so it seemed, even a few of the officials had rather vague notions of what a move or a warning or the system of scoring meant. Not so the spectators, totally involved with the grabbing and pulling and tripping and rolling-from-under. They hollered and grunted, in contrast with the horse spectators, who sat silently and restrained their oohs and eeks as the horses stumbled, riders fell, and sometimes ended pinned under their mounts, in imitation of judo.

Similarly, boxing fans would be hard-tested by the decorum of dressage watchers. No shouts of "Atta girl" (addressed to horse or rider) could be countenanced in the midst of such niceties as sidling, hoofmanship, tail prink-up, marginal prancing, and extraordinary kidney restraint. The top hat and the dress riding coat and silk ascot of the dressage competitor would be a little freaky at the fights unless, of course, the costume were some new twist in ringmaster get-ups.

Context, at the Olympics, was everything. As long as a particular sport buff occupied restricted turf, everything was okay. For the most part, the Olympics operated on the principle of "to each his own." But it wasn't economical for either a media representative or a spectator to settle for observing only one event. Therefore, the Olympics had many a weightlifting writer, say, turn up to watch field hockey or try to understand the issues in dressage. A Bulgarian I met at Bromont told me:

"Horse, only horse, horse should get gold medal."

An American from the Detroit area who was delighted to get free Olympic tickets, then found they were for preliminary fencing matches, described the foils events she witnessed as something between two electrified suits of armor set up for animation on a story board (presumably aimed at the Saturday morning television watchers of "Tom and Jerry" cartoons). There was, it's true, a certain sameness about the thrusters and parriers' pattern of *shuffle shuffle stamp stamp—lunge—pull off the mask—lament or exult.* The exciting part of most confrontations I found to be the victory toss-in-the-air which had a Jimmy-the-Greek factor built into whether the champ, landing, would be caught.

A couple of writers who had been forced to watch team handball came out screaming (they were obviously hockey fans):

"For chrissakes, doesn't the goalkeeper *ever* make a save?"

For my own part, I found salvation in the philosophical stand that one can't be in more than one place at one time: not dressage, not fencing, not team handball made a convert out of me in Montreal. Judo I regarded as an interesting slack-season variation on the clothing-store puller routine, in which salesmen from adjacent *schlockhouses*, having no customers to drag in, yank at each other's lapels in a do-or-die struggle as to who tugs whom into whose doorway. The judo floorwork didn't get to me much either. In that number the small round fatty always ended up playing turtle, while over him thrashed a seven-foot incompetent clearly unable to tell head from tails.

Water polo is a game that requires one adjustment: the spectators should be watching underwater. Not only is the action below water level, but, underwater, one would be released from that incessant and hideous whistle-blowing (that ostensibly saves many a player from drowning). Water polo is the only sport that threatens death as part of a defensive game plan. The contest itself features bobbing white hats and bobbing black hats trying to inflict reciprocal water-on-the-lung on each other in pursuit of a seemingly slippery ball (while a relatively dry referee stands on the sidelines and blows). Once in a while the water polo ball is thrown, shoved, or nosed into the goal. The game, however, had one thing in its favor: along with field hockey and team handball, it was guaranteed to be completely scalper-free.

Regardless of whether a sport was popular with scalpers or not, the same network of officialdom, in greater or smaller numbers, attended its operation. Each sport was under the aegis of an international sports federation—one for swimming, one for track and field, one for boxing, etc., etc. Each nation had its own sports federation for each of the sports in which it participated. In addition, each nation had its own national Olympic federation.

That adds up to a lot of officials. Of all the federations, the international sports federations in track and field, the equestrian sports, yachting, and swimming had the greatest impact on the Games, socially. An international sports federation (and the International Olympic Committee) is an excellent spot for exiled royalty to practice the ceremonial. Sports federations also serve a once-every-four-year function of allowing an octogenarian bearing a recognizable international robber-baron family name to stand tiptoe and buss a young woman gymnast or swimmer (the women's field-event winners the officials shook hands with).

With so many distinguished officials in town, many of them less interested in sports than in their credentials, an Olympic society calendar was needed to accommodate important after-hour social needs. Hostesses and hosts, usually out of town in

July, were imminent and generously available. The total cost of feeding and watering para-dukes and meta-aristocracies, though impressive, seemed paltry in comparison with the money Mayor Jean Drapeau's builder friends and associates ate up.

Many of those same Drapeau people were medium-rated on the local social scale—just above a shoe-firm sponsor, just below an insurance executive with a hospitality suite. They also served on the community-service front with local politicians, chamber of commerce and board of trade officials, crowding in under the Montreal social umbrella.

The clotted social calendar resulted from many countries represented in the Olympics wanting to have a national party. The pattern for entertaining was simple: a consular official from some country or a trade representative, a business official, a Montrealer (once resident in that country) would host a huge party honoring:

(1) a high political figure (in Montreal for the Games)
(2) a relative of a high political figure who didn't make it
(3) a high International Olympic Committee member
(4) a high International Sports Federation officer from the country
(5) the highest national sports federation officer from that country
(6) the country's Olympic team members.

The guest list would be sure to include the consuls of most other countries represented in Montreal, the Commissioner-General of the Games, Roger Rousseau and his wife, and whatever string of social lights were available. Competition for celebrities was brisk, resembling the stake a stop on the professional golf tour has in "getting" a Bob Hope or an Andy Williams or a Glen Campbell.

On our model night, Friday, July 23, parties were being thrown by the Mexicans, the Danes, the Egyptians, the Greeks. Celebrities were plentiful in Montreal, the celebrity of celebrities being Her Majesty, Queen Elizabeth II—and her family, gathered on Canadian soil for the very first time. Nobody Mexican, Greek, Egyptian, or Danish was able to get the Queen out to a party Friday night. The night before she had been the star of a dinner party on the royal yacht *Britannia.* The next night she and members of her family would be the honored guests at a state dinner given by Prime Minister and Mrs. Pierre Elliott Trudeau at the Beaver Club in the Queen Elizabeth Hotel.

By Friday, July 23, the queens of Montreal were Olympic stars Kornelia Ender, Nadia Comaneci, and Nelli Kim, but none of them appeared at the society parties. The members of the Mexican Olympic team, the Danish team, the Egyptian team, the Greek team did turn up at their respective national parties.

A society writer for Montreal or other newspapers had as tough a time covering all the parties as Mr. and Mrs. Roger Rousseau. For the Danish party, which was held at the Mount Stephen Club (also the location for the Greek party), the Danish Ambassador, His Excellency Hans Tabor, and his wife joined Montreal's Consul-General, Erling Birger Abrahamson, and his wife in hosting a relaxed affair for the Danish athletes.

If one examined the newspaper accounts of the parties it became clear that Egypt and Denmark failed the food, drink and celebrity tests. Neither party got much space. Neither party was the source of society quotes.

By Friday any reporter, social or otherwise, would know that the function of a journalist was to gather "quotes," i.e., obvious responses to routine questions. By Friday the word "quotes" was, in the singular, a kind of Hemingway locution: a couple of American journalists were hoping a certain athlete wouldn't win a gold medal because she was "a bad quote."

The newspaper versions of the parties worth staying at—the Mexican and the Greek—indicated that social quotes from all over were on a par with sports quotes. Mrs. Rousseau at the Mexican party told of having been at the Queen's party aboard the *Britannia* (a nice casual way to score social points). She told of having "quite a conversation with Prince Andrew. He's outstanding for his age."

Other quotes originated with Mr. Alberto Avila, former Mexican Consul-General: ". . . it's great to be back." A quote from the Greek party sounded like a publicity release. It emanated from Mr. George Savidakos, vice-president of the Greek Community:

"Saturday night our dancers will perform at the Place des Nations of Man & His World at the same time our pavilion there is being opened."

The quote-gatherers didn't do much better at the next night's state dinner, even though the Queen was but one of 2,000—*two thousand*—predinner reception guests of the Prime Minister and Mrs. Trudeau. One of the 200 stay-for-dinner guests was quoted as saying:

"The dinner was out of this world."

The dinner menu read:

> *Beavertail soup*
> *Fillet of sole*
> *Stuffed quail*
> *Pureed artichoke hearts*
> *Wild rice*
> *Peaches MacMillan*

Clearly, for many of the guests, the Prime Minister's dinner was the high point of the Olympics, far more important than any of the athletic contests to which one came as mere spectator. The social events surrounding the Games were not for sportsmen, not even for athletes, coaches, or shoe salesmen. The subject (and object) of society is society. With a week of finals and great events to go, many, having been at the Queen's party, left Montreal surfeited. The Olympic Games had fulfilled their social function—as all spectaculars must—of bringing together in a special place at a special time the special people.

The national parties could come up with a consul or an ambassador, but the gala parties featured royalty, society, cabinet ministers, philanthropists, senators, jet-setters, glamorous beautiful people. At the Trudeau party celebrities flowed. No matter what field a guest cultivated, she or he had to achieve something special to make it into the presence of the Queen.

Her Majesty knew Prime Minister Trudeau's dinner was Montreal's peak social event. She wore a diamond tiara that

Japan, winner of women's gold medal in volleyball, seen here defeating
Hungary. *(Canadian Press)*

Benjamin Peterson of the U.S., silver medalist in the 90-kilo freestyle wrestling category, punishing Bulgaria's Choukri Lutviev. *(Canadian Press)*

Canada's basketballers lost to the U.S.A., eventual gold-medal winners.
(*Canadian Press*)

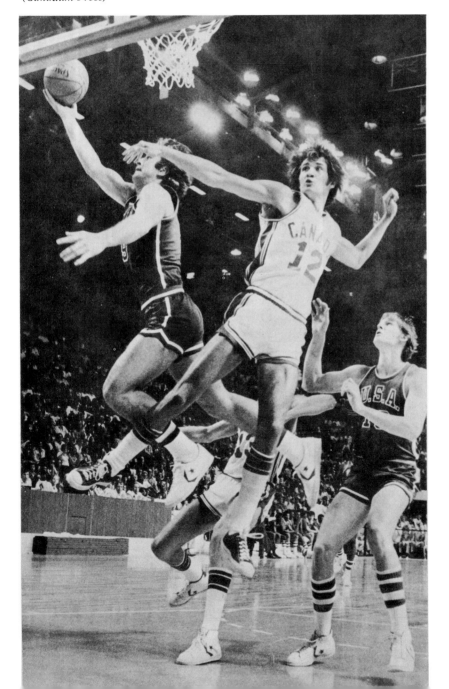

Vasilyi Alexeev, U.S.S.R., gold medalist in the
superheavyweight weightlifting division.
(*The Toronto Star*)

Mac Wilkins of the U.S.A. hurls the discus 67.50 metres for a gold medal.
(*Canadian Press*)

made her look very much a queen—in contrast to the unflashy outfits she wore at the Olympics. The emeralds and diamonds at her throat (and over her elbow-length queenly white gloves) reinforced the impression that the Queen meant state business. Her brilliant green and white gown went well with Madame Léger's unflashy basic black or Margaret Trudeau's southern-belle pale pink, pale green flowers of silk.

Mayor Drapeau didn't stop in at many of the national parties. That he left to Roger Rousseau. But for the Big Ones, he and his wife always took their places in the *cérémonie protocolaire.* Just as his opponents underestimated the effect Drapeau's formal appearances would have on Stadium spectators, so they failed to see the tremendous advantages of the station, Mayor of Montreal, in the formal hierarchy of state:

First came the Governor-General and his wife.

Next came the Prime Minister and his wife.

Then came the provincial Premier and his wife.

Finally came the Mayor of Montreal and his wife.

In other words, it was almost impossible for the Queen to appear in the city of Montreal *sans* Drapeau.

If Premier Robert Bourassa had thought himself rid of the Mayor he, too, discovered that in any formal protocol his neighbor was always Drapeau. Who would snub Jean Drapeau in his own home town? Whether the Prime Minister or the Premier was host to the Queen—whether the setting was the Place des Arts or a posh hotel ballroom—there was the Mayor. For Anglophiles, the Mayor turned up with the Queen; for Francophiles, with Governor-General Léger, or the less-than-delighted Premier Bourassa, or Prime Minister Trudeau. Or the hundreds—thousands—of Establishment figures, success stories, and donors-to-the-public-weal who thronged the big Olympic parties.

A spectacular like the Olympics is a good place for political fence-mending; political and other forms of career-building; social climbing, social escalating, social imperialism; charity pushing; ticket selling (to forthcoming society events). Social registry ultimately means being seen in the right places with the right kind of people. The Olympics provided just such a stage. It was, in addition, a clothes designer's dream set: 15 days and nights of partying, adding up to at least a dozen different ballgowns, a dozen different day outfits, sport clothes for the spectator hours, hostess gowns for the leisure moments, etc., for each society woman. If the society columnists were describing clothes (however sketchily), one could hardly have the same gown described more than once.

And so it went, parallel to the Games, tangential to the Games, a complete self-inclosed Second World—social, political, economic—sometimes touching the Olympic action, frequently quite apart but using the Olympics as the great international leap-year "there" to which everyone wanted to come.

The people at the society events, the international and national federation officials, the politicians, the promoters, had very little connection with the athletes. They had even less to do with those people who paid out precious primary ticket money so that they, like their alleged social betters, could be "there" too.

The total mix of the Olympics encompassed them all: the exploiters of products (and people), along with the exploited; the gainers and the losers; the upwardly mobile and those precipitously sliding; those (like Jean Drapeau) who would be blessed, and those (like Jean Drapeau) who would be damned; those (like Premier Bourassa) who held their criticism of the Olympics in abeyance, and those (like most of the guests at the Premier's or the Prime Minister's state functions) who publicly deplored the cost of the Games while thoroughly enjoying the almost vulgar Olympic social spin-off.

# 6 The East Germans. And Then the Cubans

Light years from the social dress-up action stood the swimmers and all the other athletes from East Germany, uninvolved with ballgowns, fancy menus, pseudo-aristocracies, and commercial exploitation.

When a country decides to participate in a series, a single contest, or a complex of games such as the Olympics, that country gives up the right to whine. If it decides to compete, it accepts the conditions of the game or series: *we* will do our best to prepare for you, *you* will do your best to prepare for us. Whatever has been labeled "amateur" is amateur; whatever has been barred as "professional" is out.

Canada did the right thing when it withdrew from Olympic hockey because its best players, its professionals, could not qualify. Had Canada decided to play according to the Olympic rules, it would have given up its right to bore the world with lamentations about barred professionals. The United States in 1972, competing with the usual pick-up team of basketball non-pros, and losing in a freak final to the U.S.S.R., got back on the treadmill theme of "Yah, but what would we have done with Jabbar, and Walt Frazier, etc., etc.?" The time to bring up a Jabbar is *before*, not after, one has agreed to participate.

All nostalgic sentimental what-might-have-been's are tedious, irrelevant second guesses after the fact. The West Germans in 1976 did not field an Olympic football team, as I've already pointed out; their stand was roughly the same as Canada's in hockey: that a team without the nation's very best players was a farce. Therefore no West German footballers. The fact that Soviet and other East European athletes are "like professionals"—supported by the state through sports organizations, universities, the army—and thus no more "amateur" than Kareem Abdul Jabbar, is an irritant. Again, the option is available. Compete or don't. Otherwise the bitching about Eastern European "professionalism" is an alibi kept in reserve: if the West wins, the alibi isn't needed; if it loses, the old "professional" line is trotted out.

Another cliché is the alibi I've already mentioned: that the East German athletes (and East Europeans generally) are something less than human. Proofs?

(1) The East Germans (Europeans) lack joy and fun in their dedication.
(2) The women have given up their femininity.
(3) The athletes are "forced" by the state to do well—and maybe fed drugs!

In many instances, I think that East German athletes appeared ominous and subversive because many of them didn't speak English.

From listening to some of the Western athletes and coaches I got the impression that *Oliver Twist, Nicholas Nickleby, David Copperfield,* and *Dombey and Son* were being rewritten to explain how East European athletes were forced to do athletics or face punishment. This dungeon view was part of the joyless-automaton complex.

The East German eruption into sports eminence is, for the West, a mystery: analogies with the put-upon Dickens children don't go far enough. One has to suggest parallels with Frankenstein's monster, and mysterious infusions, potions, and injections, to account for this new force unleashed on the world.

Solutions to the East German mystery are little different from the solutions to the Soviet sport mysteries. Intelligence in an unlikely place, i.e., sports. Those Westerners who have studied the East European sports program first hand (but only on the surface) have repeatedly run into intelligence. And knowledge—about the human body and what it can and cannot do.

I spoke with Doc Counsilman, the United States swimming coach, and to the U.S.A. swimming team's doctor, Chet Jastremski (who once swam the breast stroke for the U.S.A. in the Olympics), and found out that three of the best swimmers on the U.S.S.R. men's relay team had been working under Counsilman at Indiana University this past year (other U.S.S.R. swimmers worked with him too). From watching the Soviet program in hockey develop I suspected what Doc Counsilman confirmed: that these Soviet swimmers were part of a long-range plan he thought would bear results 12 years from now. That is, in these Olympics of 1976, in which the United States men broke all kinds of world records, the Soviet Union, an also-ran, was preparing—in Doc's words—"to be on a par with our guys in 1988, maybe sooner."

These swimmers had a double responsibility: to learn to swim, individually, with American champions and, much more importantly, gather *knowledge that converts into teaching and coaching principles*. The Soviet Union and other East European countries for many years now have concentrated on producing first-class coaches and trainers. In the West it's foolishly assumed that athletic superstars don't need coaching. A hockey cliché, for instance, suggests that the superstar can be hurt by coaching. By bad coaching, yes; by intelligent coaching, no.

For an objective evaluation of the East German achievement in 1976, Western observers must also reject the cold-war posture assumed by some of the East's sports commissars that every sports meeting is, in essence, a test not of individuals or of teams but of political and economic systems.

Hogwash.

No less hogwash when the point of view is European and North American than when it's East European. To praise Kornelia Ender or Waldemar Cierpinski is not to exalt the East German economic or political system, one of East Europe's most repressive. But anyone who spends five minutes with swimmers Roland Matthes and Roger Pyttel will see them as quite different from Udo Beyer, East Germany's gold-medal winner in the shot put. The difference between Matthes and Beyer is as great as the gap between gee-gosh swimmer John Naber and U.S. discus gold medalist Mac Wilkins.

Not speaking English, the East Germans may seem to come from another planet and perhaps have four lungs, auxiliary hearts, and philter-packs undetectable by Western testing rules.

The fundamental question is: how is it possible for a country with a population three quarters the size of Canada's to emerge as gold-medal winners second only to the U.S.S.R. (which has a population more than 30 times as large)? This particular question applies to the 1976 Olympics, but the larger issue is: what are the forces that change the relative strengths and weaknesses of athletes as measured every four years by the Olympics?

Let's start by saying that the motives of any country or system for applying its energies and resources to Olympic victories are, in the long run, a side issue. There is also no guarantee that massive expenditures will produce gold medals. If East Germany and the U.S.S.R.—and Rumania, Bulgaria, Czechoslovakia, Hungary, Poland, and Cuba—feel that their successes demonstrate the superiority of the Marxist-Leninist socialist paradise, good luck. If Western countries feel that the failure of these countries in a particular sport—basketball, say, or men's swimming—proves that the Marxist-Leninist socialist doctrine is phony, okay too.

The point is only: what did the East Germans *do? How* did they do it? What generalization emerges from a study of how one particular group of athletes escalated its Olympic accomplishment?

The conclusions of the Cincinnati research team I referred to earlier—that present time barriers in footraces are psychological rather than physical—obviously were shared by the East Germans not only about footraces. What happens when one removes John Walker's 3:49.4 in the mile as an absolute limit is that 3:45, say, or 3:40 becomes a realizable goal.

An athlete doesn't blunder into new world records. The assault on time and space and gravity has to be planned, and paced. Let's take as model the triumph of East Germany's Waldemar Cierpinski, over 1972's gold medalist, Frank Shorter. For the 26 miles, or, the Olympic distance, 42,195 metres, Shorter's previous best time was 2:11:51. Cierpinski's best was 2:12:21—the difference of half a minute in a race that took over two hours. Canada's Jerome Drayton had recorded the best time of all, 2:10:08. Karel Lismont, of Belgium, the eventual bronze medalist in the marathon, had done 2:11:13. David Chettle, of Australia, who didn't finish the race, had put up the second fastest marathon, 2:10:20.

In the actual running, Lismont was able to knock only 4/10ths of a second off his best time; Shorter was able to cut more than a minute off his best time (recording a 2:10:45.8); Cierpinski was able to reduce his best time by almost 2½ minutes (the best Olympic performance ever, 2:09:55.0). All the marathoners had to cope with rain, slippery streets, puddles, early darkness. All the contenders, with the exception of Lasse

Viren, were in only one Olympic event, the marathon. Frank Shorter had considered running the 10,000-metres, gave up the notion, and ran in only his best event.

The race hadn't gone more than five kilometres before *the* question became:

"Who's that Number 51 running with [the U.S.A.'s Bill] Rodgers?"

At 10 kilometres 51 was still there—and at 15, 20, 25, 30. At 35 kilometres he held a 13-second lead over Shorter. By then everyone knew he was Waldemar Cierpinski of East Germany, had checked out his best time, and slowly realized that nobody was going to catch Cierpinski—not even Frank Shorter.

The question remained: who was that "Number 51" named Waldemar Cierpinski? One obvious answer was *the guy who beat Frank Shorter*. The real question, though, was: *how?* That's a question I still can't answer definitively, even after hearing Cierpinski's explanations:

"A lot comes from the sense of community for me to perform well. I got a feel of success from the other athletes."

Cierpinski meant that the East German athletic community communicated the *possibility* of doing what he did.

"Until this year," Cierpinski said, "I kind of run marathons just for fun. My first was three years ago. But I've run five. This was my third for 1976."

Cierpinski had, as most athletes attempted to do, peaked for the Olympics. But strategy and an intelligent assessment of the course were important too.

"I went over course yesterday," Cierpinski explained. "I liked it because there was lot of undulation."

Did that mean Cierpinski was better suited to go up Montreal's steep hills than others whose best times were faster than his? Those best times were recorded not in Montreal but all over the world. Cierpinski's preparation was over an "undulated" course he had run in 2:12:21. The way Drayton and Shorter faded, could the hills of Montreal have been too much for them? Shorter came into the race in top shape. The course conditions did not please him:

"I don't like the rain, but you've got to get used to it."

Shorter's explanation of what happened was:

"During the marathon, you have spurts of feeling good and feeling bad. Just before 20 kilometres I started feeling good. But after 20 kilometres I had a wave of feeling bad. Then I had a lapse, a physical lapse, and he [Cierpinski] left me. . . . He got his whole lead within a half-mile near McGill University [i.e., where the course undulated significantly]. With three miles left, I knew I had had it."

Cierpinski's explanation fitted in with Shorter's, but first Cierpinski had to explain that "Before [the race began] I didn't think I had much chance." Something—not Shorter's admitted "physical lapse," but a sign that came much earlier—convinced Cierpinski that he could possibly beat Shorter:

"Shorter did a lot to make good fast race. Up to 10 kilometres Shorter provided lot of speed. There were 18 people then. It stayed even till 20 kilometres. Then Shorter picked it up. I was the only one to go with him. I finally broke away from Shorter at 32 kilometres."

If Cierpinski had seen films of Shorter's 1972 Munich win, or studied the pattern of Shorter's marathon runs, he could have prepared himself for Shorter's big move—pour it on close to the 25-kilometre mark and do a Vladimir Kuts on his opponent. Cierpinski was obviously ready for the Shorter escalation. The psychology of that turn-on is effective only when the runner keeps it going harder and longer than his opponent. But what if his opponent has structured *his* race not only to meet the new pace but to ante it up?

In the marathon, Shorter took over the lead at about 13 kilometres, with Rodgers, Viren, and Drayton between him and Cierpinski. At 15 kilometres Shorter led, looking relaxed and easy. Rodgers seemed to be blocking for Shorter, making sure that Cierpinski didn't pass (and upset the race plan). At 20 kilometres Shorter was still in front, still looking relaxed, though wet. The people the marathoners threaded their way through were under umbrellas or wrapped in raincoats. Cars had their lights on (at 6:30 P.M.), the roads gleamed and reflected the marathoners' quickly passing shadowy forms.

At 25 kilometres Shorter stopped to grab some juice, looked behind, and there, just a second off his pace, was Cierpinski. Shorter could take that juice break, he thought, because his spurt had just disposed of Lasse Viren (and Rodgers). A few minutes later Shorter tried to bury Cierpinski, but at 30 kilometres the images that flashed up on the Stadium electronic board showed Cierpinski running with him—and easily. Both runners had identical times for the 30 kilometres: 1:32:08.0. Shorter had been trying to knock Cierpinski off for some 10 kilometres, but Cierpinski wouldn't ease back. Rain began to fall harder, which didn't stop Cierpinski's East German teammates, the women's 4 x 400 metres relay team from breaking the world record just as Cierpinski went into the lead.

Though rain was pouring down, Shorter grabbed a sponge and squeezed water over his face and head and neck. Suddenly his head began swinging back and forth—it's called "breaking up" when a cyclist or a horse does it. He had tried to sustain his punishing pressure tactic longer than he himself could stand it. A minute later, Cierpinski was 50 metres in front. Then 70, 80. At the next Stadium board check-off, 35 kilometres, Shorter wasn't in sight. Cierpinski was running in the same steady—and, from Shorter's point of view, relentless —pace. One last time Shorter tried to get to Cierpinski (at about the 38-kilometre point). It was Cierpinski's turn to do the Vladimir Kuts. He spurted away from Shorter, whose face registered resigned acceptance. The race was Cierpinski's. Shorter flagged. Cierpinski pulled away, 100 metres in front. He finished almost 50 seconds ahead of Shorter.

Was this a victory for Marxist-Leninism over American free-enterprise capitalism? Was it in any way a national "high noon"? Shorter, alas, had the bad taste to come to the medal ceremony with a small American flag in his hand. He planted it in Canadian soil as if *he* were the gold-medal winner or some jingoistic astronaut come to the moon.

The race, however, was only between two men. One man was 26, the other near 29. The 26-year-old, Cierpinski, was 5 feet 7 inches tall; Shorter was just under 5 feet 11 inches. They weighed just about the same. In other words, their statistics revealed nothing.

The answer had to be sought somewhere else: before this marathon night was over, Cierpinski and his East German teammates would have won 40 gold medals, 25 silver, 25 bronze—90 in all. In 1968 the country won a total of seven.

What those statistics revealed, and what Cierpinski had seen in the 14 days of competition that preceded his race, was possibility turned into actuality. *Nothing*, his teammates' victories seemed to indicate, *is beyond us*. Nobody was invincible, not even Frank Shorter. If Cierpinski had trained up for his event as Kornelia Ender had for her events, as boxer Jochen Bachfeld (an admirable, courageous fighter) had prepped for his, as cyclist Klaus-Jurgen Grunke had for his 1,000-metre race—not to mention 30 (plus) other gold medalists—why couldn't his effort, his strategy, his hope lead to victory over Frank Shorter? And what if, for argument's sake, Cierpinski *knew* that his best time had been set over a course just as difficult as Montreal's? Couldn't his year-long preparation have guaranteed that this race would be run one, two, or three minutes *faster*?

Once Cierpinski saw the whites of Frank Shorter's eyes, saw Shorter's stride, pace, rhythm, he realized that he did indeed have "much chance."

It wasn't simply that the East Germans won 40 gold medals: what they accomplished in winning was most impressive:

*In Track and Field: Women Gold Medal Winners*

| | | |
|---|---|---|
| Baerbel Eckert | *200-metres* | New Olympic Record |
| | *4 x 100 metre relay* | New Olympic Record |
| | *4 x 400 metre relay* | New World Record |
| Rosemarie Ackermann | *high jump* | New Olympic Record |
| Evelin Schlaak | *discus* | New Olympic Record |
| Ruth Fuchs | *javelin* | New Olympic Record |

In the pentathlon, the East Germans took the gold, silver, and bronze, with Siegrun Siegl and Christine Laser finishing with identical scores (and Siegl being awarded the gold because she had finished ahead of Laser in three out of the five events).

*In Swimming: Women Gold Medal Winners*

| | | |
|---|---|---|
| Kornelia Ender | *100-metre freestyle* | New World Record |
| Kornelia Ender | *200-metre freestyle* | New World Record |
| Kornelia Ender | *100-metre butterfly* | Equaled (Own) World Record |
| Petra Thumer | *400-metre freestyle* | New World Record |
| Petra Thumer | *800-metre freestyle* | New World Record |
| Ulrike Tauber | *400-metre indiv. medley* | New World Record |
| | *4 x 100 metre relay* | New World Record |
| Ulrike Richter | *100-metre backstroke* | New Olympic Record |
| Ulrike Richter | *200-metre backstroke* | New Olympic Record |
| Andrea Pollack | *200-metre butterfly* | New Olympic Record |

In rowing the East Germans were almost as impressive. The women won gold medals in:

*Single scull*    Christine Scheiblich
*Four sculls with coxswain*
*Quadruple sculls with coxswain*
*Eights with coxswain*

The men won gold medals in:

*Pairs with coxswain*
*Pairs without coxswain*
*Four sculls*
*Fours without coxswain*
*Eights with coxswain*

In total, nine out of a possible 13 gold medals. Carola Zirzow won the 500-metre kayak singles (there were only two women's canoe races); the East German men won the 500-metre kayak doubles and 1,000-metre kayak singles (spectacularly, with Rudiger Helm).

In shooting, the East Germans took two of seven medals, in cycling one of six. In yachting, Jochen Shumann won the Finn class. East Germany won the football championship.

The East German Olympic Committee president, Manfred Ewald, with so much to brag about, didn't come on at all pushy. He linked East Germany's Olympic achievement with the "socialist state's" encouragement of other things:

"The athletes we send to Montreal do not perform miracles. They have shown that in our socialist state, man can develop his physical *and intellectual* [my italics] abilities to the fullest."

Ewald had statistics to demonstrate East Germany's commitment to sports: 15 percent of its population—about 2.6 million people, children and adults—belong to the over 8,000 sports clubs (whose secondary function is to produce pins for trading). Sixty percent of East German kids add to their compulsory school sports program by participating in organized after-school sports. Ewald said that over five million people—30 percent of the country's total population—"took part in mass sports competitions in 1975." This mass competition produced the magnificent East German achievements of 1976. But like the U.S.S.R., the East Germans wanted to make sports not only a system that searches for, discovers, trains, and coaches "top-class athletes"; it wanted also to connect that huge effort with the physical well-being of the entire population.

Perhaps because it was so new to the game of Games, Cuba came on much more aggressively than East Germany, promoting the island paradise and the blessings of life under Fidel Castro. Cuba's athletes obviously wanted to mimic Chinese gratitude toward Mao. All their heroes had prepped in ideology. Gold medalists such as Alberto Juantorena and Teofilo Stevenson had mini-lectures ready for their press conferences. Juantorena and Stevenson wanted not only to exalt Cuba and Castro but to connect Cuban victory with the brotherhood of socialist states. More important than competition was international socialist cooperation and, again, sense of community. Polish experts such as Juantorena's coach, Zygmunt Zabierzowski, helped the runners; Soviet coaches helped the Cuban boxers. Juantorena indicated that Cuban accomplishment in Montreal meant the country no longer had "to depend on the fraternal help."

When Juantorena won the 800-metres he dedicated his victory to both the Cuban Revolution and Castro. After his victory in the 400-metres, he dedicated that medal "to the people of Cuba, and comrade Fidel Castro, and to everyone who made possible our revolution in sports and our coming to the Olympic Games."

That revolution in sports in this tiny country produced six gold medals in Montreal (and four silver medals and three bronze). The concentration was in track and field (Juantorena's two gold medals) and, even more so, in boxing. In addition to Stevenson, Cuban boxers who won gold medals were Jorge Hernandez (48 kilograms—106-pound class), Angel Herrera (57 kilograms, 126 pounds). In judo (another sport helped by U.S.S.R. coaching) Hector Rodriguez was the lightweight (63 kilograms) gold.

The flamboyant style of Juantorena and Stevenson, the excellent boxing performances not only of the gold medalists but of, say, Sixto Soria (who looked just as lethal as Stevenson before he, alas, ran into the incredible U.S. light heavyweight, Leon Spinks) made Cuba one of the Games' most exciting participants. The Olympics had brought Castro's athletes to Canada, mere miles from the United States Cuba considered its great enemy. Cuba's real opponent in the Olympics was the United States—even the black American athletes.

"The United States athletes are strong," Juantorena pronounced after his 400-metre win, "but not invincible."

The American attitude to Juantorena, on the other hand, was that he had proved himself strong *and* invincible. In the Stadium press section, veteran track and field writers referred to him as "The Stud." His nine-foot stride was treated as if Juantorena were a track-shoe Dick Wittington. Bob Seagren, a gold-medal winner in the pole vault some years back, said that

Juantorena wasn't like other athletes, but a "freak, an oddity. He's so incredibly fantastic he frightens me."

Juantorena was another of Montreal's fabulous images, a tall long-legged man with an afro and mutton-chop whiskers, who loped beside his opponents in the heats, and turned on just as much power as he needed to win. He set a world's record in the 800-metres, fell short in the 400-metres, but in both races gave the impression that nobody could possibly beat him. When he won the 400, whizzing by the U.S.A.'s Fred Newhouse and Herman Frazier, he didn't seem to be breathing at all heavily. Maxie Parks and the other Americans, and, in fact, all the other runners were doubled over, gasping, collapsed. Juantorena did his victory lap and came back talking:

"I like to attack with 150 metres to go. In the last 50 metres I thought I showed a little power, no? But I have this power, no? It is a power race, no?"

Juantorena's 400 was a power race that obliterated the ordinary performances of Hasely Crawford in the 100-metres and Donald Quarrie in the 200-metres; more than that, Juantorena's world-record win in the 800-metres made it the glamour event of these Games—and possibly stole the glory mantle from the 1,500-metres. With no Filbert Bayi and a mediocre run by John Walker, the 1,500-metres dropped several notches; Juantorena made the 800-metres the most exciting shorter distance race in the Games while winning it and the 400 for the first time in the history of the Olympics. Juantoreno was a subject for a coin or a commemorative stamp, striding long and victoriously, his head to one side, quizzically observing the mere mortals left in his wake.

Teofilo Stevenson was another mythic athlete caught in Olympic history. The stop-action was always the same—that instant of Stevenson's right making contact with the doomed. He and Juantorena were close friends, socially realistic living statues dramatizing the accomplishments of Castro's Cuba: what Juantorena did figuratively to his oppenents, Stevenson did literally. His murderous precision made even one extra punch seem wasteful.

Pow! went Cuba's comic-strip superfighter and zapped Mamadou Drame of Senegal. Pow! took care of Pekka Ruokola of Finland—the referee stopped the fight because of a not-so-mysterious blow to Ruokola's head. Perhaps the most terrifying moment of all the boxing matches came when the U.S.A.'s Johnny Tate, a strong, big truckdriver fairly new to boxing (and subject, like all the American boxers, to that sticky lugubrious build-up known as the Howard Cosell treatment) ran into that Pow! For a second Tate did a blank-face imitation of a comic character bopped on the head. He staggered, shuffle-marched in a slow round, tried to get to a corner, grabbed the ropes, and only then sustained the full force of Stevenson's blow—a slow take of five or six seconds.

For a minute or so it looked as if Tate had been seriously injured, and might even have been in a several-second coma. No wonder then that Stevenson's Rumanian opponent in the final—Mircea Simon—came into the ring under pressure. By that time Stevenson's lightning zap had annihilated three grown men. Simon went into a protective crouch at the opening bell, almost keeping his legs crossed. It was the closest thing to total paralysis one could observe in a public match. Yet nobody booed. Simon was simply observing the discretion his three predecessors had held in reserve.

The first round looked like an Arthur Murray beginners' class in medley dancing. Stevenson stepped forward, Simon moved back. A couple of times Stevenson aimed a left and a right in Simon's general vicinity. By the end of the first round Simon hadn't once demonstrated that he could even straighten his arms. The referee would undoubtedly have stopped the fight, or done something to make the two men mix it up, had he not known what every person in that Forum knew—including Simon—that something terrible was going to happen. The Forum still resounded from the tremendous blow Stevenson had landed to the head of John Tate.

At the beginning of the second round Simon, obviously responding to instructions from his corner to come out of this fight alive, responded to the bell in the prescribed Pavlovian manner. He salivated a little, stiff with fear. Stevenson, to make matters worse, sighted Simon over his outstretched arm as if he were using a catapult.

Nothing was happening.

Pull this sort of thing and you get thrown out of even a YMCA gym. Stevenson was cursing Simon (one supposes in Spanish) but made no move to wade in and finish it. Simon was, in any other setting, not a bad fighter. He clearly had the capacity to land a lucky punch. Stevenson didn't give suckers even breaks.

After round two, the crowd's patience and compassion was gone. The booing started. Simon sat on his stool looking depressed. He hadn't been so much as nudged by Stevenson during those two disengaged rounds.

The third round began with Stevenson turned fencer, poking that left forward, dancing back, thrusting, thrusting again. Fencing rules would have had to be invoked to declare a winner at that moment.

At two minutes 35 seconds of the third and final round, Simon threw his first real punch, a right. Then Stevenson unloaded. The referee looked at Simon. The fight was over.

For his gold-medal ceremony, Stevenson came out with little Cuban flags and gifts he handed out to women and children. From the very beginning, when Stevenson marched into the Stadium at the head of the Cuban delegation, their national presence was athletic theater. The white and red of their street costumes, the pride in their bearing, the almost comic way Stevenson ice-cream-coned the Cuban flag would have been absurd had they not been prelude to the attention-fixing championship performances that followed.

The U.S.S.R. may have won more medals and more points than any other country in the Games. But the winners as far as interest and respect were concerned had to be the East Germans and the Cubans. In both cases, intelligence in discovering talent, nurturing it, respecting it, coveting it, was obvious. An intelligent coach is less likely to have his star athletes injured. Much of North American and European injury can be related to ground conditions, poor equipment, and, more frequently, the ignorance of coaches and trainers who, more often then not, fail to bring that body along so that it will be prepared for whatever is demanded of it.

The East German and Cuban medal performances derived from applying Soviet sport and physical culture programs and methods of analysis. Other countries, too, had adopted and then adapted the Soviet methods.

One should pause a moment and say that the all-out commitment to sports may be, for many a country, something of a disaster. A jockocracy is no different from a rockocracy or a theocracy. The desire to solve national problems through massive athletic programs is a form of contemporary jingoistic hysteria. There are some who consider the excessive involvement with sports in most parts of the world anti-intellectual, anti-political, anti-the-arts. Some of these people would consider it a disaster were the West to make of sports the icon worshiped in the East.

That, then, is another option. Not to get involved in the competition the Soviets, the East Germans, the Cubans, the Rumanians, the Czechoslovakians, the Hungarians, the Poles, the Bulgarians have thrived on. Not to allow any greater portion of a nation's resources to be spent on sports programs. To spurn the accomplishments, and the motives, of East Europe in the Olympics.

I suggest that it isn't the money so much as the intelligence that has allowed East European countries and Cuba to do so well in the Montreal Games. Perhaps not much more money will have to be allotted by Western countries that don't exercise the option of *no!* Perhaps the East German and Cuban models demonstrate how much more important good coaching and good training are than massive national programs that spend great sums of money—with high hopes and athletic ignorance.

The opposite of Cuba's success was Canada's so-called failure. Canada had something it tagged with a 1976 hup-hup-hup name, "Game Plan" (one of former U.S. President Richard M.

Nixon's favorite terms). Anything so cleverly titled obviously couldn't go wrong. "Game Plan" assumed that if you dropped a certain amount of dollars on athletes—five million dollars—such unprecedented governmental largesse would produce million-dollar achievements. The money turned out to be vulgar and irrelevant. When Canada became the first host nation in the history of the Olympics not to win a gold, the "Game Plan" commissars, instead of confessing that they didn't know their javelins from a discus, jumped on the athletes for "not trying."

"Game Plan" allowed just a bit over a year for an athlete to take the money injection and respond with gold. It did little to search for athletes (the way Rumania did to turn up Nadia Comaneci, or the way the U.S.S.R. did to find Nelli Kim). Therefore it had to make champions of what was. That meant an incredible amount of bilge had to be written about Canadian Olympic chances; a lot of puffing and build-up went into the program, helped by well-meaning Canadian journalists burdened with the enormous task of grinding out Canadian-content Olympic copy for almost a year.

The program did not, on the whole, develop coaches, trainers, training facilities; nor did it develop a long-range policy of borrowing coaches from other countries in events new to Canada. The program was patchy, the hopes unrealistic, the intelligence displayed minimal. The Canadian achievement, given the conditions the athletes worked under, was praise-worthy. And in the events that had intelligent coaching, a worked-out program, and a sense of community—notably, swimming—the Canadian athletes did very well indeed. That Canadians didn't do as well as East Germans or Cubans didn't mean the Canadian athletes weren't trying. No amount of trying is going to make someone into a Kornelia Ender, a Waldemar Cierpinski, an Alberto Juantorena, a Teofilo Stevenson. Canada, in most events, was up against extraordinary talent—well coached, well protected against injury, and well inclined to do well. Those qualities emerged from an intelligent sports program which, once you decide sports is the thing, is the only way to go.

# 7 What If You Gave a Party and Everyone Else Went Home with the Prizes...

Early in spring the Toronto *Globe and Mail* published a review of Canada's prospects entitled "Our Olympic Athletes 1976," prefaced by a "buck up, kids" piece by one Christie Blatchford, the kind of pep talk parents give Little Leaguers who are down 18-0 in the first inning with little prospect of getting the other side out. It was an overture on the theme of "losers":

". . . Trite and common it may be; there are no losers in these [Winter Olympic] Games, least of all Canadian losers.

"Losers do not make it this far, do not have the courage and the talent and the magical ingredient that puts the two together.

"Losers, perhaps, are the kids at home, the young in dozens of countries who grow fat and slow and bored—and unhappy. The Olympians, the lithe, lean-thighed athletes, are all winners."

Then followed a sport-by-sport prognostication by other writers lacking the 1984 consolation touch about losing equals winning. These pieces lacked inspiration but were terribly realistic: Canada's archers, one article said, though shooting at a target, were actually "aiming for respectability"; on women's track and field: "Canada will not have the same national embarrassment on the Olympic track-and-field site that it had in trying to build it." The article summing up the modern pentathlon asserted that "[r]ight now, the country's imaginary couriers would place second to the Canada Post Office" (offering little comfort even to the "lithe, lean-thighed").

Hope ranging from "wan" to "faint" was expressed for Canadian prospects in wrestling, boxing, judo, cycling (Jocelyn Lovell), weightlifting, volleyball, fencing, gymnastics, team handball, rowing, football (soccer), water polo, field hockey; moderate optimism attended a review of canoeing (John Wood and Susan Holloway), basketball (men's), yachting (Tempest and Flying Dutchman classes), diving (women's); medal hopes centered on Jerome Drayton in the marathon; Canada's excellent high jumpers (men and Debbie Brill); Diane Jones in the women's pentathlon; Susan Nattrass and John Primrose in trapshooting; equestrian jumping; dressage (Christilot Boylen).

The greatest concentration of A-card holders in Canada's Game Plan was in swimming, the women swimmers ranking slightly higher than the men. To be an A-card holder, and get the most money, a competitor had to stand among the world's top eight in her or his event; to be a B-card holder (and get less Game Plan support) a competitor had to rank among the top 16. In swimming Canada had a major development plan under two excellent coaches, ex-Australian Don Talbot (Thunder Bay) and Deryk Snelling (Vancouver).

Though a few other publications in the interim grew slightly shrill with positive thinking, the Canadian achievement in July almost fitted the *The Globe and Mail* anticipation: five silver medals, six bronze, no gold. Three of the silver medals were won, respectively, in canoeing (John Wood), Grand Prix jumping individual (Michel Vaillancourt on Branch County), and, of course, the high jump (Greg Joy): the rest of the medals were won by the women and the men swimmers (the women getting a silver and six bronzes) the men's 4 x 100 metre medley relay team Canada's other silver).

Canadian television (more so the English than the French network coverage) tended to emphasize the Canadian "angle," the approach of Canada's media in general. Media representatives from all over the world generally tended to concentrate on those events in which their countries had entries, not just medal hopes. Working the national "angle" sometimes tended to distort an event: following Canadian wrestlers and boxers, for instance, meant losing sight of the great athletes from other countries in those two sports. If the eventual gold medalist was performing at the same time as a Canadian, the Canadian was covered. The gold medalist might be picked up later, almost as an afterthought. In some sports when the Canadians were eliminated, the sport itself was downgraded. Some of the European or South American coverage was even more startling: when the national representative was knocked out, the media dropped the sport altogether.

The best coverage of the Olympics, from its beginnings to the follow-up, occurred in the locally based Montreal *Gazette*, largely due to the concentration of its sports editor, Doug Gilbert, and, during the Games proper, a number of involved, talented writers such as Tim Burke, Ian MacDonald, etc. Aislin's *Gazette* Olympic sketchbook caught the images, bizarre or straight, of what was happening among the spectators as well as among the athletes. *The Gazette* made sure that Canadian participants were followed but also kept watch on the Nabers and Walkers and Juantorenas and Kazankinas and Szewinskas and Virens (Comaneci, Kim, Ender, Alexeev, Jenner, Joy, Cierpinski, nobody could miss).

Though some coaches, some spectators, some writers would lament the Canadian performance and blame this or that participant, the Canadian accomplishment coincided with realistic expectations, given the talent, the time, the preparation, the facilities. Perhaps the men swimmers might have picked up an additional medal (they were disqualified in the 4 x 200 metre freestyle relay preliminaries because Steve Pickell left too soon).

Gold medals were simply out of reach for Canada in Montreal: the men swimmers couldn't possibly beat the United States, powerful in all but one event (David Wilkie's gold, the 200-metre breaststroke). The women couldn't possibly beat the East Germans in the individual events (victorious in all but, again, the 200-metre breaststroke). Except for the American women's 4 x 100 metre freestyle relay win (tarnished only a little by what looked, on replay, like a flying start by Shirley Babashoff that might not have affected the race), the best showdowns were between two or more East German women just as, in the men's competition, the best races were between or among Americans. Canada competed in a mini-Olympics, in which silver medals were the highest prize, and did quite well.

In the 400-metre individual medley Cheryl Gibson broke the world record by 69/100ths of a second, a wonderful effort; it won her a silver. The East German winner, Ulrike Tauber, broke that same record by *6.02 seconds!* Two-and-a-half seconds behind Cheryl Gibson came Becky Smith to win a bronze for Canada.

In the 4 x 100 metre medley relay, in which the Canadian women won another bronze, the team made up of Wendy Hogg, Robin Corsiglia, Susan Sloan, and Anne Jardin finished 67/100ths of a second behind the American women; but the East Germans won the gold by *6.60 seconds.*

In the 4 x 100 metre freestyle relay the Canadian team of Gail Amunrud, Barbara Clark, Becky Smith, and Anne Jardin finished just 1/100th of a second off the world record—for a bronze—while the winning American women broke the world record by almost 4 seconds.

Nancy Garapick, who won two backstroke bronzes—in the 100-metres and 200-metres—finished a good number of lengths behind the silver medalist in both races, Birgit Treiber, who was a respectable distance back of the gold medalist in both backstroke contests, Ulrike Richter. The Canadian swimmers were in their early teens, but so were the East Germans.

In the men's 4 x 100 medley relay, every Canadian swimmer did his best 100 metres ever, the team broke the world and Olympic record by more than 1½ seconds—a gold-medal achievement. But Steve Pickell, Graham Smith, Clay Evans, Gary MacDonald, had the bad luck the American women and all Canadian swimmers ran into throughout the Games: the men's bad luck was called "American"; the women's bad luck was called "East German." That tremendous effort by the Canadian men left them over 3½ seconds behind the American men—who broke the world and Olympic record by *5.06 seconds.*

At Bromont, Michel Vaillancourt's silver medal, won after a ride-off, was a splendid accomplishment. But the gap between the gold-medal winner, Alwin Schockemoehle of West Germany on Warwick Rex, and the rest of the field was huge. Schockemoehle was the only rider to record zero faults and zero time faults.

The course was wet and, in spots, dangerous. Numerous riders smashed barriers, splintering them. Horses skidded, fell, their riders beneath them, then up, shaky, but soon remounted, waiting for the bell that meant the disaster ride could continue. Photographers early on concluded that jump 14 was the place most cordial to catastrophe, so clustered there waiting anxiously for the next horse and rider to fall. Into all of this came Schockemoehle, cool, unperturbed, and, after 1:34—not a hurried ride—emerged as The Faultless. The skies broke a mean July storm over Bromont just as Schockemoehle began his second round (Schockemoehle was an Olympic veteran, 39 years old, and a gold medalist for West Germany in the 1960 Olympics).

Vaillancourt had turned 22 the day before the Grand Prix jump; Canada had never won a medal in this equestrian event. Vaillancourt's horse, Branch County, an ex-pacer out of Winnipeg, steady, reliable, but not flashy, wasn't in the same class as the jumper many expected Jim Day to ride to a Canadian medal, even the gold—Sympatico, a horse purchased for a quarter of a million dollars.

Grand Prix jumping allows for barriers to be set at a maximum height of 5 feet 7 inches (the size of Marcel Dionne on skates) and permits maximum spreads of 7 feet 5 inches (the size of your average Soviet Union basketball center). Vaillancourt performed his first 14 jumps faultlessly, with everyone wondering if he would indeed record a perfect ride. The fifteenth jump stopped him. Branch County seemed just too strained and too tired to go over the brush oxer spread at that widest 7 feet 5 inches.

In the afternoon jumping Vaillancourt had two faults, so that he and the young English woman with the girls' book name, Debbie Johnsey (riding, would you believe it, a horse called Moxy?), and François Mathy of Belgium (on Gai Luron—trans. "jolly jolly chap"), each ended with a total of 12 fault points, forcing the jump-off. In this late-afternoon event—their third go-round in a day that began at dawn—Debbie Johnsey's ride fell apart. She had 15 fault points and .25 time faults; Mathy had eight faults. Vaillancourt had four. The people who do the Grand Prix circuit had been complaining about the mud and sand of the Bromont course; if the course had been the usual turf it would have been fierce and slippery after the heavy rains.

It wasn't simply that Vaillancourt had won an unexpected medal; Canadian equestrians wanted to use the Olympics to publicize their events and to get government and other money for the purchase of horses and the leasing of training facilities. Vaillancourt's trainer, Pierre Jolicoeur, read Vaillancourt's triumph as a Canadian breakthrough into European jumping.

Vaillancourt "put Quebec on the equestrian map," Jolicoeur said. "He was up against the wall—being in his home town and riding a green horse." Jolicoeur had wanted to buy Branch County for Vaillancourt—but the asking price, 100,000 dollars, was beyond their means; so, too, was the 15,000 dollars they had to come up with to rent the horse for the three months Vaillancourt needed to ride it.

"The Quebec government was supposed to give us money," Jolicoeur said matter-of-factly, "we're still waiting. They did help us train in Florida, though."

Then Jolicoeur added the greatest line I heard about these billion-dollar Olympics: "Anyway the Olympics is no time to talk money."

John Wood, of Port Credit, who won a silver medal for Canada in the 500-metre canoe event, wanted his victory used to promote canoeing, and all other Olympic sports. His silver medal, like Vaillancourt's, was a gift to "the Canadian public," part of that public's liberation from athletic ignorance. At Bromont more than 20,000 were in the stands, sitting on camp chairs, rickety bleacher seats, on the wet grass spread with groundsheets, huddled under umbrellas. Some had come out to Bromont because it was Prince Philip's turf and the place where Princess Anne competed (when vertical). The crowd at the Olympic basin to watch Wood added up to about 5,000 people, a huge turnout for a sport that most frequently is watched by fewer than a hundred spectators.

In Helsinki, in 1952, Canada won its last canoeing medal—a long nostalgic paddle with no medal pay-offs. Wood's 500-metre "sprint" race was one of the most exciting of the Games: three paddlers came down to the finish line separated by 37/100ths of a second. The gold went to the favorite, Aleksandr Rogov of the U.S.S.R.; only 2/100ths of a second behind Wood came Matija Ljubek of Yugoslavia.

Just as Waldemar Cierpinski, before the marathon began, didn't think he had much of a chance to beat his event's favorite, so both Wood and Vaillancourt had to realize, in the middle of the competition, that they could not only win a medal but might, just possibly, luck into a gold. After Schockemoehle's ride, Vaillancourt was going for silver; Wood, however, came into the final thinking: "If I feel pressed I'm going to concentrate, slow down and paddle my own race." When he reviewed the entire race he was satisfied with his work up to the last six strokes, he said—but those last strokes were part of his finishing kick, and Rogov's kick proved to be the race's strongest.

In the canoe and kayak races, as in the rowing events, the beautiful blue fiberglass boats of the East Germans were always at that finish line (though in Wood's event the best an East German could do was fifth). The other rowers and paddlers felt that the East Germans operated with a technological advantage in both the rowing and the canoe events (their boats evidently grew slimmer and longer in the water—boat doping it will soon be called, I'm sure).

The canoe events—both men's and women's—found not East German but East European dominance complete: every gold went to the Soviet Union (six), the Rumanians (one), the Yugoslavians (one), or those ubiquitous East Germans (three). Each of those countries either had a region that is temperate 12 months a year or belonged to the socialist brotherhood Alberto Juantorena referred to: the interchange of athletic information and coaching techniques among socialist countries also extended to sports facilities. A country with inadequate facilities could, through sports exchanges, arrange for the use of facilities in another country.

[I well remember seeing the Bulgarian national hockey team working out at the Army Club in Moscow. Bulgaria needed the facilities of an artificial ice plant, and needed even more the special talents of the Soviet Union's hockey coaches.]

An intelligent plan for Canadian athletes was needed if Canada wanted to compete at the highest, gold-medal, levels in future Olympics. But, as I pointed out earlier, this is an option. A country might have as much satisfaction just having a delegation of athletes at the Olympics (another option is no athletes at all). Should a country decide to compete, and should the country lack those temperate Black Sea and southern Asian regions the Soviet Union has, its training program in outdoor events will be terribly expensive. Canada had to send its athletes to Florida or other areas of the southern United States. Even when the athletes worked out on university campuses and lived in college dorms, the cost was high. For Canadians to become competitive in track and field, for instance, the athletes would have to be supported for two or perhaps three years between Olympics, and supported while traveling all over the world in search of the Olympic-level competition that leads to gold medals being won.

I repeat: it's an option. And I must report what happened in Montreal, among the Canadian spectators if not among the Canadian broadcasters and writers. It took only a few days, as I've already suggested, for the spectators to catch on to the facts of Canadian athletic life. They did not turn on the athletes. What happened, instead, was rather charming: Canadians turned themselves into a claque, a cheering section, an encouragement-chanting results-ignoring happy mass, delighted to be in Montreal, delighted to see suited-up Canadians competing against the Enders and the Nabers and the Jenners. "Losers" and "winners" didn't matter much to these people in the stands; they didn't even submit anybody to the "lithe, lean-thighed" test before applauding.

To them this was an amateur gala full of spectacular stars their countrymen and countrywomen were having a tough time keeping up with. Early in the track and field competition—on its very first day, in fact—when, in the midst of many other events going on in various parts of the Olympic Stadium, the walkers came wiggly-waggling out, lickety-split, in their midst was old Alex Oakley, whose year of birth must have looked like a misprint—1928. Oakley had labored long in the service of the walk.

Like a swarm of men suffering from both tight shoes and delusions of grand military marches the walkers left the Stadium just after 5:30 P.M.. At close to 7:00 P.M. the first walker, the gold medalist, Mexico's Daniel Bautista, who had gone into the lead at the gun and didn't give it over, returned to the Stadium, his image up on the electronic board. His time, 1:24:40.6, set records for world and Olympic walks over the 20-kilometre route. Less than a minute later the East German winners of the silver and the bronze entered—while the 10,000-metre heats were still being run.

No matter what was happening, that crowd sat back, waiting. Almost 20 minutes after Bautista crossed the finish line, 48-year-old Alex Oakley was announced entering the Stadium, his hurrying form massive on the electronic scoreboard, almost the same as Bautista's when he came in. At the mention of his name a great handclapping began, followed by a cheer, and then, as Oakley passed the stands in his "victory" lap, a standing ovation (that made non-Canadians wonder what was happening in the 10,000-metre lanes flagged off from those of the walkers).

The pattern was set. In the 10,000-metres, Canadians like Christopher McCubbins, were cheered every time they passed the Canadian fans concentrated in the east and west sections of the Stadium. Dan Shaughnessy understood what the applause was all about and, at one point, took the early lead in his 10,000 heat. Jerome Drayton, with greater hope than McCubbins and Shaughnessy, took the lead in the marathon just long enough for his form to appear on the Stadium board. He, too, coming into the Stadium the last night of track and field competition got a tremendous reception from the Canadian fans anxious to get home in the drenching rain.

Those fans stuck with Diane Jones in the pentathlon, watched her warm up for her various events, cheered her wildly when she began to take off her sweatsuit in readiness for another try. Groaned when she missed at high jump, groaned when she fouled or made a bad shot-put throw, groaned even louder when she failed to finish in front of any of her race heats. Diane Jones was, of course, one of Canada's medal hopes; but as she slipped behind Andrea Bruce of Jamaica even in her best event, the high jump, the spectators saw the consequences yet did not stop cheering and applauding.

Julie White and Louise Walker, who qualified for the high-jump final after the Canadian favorite, Debbie Brill, failed her three jumps, were welcomed by the Canadian crowd no less enthusiastically than Greg Joy and Claude Ferragne and Robert Forget (who missed his three attempts while his mother and father sat in the VIP-est part of the VIP section with Premier and Mrs. Robert Bourassa). Julie White became an instant favorite of the Canadians, taking over where Debbie Brill hadn't begun to leave off.

Perhaps some people had in mind the Kathy Kreiner gold medal in the downhill at Innsbruck during the Winter Olympics, a totally unexpected victory over all the great names in European skiing. Maybe someone else would do something way over her head. One by one the Canadians fell. Most didn't even get into the finals of their events. Those who did were usually eliminated long before competition began among those certain to win some kind of medal.

Canada's only Kathy Kreiner in the Summer Games was Greg Joy. It was if he had skied down on the torrents of rain. If those who had cheered Jocelyn Lovell in the Velodrome were in the Stadium that wet last-competition night, Greg Joy might have made up for their disappointment. To those that followed Canada's basketball team into the Forum (in hopes that it could defeat the U.S.S.R. and come off with a bronze) and watched it lose, Greg Joy might have offered consolation.

His clear clean last-minute leap made up for Jerome Drayton, and Diane Jones, and Debbie Brill, and Bruce Simpson (who couldn't make the qualifying height in the pole vault). Had he missed, the cheering and clapping would probably have been reduced only a little. Greg Joy was all of Canada's participating athletes come down to the last event that could qualify as a precious moment, the last snap of the final frame illuminated by the only flashcube left.

When he failed at the heights that could have given him the gold, he was celebrated again—even on his third and last miss, when he hit the bar with his thigh. By that time Greg Joy was part of the ceremonial Olympics. By that time the applause for him was like the end of a five-ring circus, when one by one all the performers came out to take that last standing ovation and make that final bow.

Let's face it: most of the Canadians at the Olympics were losers. And losers aren't winners. It's demeaning to tell them so. Losers aren't better or even different from those who stay at home. There is a consolation to losing, and it's not verbal sophistry. It's old Alex Oakley, *participating* in the grandest of all athletic events, the Olympics, and doing the business of any participant in anything begun—finishing. The word "loser" or the word "winner" would sound paltry describing what Alex Oakley was all about. Alex Oakley was the amateur. Alex Oakley walked his 20 kilometres because in the Montreal Olympics of 1976 he and that space were there. I saw him enter the Stadium, perk himself up to sashay in jauntily, and finish in a burst of pure style.

He was exercising one of the real Olympic options: to participate. If medals came, they came. If they didn't, the meaning of that participation didn't change. Canada could choose to go the way of East Germany or not; to go the way of the U.S.S.R. or not; to go the way of the U.S.A. or not. Greg Joy's way was doubtlessly more dramatic and more exciting than Alex Oakley's. Kathy Kreiner's may have been the most exciting way of all. But as I watched those people in the stands respond to the achievements and the attempts by Canadian athletes day after day, I had the distinct feeling that masses of medals would probably carry them no higher. That the great experience they were having was being there—at a Canadian Olympics. And that the greatest contribution to that experience was the presence of those athletes in white and red—their presence and, quite possibly, nothing else.

It seemed to me that after the year or more of medal talk and medal hopes, the people in the stands, and watching on television, remained uncoerced, and still amateur. There was something familial about it all, something rather touching—a sense of community which, unlike Juantorena's or Cierpinski's,

Leon Spinks, U.S.A., gold medalist in the light heavyweight boxing division, throws a right at Sixto Soria of Cuba. (The referee stopped the fight.) *(Canadian Press)*

Isamu Sonada of Japan tosses his opponent Paul Buganey of Australia in a middleweight judo match. *(Canadian Press)*

Lasse Viren of Finalnd winning the 5,000-metre run as Klaus Hildenbrand of West Germany dives for the bronze. (*Canadian Press*)

Bruce Jenner, U.S.A., was gold medalist in the decathlon. (*The Toronto Star*)

Alberto Juantorena of Cuba, gold medalist in the 400- and 800-metres. Rick Wohlhuter, U.S.A., won the bronze in this 800-metre run. *(Wide World Photos)*

John Wood, Canada, silver medalist in the men's 500-metre canoe singles event. *(Canadian Press)*

wasn't pushing much of anything. That Canada was the first host nation in the history of the Olympics not to win a gold medal might be the story of the Games to some. Not, I submit, to those dedicated watchers.

"I just loved seein' us out there," an older woman told me after the opening ceremonies. She of course was referring to all those athletes strolling behind the Canadian flag Abby Hoffman was carrying.

Alex Oakley to her undoubtedly was "us out there," and so was Greg Joy. She probably summed up the Canadian "angle" on the Olympics.

# 8 The Flip Side of the Iron Curtain

Some Americans were clearly unhappy with the American performance at the Games—third to the U.S.S.R. and East Germany in gold medals; far behind the U.S.S.R. in the category of points. There was dissension in certain areas of American participation: different sports represented different life styles; sometimes within a sport the athletes mirrored the wide range of differences in American society. Regional variations had an effect on team unity too. Racial attitudes affected solidarity and, I suspect, performance.

But on the whole this was a quiescent time for American Olympic involvement: the first Games since 1960 that didn't have as a backdrop war in Vietnam and other areas of southeastern Asia: the first Games since 1960, say, that didn't reflect the split between black radicals and the white majority.

If one began with American men's swimming, the total accomplishment stood as one of the awesome triumphs of the Games. Men's swimming was a private party to which competitors from other countries were invited as observers. Americans vied with other Americans. David Wilkie of Great Britain slipped in and stole a medal in the 200-metre breaststroke—otherwise American domination was almost imperialistic. The swimming team came on like a boys' camp reunion. The talent was so impressive, the records set so astounding, the team spirit so cohesive, other athletes suffered from comparisons with that swim team.

The American men came to Montreal with Mark Spitz's Munich achievement fresh in everyone's mind: seven gold medals in individual and relay events. Most of Spitz's records had been broken before the Olympics—several during the Olympic tryouts—but a few remained (only his record in the 100-metre butterfly stood up at the Games). The relay times that gave Spitz two gold medals in Munich were smithereened by the New Swim Gang. They were college buddies taking a victory walk around the pool, leaning into the stands to hug and kiss mothers and fathers, sisters and brothers (Gary Hall brought out his small child). They marched in and out, waving, clowning, John Naber the objectification of the casual style, shuffling out of martial step, grinning at the American women swimmers sitting in the stands and shouting "Go, John, go!"

The Swimming Pool was the family place during the Games, full of kids, babies, close relatives, and distant relatives of the swimmers. Americans on most days outnumbered Canadians.

John Naber didn't clown in the Pool. From his first appearance in the 100-metre backstroke he established himself as the male counterpart of Kornelia Ender. Like her, he seemed to have unlimited reserves of energy; like her, he was tall, long-armed, long-wristed, long-legged, broad-shouldered, smooth-muscled, supple, relaxed. Like her, he delighted in winning, *and* in breaking records. Unlike her, Naber connected his achievements with God's will and American destiny. God, flag, family, the middle-class virtues did extremely well when the American men were in the Pool, less well when the American women took over.

Those men were beach lifeguards frolicking after hours—Joe Bottom and Matt Vogel with their heads shaved, Vogel wearing a black-and-white touque modestly hiding his head's nakedness till it could be anointed in water. Jim Montgomery, who made a shambles of Mark Spitz's 100-metre freestyle record, like Naber broke swim barriers once considered as invincible as the four-minute mile: the 50-second barrier in the 100-metre freestyle, for instance. In races won by the American men 1-2 or 1-2-3-, more than one swimmer usually broke the world record. As good as the East German women's accomplishment was, it did not match the performance of the American men: they broke records in every event but, to repeat, the 100-metre butterfly (in the 200-metre breaststroke, though David Wilkie won the gold; though John Hencken swam in world record time while winning a silver). Nobody in FINA (the international swimming committee) had to tell the American men "to show a little more enthusiasm and happiness during the medal presentations" (an actual memo). They pounded each other on the back getting up on the medal winners' platform, embraced, shook the victory fist in the air, jumped and skipped, yahooed, pausing only long enough to treat the American national anthem as if it were a requiem.

I sat with the American coaches during the competition one night (July 21). Doc Counsilman and Dr. Chet Jastremski said they welcomed the emergence of the East German women in swimming. They foresaw competition increasing from the U.S.S.R. in both men's and women's swimming and diving; from the East German men; from the Hungarian men.

"I'm glad the other countries are pushing us," Jastremski said. "It's the way we get better."

[As far back as 1961, when Jastremski was participating in national and international swim meets, the American swimmers were followed around by three Soviet coaches who watched everything they did, took notes, asked questions, and followed up their interest year after year—culminating in those Soviet swimmers coming to Indiana University, which, coincidentally, had one of the best Russian programs in the U.S.A., as well as one of the best swimming teams.]

The U.S.A. swimming officials, like those in basketball and boxing, could consider the Olympics a great success. Other sports were not so fortunate.

"The American sports commitment is to non-Olympic things like baseball and football," Jastremski said. "That's where the interest is, that's where the fans turn out, so that's where the money is. In Europe almost all the popular sports are Olympic sports. Canada suffers from this difference as much as we do."

On the fourth day of swim competition, some Olympics officials from the U.S.A. were already resigned to a poor showing; i.e., running second to the Soviet Union in gold medals and points. But what was happening in the Swimming Pool made 1976 as successful as Spitz's one-man show of 1972.

This was the American men's achievement:

| | |
|---|---|
| *John Naber:* | four gold medals, one silver; two world records (in the 100- and 200-metre backstroke); two relay world records (in the 4 x 200 metre freestyle and the 4 x 100 metre medley relay). |
| *Brian Goodell:* | two gold medals; two world records (in the 400- and 1,500-metre freestyle). |

| | |
|---|---|
| *Jim Montgomery:* | three gold medals, one bronze; that world record in the 100-metre freestyle and two relay world records for which he swam the anchor leg. |
| *Bruce Furniss:* | two gold medals; a world record in the 200-metre freestyle; another in the 4 x 200 metre freestyle. |
| *John Hencken:* | two gold medals and a silver; a world record in the 100-metre breaststroke. |
| *Mike Bruner:* | two gold medals; a world record in the 200-metre butterfly and in the 4 x 200 metre freestyle relay. |
| *Matt Vogel:* | two gold medals; swam the butterfly leg in the world record medley relay. |
| *Rod Strachan:* | a gold medal and world record in the 400-metre individual medley. |

Steven Gregg, Tim McKee, Jack Babashoff, Tim Shaw, Bobby Hackett, Joe Bottom, and Peter Rocca won silver medals (Rocca winning two). Dan Harrigan, Gary Hall, Rick Colella, Bill Forrester won bronzes.

Though the American women ran far behind the East Germans, their accomplishment was not unimpressive: there was that gold medal in the 4 x 100 freestyle relay for Shirley Babashoff, Kim Peyton, Wendy Boglioli, and Jill Sterkel. Other medalists ended up with silvers and bronzes:

| | |
|---|---|
| *Shirley Babashoff:* | four silver medals and that gold; swam the anchor laps in the 4 x 100 metre freestyle relay (for a new world record). |
| *Kim Peyton:* | one relay gold medal. |
| *Wendy Boglioli:* | one relay gold and a bronze in the 100-metre butterfly. |
| *Jill Sterkel:* | one relay gold medal. |

Linda Jezek, Lauri Siering, Camille Wright won silver medals in the 4 x 100 metre medley relay; Wendy Weinberg won a bronze in the 800-metre freestyle.

The Pool was also the locus of American gold medals in diving, Jennifer Chandler finishing far ahead of East Germany's Christa Kohler in women's springboard diving, an event full of charges and countercharges about politically motivated judging (the American judges came off as poorly as the East European). The consensus seemed to be that if Christa Kohler ever put the parts of her diving performance together she would emerge as the next Olympic champion. A sign of new things happening appeared in women's platform diving. The gold medal went to the U.S.S.R.'s Elena Vaytsekhovskaia, with Sweden's Ulrike Knape winning the silver. In both the springboard and platform events the United States won bronzes— Cynthia McIngvale in springboard, Deborah Wilson in platform.

In the men's springboard event Philip Boggs easily held onto his position as the world's leading springboard diver, but again a Soviet diver won a medal—Aleksandr Kosenkov taking the bronze behind Italy's Franco Cagnotto. In platform diving Italy's Klaus Dibiasi repeated his gold-medal performance of 1972, with the U.S.A.'s Greg Louganis getting the silver medal and the U.S.S.R.'s Vladimir Aleynik the bronze.

The Americans were the champions of the Swimming Pool. They were also able to take back the men's basketball gold medal, which with only few interruptions had been American property since the game's Olympic beginnings. The team that represented the United States was, at most, three to three and a half men strong. Not only were the stars of the National Basketball and American Basketball Associations ineligible; most of the United States college basketball standouts didn't want to get involved with the Olympics for a variety of reasons. Some claimed to have had other commitments; some objected to risking a professional basketball career for something so bush as an Olympic gold medal; still others felt they weren't being covered adequately by Olympic-play insurance. There may have even been a few who felt that losing, again, to the Soviet Union would tarnish one's individual value on the professional basketball market.

The team had three first-rate players—college basketball's number-one man from the 1976 NCAA Indiana University champions, Scott May; his excellent backcourt teammate, Quinn Buckner; and Notre Dame's fine forward, Adrian Dantley. A few notches down were Phil Ford, Walter Davis, Mitch Kupchak. The consensus seemed to be that though the United States men lacked a first-class center, they would make up for it with ball handling and the shooting of May and Dantley. Which is how things turned out.

The drama of the Olympics called for the United States to avenge its weird loss to the U.S.S.R. in Munich. The 1976 final observers had been anticipating in the intervening years. That's not the way things turned out. The Montreal Forum was the site of one of the Games' great upsets: the U.S.S.R. team, probably the best all-around squad in the men's touarment, was knocked off by Yugoslavia, not even given a chance to get into the medals ahead of Italy and Czechoslovakia.

I watched the U.S.S.R. beat Canada in the playoff for the bronze medal, and couldn't believe that this Soviet team had lost to anyone. They were the only Olympic basketballers with roughly 10 men of NBA stature. Canada could come up with perhaps two, Yugoslavia with the same number. An NBA team finishing at the bottom of the league during 1975-76 could well improve its position if it swapped squads with the U.S.S.R.

But Yugoslavia knocked the U.S.S.R. out of the finals, 89-84, then went on to lose to the U.S.A. in one of the great romps of the Games, 95-74. The United States team had keyed on the U.S.S.R., but getting back the Olympic gold medal was even more important. As the game clock wound down, the entire team went into a kind of boogie, throwing the ball high into the air at the final buzzer. I couldn't but wonder, when I compared the Yugoslav performance with the deadly 100-point shooting of the U.S.S.R. against Canada earlier that day, what the outcome might have been if the U.S.A. and the U.S.S.R. had

*129*

met in the final. In group A, the weaker of the two basketball divisions, the U.S.S.R. scored 548 points, 150 more than the United States in the stronger group B. With Dantley or May or Buckner on the bench, the U.S.A. team sagged noticeably; the U.S.S.R. had two men of exceptional talent for each position (most strikingly at center).

The American victory was earned, and exciting. For the second Olympics in a row, however, the American method of team selection was called into question. The entire Indiana University team playing as a unit would undoubtedly have been a stronger side to represent the country. Canada didn't have a single team strong enough to go to the Olympics; the United States had not one but four or five. Unless ways could be found to get the very best college basketballers to turn out for the Olympics, basketball might well go the way of hockey in the winter Games—East. For 1976, though, the United States was the undisputed Olympic champion.

In women's basketball the United States did better than its critics had anticipated. The U.S.S.R. women were rated head and shoulders above all other competition, which they literally were. The Japanese and Czech women were expected to fight it out for the silver and bronze medals. The American women, though having little international play behind them, had a tough fast team able to cope with everyone but the exceptionally small Japanese and the exceptionally tall Soviets. The U.S.S.R. scored 504 points in the championship pool, annihilating Canada 115-51 before doing in the U.S.A. 112-77. The only team that made it a game for the U.S.S.R. were the Czechs, who lost by 13 points, 88-75. The United States and the surprise of the entire tournament, the Bulgarians, finished with identical records of 3-2, but the United States was given the silver because of its 95-79 win over Bulgaria. Julie Simpson, Nancy Lieberman, Lusia Harris, and Ann Myers played extremely well in the games that brought the silver medal, against Canada, Bulgaria, and Czechoslovakia.

Right up with the men swimmers and the men basketballers were the United States boxers, possibly the toughest bunch of punchers to represent any one country in the Olympics. *The New York Times* in its pre-Games projections saw four Americans as gold-medal possibilities, Davey Armstrong in the featherweight division (he won a bronze, losing on points to Cuba's Angel Herrera, the eventual gold-medal winner); welterweight Clint Jackson, who was knocked out of the medals by Venezuelan Pedro Gammarro (who went on to win the silver); lightweight Howard Davis, one of the most impressive boxers of the Games, who won the gold in a unanimous decision over Rumanian Simon Cutov; light welterweight Sugar Ray Leonard, who carried Howard Cosell on his back most of the Games but overcame the build-up to win the gold against Cuba's Andres Aldama.

Overlooked in the selections, however, were the Spinks brothers, Michael and Leon, who turned out to be gold-medal winners in the middleweight and light heavyweight divisions respectively. Both emerged as Olympic champions, Michael pounding away at tough U.S.S.R. fighter Rufat Riskiev in the final till the referee stopped the fight; Leon beating the hard-punching Cuban Sixto Soria in another fight the referee had to stop. Overlooked, too, was Leo Randolph in the flyweight division, who boxed his way to wins over a variety of talented opponents, climaxed by his 3-2 decision over another Cuban, Ramon Duvalon, in the final.

The effect of the African boycott on the boxing championships is impossible to determine. Archie Moore, the former world light heavyweight champion who had been coaching the Nigerian boxing team, claimed that two Nigerian boxers had a chance at gold medals. Others thought Togo had medal chances, or Ghana or Egypt or Kenya or Ethiopia or Uganda. There were a large number of African boxers entered in every division; their failure to appear made a shambles of the early rounds of the eliminations. Hundreds of thousands of dollars in ticket money had to be refunded; the 'walkovers' affected boxing more than any other Olympic sport.

The American boxing accomplishment of five gold medals, a silver, and two bronzes in the 11 divisions was an exceptional achievement not to be tarnished by an asterisk explaining the African absence.

In 1972 the Americans won the gold medal in both men's and women's archery. The *Times*, for example, picked Darrell Pace to win the men's gold, and Richard McKinney the silver. Its charts indicated that Linda Myers would lead the American women but would not be able to beat "the Russians."

Pace, though still in his teens, had emerged to dominate archery competition in the years since Munich. His reputation as an archer was paralleled by his reputation as an intellectual Whiz Kid. He looked like a smart-ass kid, his hair combed back off his perky face as he stood around in his starred-up T-shirt, chatting. He seemed to know everything about the effect of temperature, atmospheric pressure, humidity, on archery scores. He could outtalk even Dwight Stones, but unlike Stones, Pace delivered in Montreal. He won the men's gold medal easily, while McKinney, with a score of 100 behind Pace, didn't make it into the medals at all. Pace had an amazing confidence in his ability, and none could dispute him: he believed that he had mastered the archer's art, and his perfection was disturbed only by outside factors such as the weather.

Overlooked in many of the archery predictions was the eventual women's gold-medal winner, Luann Ryon, who out-shot Linda Myers and, in doing so, beat the favored "Russians," Valentina Kovpan and Zebiniso Rustamova. Unlike Pace, who never scored worse than second at all the distances, Ryon survived a tenth-place ranking in the 70-metre range; her second go at 70 metres brought her up to first; two more firsts and three seconds in the shorter ranges gave her a gold-medal score of 2499, a new Olympic record. Darrell Pace's 2571 was also a new Olympic record.

In the shooting competition the United States again did well. The Soviet Union was favored to win in most of the shooting categories, but managed a gold in only the Running Game Target. The scoop was that the United States should come up with several medals, but only one gold. In actuality the East Germans won the Free Pistol competition, the Rapid-Fire Pistol event; the West Germans took the Small-Bore Rifle Prone Position gold and silver; the Czechs. won the Skeet Shooting.

One of the most charming moments of the Games occurred in the Small-Bore Rifle Three Positions—prone, standing, kneeling. Here Margaret Murdock, the first woman ever to make the American Olympic shooting team, was favored to win a medal—possibly even a gold. In the competition she and Lanny Bassham and West German Werner Seibold finished with scores of 1162, 1162, and 1160 respectively. But Lanny Bassham had three perfect targets and Margaret Murdoch only two. Therefore, though they had finished with identical scores, Bassham was awarded the gold medal and Margaret Murdoch the silver. At the *cérémonie protocolaire*, however, Bassham insisted that Margaret Murdoch be treated as if she too had won a gold medal: the two of them stood in the honored "gold" place on the award platform (one of the great Olympic photographs).

In the Olympic Trap Shooting competition, Don Haldeman won the gold medal by scoring 190 (out of a possible 200) against 189 by the silver and bronze medalists. In all other medal categories the United States was shut out.

Joan Lind came up with a rowing silver in the women's single sculls at the Olympic basin; Calvin Coffey and Michael Staines with another in the men's pairs without cox event. In the women's eight with cox competition the American women won a bronze. Otherwise, nothing. I've already indicated that rowing in Montreal turned into an East German sport.

Canoeing yielded no medals. Nor did cycling. Or fencing. In gymnastics Peter Kormann came up with a bronze medal in the men's floor exercises. In weightlifting James Lee won a silver in the light heavyweight group, finishing almost 50 pounds behind the U.S.S.R.'s David Rigert (the U.S.S.R.'s best-known lifter after Alexeev).

In freestyle wrestling Gene Davis and Stanley Dziedzic each won bronze medals; Lloyd Keaser, Ben Peterson, and Russell Hellickson each won silver medals. Only Ben Peterson's brother John managed a gold medal. The total of six medals was the same as 1972's except that in 1972 the United States was able to win three gold medals. In 1976 the Soviet Union dominated freestyle wrestling, winning five gold medals—three in the top weight classes. In Graeco-Roman wrestling the United States was shut out: the Soviet Union won seven gold medals.

In yachting the United States team in the Soling class—John Kolius, Walter Glasgow, Richard Hoepfner—won a silver medal. In the Tornado class the Americans won another silver medal (David McFaull and Michael Rothwell). In the Tempest class Dennis Connor and Conn Findlay finished with a bronze. For any other country but West Germany—winner of two gold medals—those results would have been sufficient. The Americans, though, had to consider the yachting results a disappointment.

The United States equestrians were led by Bruce Davidson, the world champion rider in the three-day event; the team had excellent riders, excellent horses, and should have swept the equestrian competition. But Bruce Davidson failed to perform well in the individual three-day competition, finishing a poor tenth. The United States did, however, win the gold and silver medals with Edmund Coffin (on Bally-Cor) and John Plumb (on Better & Better).

Coffin, Plumb, Davidson combined with Mary Tauskey to win the gold medal in the three-day team event. They won by a wide margin over the West German team. But over-all the West Germans outdid the Americans in the Olympics.

The two gold medals in equestrian sports were a respectable achievement. In retrospect the gold medals in track and field were, in the men's events, more than respectable. Yet, given the

American Olympic past and its Montreal hopes, the 1976 Games came off as an anticlimax.

Take the 100-metres and 200-metres. Those were once automatic American wins. American black runners dominated those events, the 110-metre and 400-metre hurdles, the 400-metres. In 1976 only Edwin Moses in the 400-metre hurdles was able to come up with a gold medal. The sprinter with the best 1975 and 1976 times, Steve Williams, tore his hamstring muscle—and reinjured it during the Trials in Eugene (where he was unable to qualify). He tried running after the Olympics, but was clearly not up to winning. His career might well be over. The great schoolboy sensation, Houston McTear, who had done a nine-second 100 yards, was also injured, and didn't make the team. Harvey Glance, whose times equaled theirs, finished fourth in the 100-metres—just behind the U.S.S.R.'s Valery Borzov, surprise winner of the 100-metre gold medal in Munich. East European coaches were wondering if American training technique took sufficient care of runners like Williams and McTear.

In 1976 Trinidad and Jamaica won the sprint gold medals, Hasely Crawford in the 100-metres and Donald Quarrie in the 200-metres recording unremarkable times far off the respective world records. In both the 400-metres and the 800-metres Alberto Juantorena whipped the American contenders—Fred Newhouse, Herman Frazier, Maxie Parks in the 400-metres; and Rick Wolhuter, the overwhelming favorite to win the 800-metres. The best Wolhuter could do was a bronze in the 800-metres; in the 1,500-metres he could do no better than sixth. Juantorena's world record in the 800-metres came as a surprise to many track and field observers who saw him mainly as a 400-metre man. The American 400-metre runners, on the other hand, thought of Juantorena as a 800-metre man just trying the 400-metre race as an experiment. Both were, alas, right. Both were, alas, wrong. In any event, Juantorena was the double winner in the longest sprint, the shortest distance race.

Willie Davenport, the old man of the American track team, managed a bronze in the 110-metre hurdles won by Guy Drut of France (who less than charmed Montreal by saying that he got his competitive courage from his English mother; he of course has a French father). Willie's great days were behind him: in Munich and Mexico City. Where the other hurdling Americans' great days were remained uncertain—Charles Foster finished fourth, James Owens sixth.

In the 400-metre hurdles, however, Moses beat his teammate, Mike Shine, by more than a second while setting a new world record; Quentin Wheeler finished fourth in this race, which had been all but conceded to John Akii-Bua of Uganda, one of track and field's leading "ghosts." John Walker's poor time in winning the 1,500-metres raised all kinds of questions about what might have happened between him and Filbert Bayi, the Tanzanian world-record holder at that distance. Moses, however, broke Akii-Bua's best times in setting a new world record. His win was classy and clean and, as it turned out, unique among the Americans.

In *The New York Times* the predictions in the field events were interesting. Dwight Stones and Bill Jankunis would come first and third in the high jump, with Jacek Wszola of Poland in between; Dave Roberts and Earl Bell would finish 1-2 in the pole vault; Arnie Robinson would win the long jump, Victor Saneev of the U.S.S.R. the triple jump for the third consecutive Olympics. Geoffrey Capes of Great Britain was supposed to win the shot put with George Woods second; Wolfgang Schmidt of East Germany was picked for the gold medal in the discus, with Mac Wilkins and John Powell right behind. Americans weren't given much of a chance in the hammer throw (the U.S.S.R. won all three medals); nor was much expected in the javelin.

The Dwight Stones fiasco I've discussed. The Dave Roberts—Earl Bell failure is almost as shocking. Here were the two leading polevaulters not just in the United States but in the world. They played with world records, a kind of "after you; no, after you" game that had carried the polevault world mark up to 18 feet 6½ inches. Roberts in the Olympic competition wasn't going to waste valuable energy jumping at the piddling heights. His strategy was to pass, and pass, and pass again—till the bar was set far above the qualifying height of 17 feet ¾ inches, something Roberts could go over with an old broomstick.

If Dwight Stones could blame the weather for his poor showing in the high jump, so could Dave Roberts and Earl Bell. If Dwight Stones could put the rap on the interminable Olympic qualifying and final jumps (he did it long before the Games opened), Dave Roberts and Earl Bell could have done the same with reference to the pole vault. Except that all jumpers shared the same weather, and all jumpers shared the same tedious wait between attempts.

It was close to noon when the polevault finals began, dark when the winner was decided. In between it drizzled. Vaulters covered their pole grips, used plastic, terry toweling, warm-up pants, jackets—anything—for protection. Trying to keep limber for eight or nine hours is a challenge: even the marathon runner calls it quits in a little more than two hours. Two landing mattresses were used to begin with. Two groups of finalists chose to cope with different heights.

In succession the vaulters dropped out—a slow time that seemed to move in stop-action from frame to frame. At last only enough jumpers remained to need one landing mattress. The other became an instant ottoman for vaulters lolling and, in the early hours, sunning. The northwest corner of the Olympic Stadium resembled the exercise yard of a prison. The vaulters would suddenly sprint down the track, stop, leap, twist, turn back, crouch, run upright, make phantom passes at imaginary runways.

Dave Roberts and Earl Bell all but disappeared during the mid-afternoon, slumped out of sight, watching their competitors diminish. Roberts, with his reddish hair thinning, looked like somebody's suddenly-aged young brother. He and Bell kept glancing up at the sky, watching the clouds close out the sun. A fine mist began falling and soon covered their approach and the used and unused landing mattresses.

Time dragged. Earl Bell made his try at 18 feet ½ inches, and failed. Roberts didn't give up his passing game plan, as he called it. After he and Poland's Tadeusz Slusarski and Finland's Antti Kalliomaki all had made 18 feet ½ inches (Roberts had missed once at the height), Roberts passed up 18 feet 2½ inches in order to set a real new Olympic record of 18 feet 4½ inches. It was the act of a champion. Roberts was not out to win an easy gold medal. He had forced a direct confrontation with space and gravity. His rivals seemed almost unimportant.

The rain began to fall harder. The air grew chilly. Roberts, like Stones later in the week, found himself asking the track attendants to squeegee water off his run. It was almost 8:00 P.M. The rain came down from the open roof in thin spaghetti strands. Roberts had a faithful band of fans waiting for him to do his height and then go on to break the *world* record.

Once he missed. A second time he sailed *under* the bar and his fans went wild, thinking he had gone over. The third time Roberts looked straight ahead, rocked back and forth only an instant, raised his pole, began his run over the wet approach, planted the pole, rose up as the pole bent, then shot toward the bar trying to inch over. He brushed it. The bar fell. Roberts was left with his last successful jump of 18 feet ½ inches—for him almost a warm-up height—and his crucial earlier miss. The world's best polevaulter, like the world's best high jumper a few days later, had to settle for a bronze medal. Earl Bell didn't get into the medals at all.

In that American men's track and field delegation two athletes stood poles apart, Frank Shorter, the favorite to win the marathon gold medal, and Mac Wilkins, a top contender for the gold medal in the discus. Shorter was the proud American, a nice chap, rather square; Wilkins was the international athlete sick of flagwaving and medal-reckoning. Before the Games began he was quoted as saying he hoped that the United States lost *all* the gold-medal contests, excluding his own discus event. Shorter in interviews referred to training, getting the right amount of sleep, eating the right food. Wilkins liked to leave the impression that his diet contained nothing but anabolic steroids which he popped like sunflower seeds. Wilkins, far from being the okay team player Shorter was, hoped aloud that his country-man in the discus competition, John Powell, would have bad cess.

It all looked like a great put-on, except that in the final competition Mac Wilkins proved he wasn't kidding. Throwing eleventh (among 15 competitors) he swung into his stride on his second go, let out a loud primal roar as the discus sailed out of the cage high and fast, coming to earth at the 221 foot-5½ inch mark. The American crowd was with Wilkins all the way, either unaware of what he had been saying or more concerned with his performance than with his "quotes." On his second throw, Wolfgang Schmidt of East Germany fouled. He fouled again on his fourth throw. Wilkins rushed out to comfort Schmidt and show him what he had been doing wrong. Wilkins and Schmidt remained in a coaching huddle, then Schmidt did a few shadow tosses, nodding vigorously. He got Wilkins' message.

On the third throw, before Schmidt fouled for the second time, the U.S.A.'s John Powell sent out a toss that put him in second place behind Wilkins. If everything remained as it was, Wilkins would win the gold and Powell the silver. Obviously Wilkins was coaching Schmidt to beat Powell, but just as obviously Wilkins was taking a chance that Schmidt, who had thrown farther than Wilkins' 221 feet 5½ inches on several occasions, would unleash a toss that would give Schmidt the gold.

On his final throw, Schmidt fell into place between Wilkins and Powell, changing Powell's seemingly safe silver into the baser bronze. As soon as Schmidt's throw was measured, Mac Wilkins ran toward the East German, threw his arms around him, danced him around while John Powell stood by wondering how come his uniform and Wilkins' were the same color. When the discus competitors marched out of the Stadium, Wilkins marched arm in arm with Schmidt. When they returned a short time later for the medal ceremonies, Wilkins and Schmidt were still behaving like teammates. John Powell, shut out, lagged behind.

The victory of Bruce Jenner in the decathlon I've already described; so, too, the defeat of Frank Shorter. The long jump brought the U.S.A. a gold medal on Arnie Robinson's very first jump of 27 feet 4¾ inches. The first jump of Randy Williams, 26 feet 7¼ inches, held up to get him the silver. Robinson didn't break the world record, but his jump at sea level had to be regarded as the world's record everywhere but in mile-high Mexico City (or Denver). In the triple jump, the U.S.S.R.'s veteran Victor Saneev was able to do 56 feet 8¾ inches even though he fouled on three of his six jumps. James Butts of the U.S.A. won the silver medal with a leap of 56 feet 4½ inches.

It was in the relays that the American men, all of them black, made up for the lack of gold medals in the individual sprint races. First came the performance of the 4 x 100 metre team of Harvey Glance, John Jones, Millard Hampton, and Steve Riddick. Less than an hour later, the 4 x 400 metre team of Herman Frazier, Ben Brown, Fred Newhouse, and Maxie Parks won by a wide margin over the Polish relay team. Alberto Juantorena ran the anchor leg for the Cuban 4 x 400 metre relay team, but ended up in second-last place. Both relay teams took their victory lap together, dancing over to the stands to wave at friends and family, backing away, jogging a few yards, then turning to the stands again, fisting the air in every variation of the victory salute. All eight relay runners held press conferences. As winners they could say something about how it was done.

In the women's 4 x 400 metre relay the United States on the last day of track and field competition won its third medal—but only its second silver—and so came out of the Olympics without a gold medal, with the same medal total the women had won in 1972. That relay team of Debra Sapenter, Shelia Ingram, Pam Jiles, and Roz Bryant broke the world record by 19/100ths of a second, but far ahead of them were the inevitable East Germans, who smashed that same record by almost *four* seconds. In the interview room, the women had a chance to explain how much this last race meant to them all. Without the win the American women's performance would have fallen from weak to puny.

In the track events, no American woman came close to winning a medal: but look who the American and Canadian women were up against:

- Annegret Richter of West Germany in the 100-metres.
- Baerbel Eckert of East Germany in the 200-metres.
- the great Irena Szewinska of Poland, who switched from the 100-metres and 200-metres to the 400-metres and at age 30 set a new world record of 49.29 seconds.
- the double-gold winner, Tatiana Kazankina of the U.S.S.R., who set a new world record in the 800-metres and won the 1,500-metres in her characteristic run-from-behind-in-the-outside-lane finish.

In the field events things weren't that much easier. Here the Americans were able to get their second silver by way of Kathy McMillan's extraordinary effort in the long jump (which left her only around two inches shy of the gold). In the javelin, Kathy Schmidt, on her last throw, got up to pick up the bronze.

But again, in the field events, the American and Canadian women faced some of the greatest athletes in the world:

- Rosemarie Ackermann of East Germany, the world-record holder in the high jump.
- Ruth Fuchs of East Germany, the best javelin thrower in the world.
- Evelin Schlaak of East Germany in the discus.
- Ivanka Christova of Bulgaria in the shot put.
- Siegrun Siegl and Christine Laser, both of East Germany, in the women's pentathlon.

To sum up the American achievement, it had to be considered uneven. Bruce Jenner had recorded one of the great performances of the Games; Frank Shorter, Dave Roberts, Dwight Stones had come through with American bummers. The same kinds of questions Canadians were starting to ask about their Olympic "plan" had been raised in the United States for years. In those sports with a plan and facilities—swimming, boxing, certain areas of track and field, yachting, archery, shooting—gold medals were won or narrowly missed. The tremendous achievement of the men's swimming team served as a measure by which to test what could be done in all other sports. John Naber, Bruce Furniss, Joe Bottom, Rod Strachan, for instance, all swam under the colors of the University of Southern California. As someone pointed out, had USC been competing as a nation, its swimmers would have taken fifth place with their huge number of gold medals. Indiana University was the other place for champion swimmers to gather. Competition and training and excellent coaching went on in swimming between Olympic years. The American swimmers, as Chet Jastremski pointed out to me, were, like champion women swimmers everywhere, getting younger; the European swimmers, though improving, were taking a long time to develop (and so reached the highest levels of competition older than the Americans).

The same consistency of coaching and performance found in swimming is hard to duplicate even in track and field, another sport with excellent college and university connections. The United States has the all-year-round weather facilities to offer its athletes in every Olympic sport. The United States, like Canada, has the option—to go at the East Europeans as if American life depended on victory; to continue cultivating the American garden and treating whatever grows as a gift and bonus.

The American spectators who took on the role of co-hosts in Montreal wanted to see Americans win. Even more, it seemed to me, they wanted Americans to participate in the Olympics. The "winning isn't everything; it's the only thing" credo didn't seem to govern either the Canadian or the American spectator's view of Olympic sports.

The degree of Olympic involvement a country chooses is perhaps a register of what it wants to do with athletics in its everyday life. The intelligent coaching, training, and physical care of athletes must be included in that option to compete. Americans are unlikely to turn to team handball and judo and field hockey while discarding baseball and football and horseracing simply because the former are, and the latter aren't Olympic sports. Almost every athlete who spoke out in Montreal thought that the U.S.A., once committed to participation on the Olympic level, could do better than it had in 1976.

Even East German athletes and coaches thought their national team could have done better in certain areas. The U.S.S.R. was upset with the performance of its men's basketball team, even more upset with its football team, which allowed two other East European countries, East Germany and Poland, to walk off with the gold and silver medals. India and Pakistan suffered cultural shock from the defeat of the two field hockey teams once used to facing each other in the finals.

Australia, which, like Canada, did not come up with a gold medal, found little consolation from reaching the field hockey finals with New Zealand—and losing. No Australian athlete got the international media coverage of New Zealand's gold-medal winner in the 1,500-metres, John Walker. New Zealand, the direct cause of the African boycott, came out of the Olympics golden.

In the end, nations made national evaluations. Mac Wilkins may have been against the politicization of the Olympics and the conversion of athletes into so many points or medals on a country's tally sheet. Yet his gold medal led to the playing of not some world anthem but the American "Star-spangled Banner": his medal was counted in as one of the 20 golds the United States won: his gold was converted to the coinage of points in the *American* column, not the column of *Countries in General*. The committee set-up accents the national identification of every sport and every athlete; the ceremonial pomp of the opening and the closing is also emphatically national. Dr. Chet Jastremski, during medal-awarding ceremonies, whispered to me:

"The Olympics should be for the athletes and by the athletes. The athletes themselves should be the administrators of these Games."

At that moment some swimming official, puffed up and proud, led another old gent in for the awarding of medals. Both men were having the time of their official lives. Space, time, and gravity weren't included in their old old scenario. The athletes who had just fought through their medium of water seemed only incidental, a necessary stimulus so these historical anachronisms called officials could make their ceremonial moves. The bureaucrats were having their Olympics. The coaches were having theirs. So, too, the athletes. The spectators. The media and the media-followers. The scalpers. Those even further out on the periphery.

During the magical competitive days everything came together and seemed unified. But on August 1, 1976, it was "Farewell Montreal 1976" and "Rendezvous in Moscow 1980." One thing was certain: everything in Moscow would change; everything in Moscow would be the same.

# 9 *Games Within Games Within Games...*

To write about the Montreal Olympics finally is to write about athletic achievement—and, alas, Mayor Jean Drapeau. Drapeau dreamed up the Montreal Olympics, he saw its buildings reach a climactic incompletion, he heard the crowd chant his name as though he were the Canadian to come up with an Olympic gold medal. The Olympic flame became

Drapeau's personal promethean gift to the citizens of Montreal; singlehandedly he stole the Athenian fire and delivered it on a laser beam to the citizens of Canada. His enemies wanted to chant:

*"Drapeau au poteau"*

which suggested this mayor was only for hanging. The rhyme most frequently found for Drapeau during the Olympics, however, was "Bravo!" and, with reference to his Olympic complex, *"C'est beau!"*

To figure out what was done in order for public land to be annexed, for public parks to be destroyed, for public golf-courses to be dug up would take the concerted labor of a regiment of investigative reporters dogging every Olympic site and Olympic Village trail. Graduate and undergraduate students at McGill University and the University of Montreal could find term papers, master's theses, doctoral dissertations in the politics and economics of Jean Drapeau's Olympics. Lawyers and accountants could enter the labyrinthine depths of Olympic building and financing and be lost in twisting intricacies forever.

Drapeau's great invention, never to "close the books" on his big-bang projects, would not work with the Olympics. He had forfeited possession of those books to the Quebec government. Premier Bourassa was calling the shots. Pemier Bourassa was a straightforward man. In response to Drapeau's vow that the Montreal Olympics would be self-financing and thus never incur a deficit—any more than a man could have a baby—Bourassa came up with a figure written boldly in red ink:

$1,000,000,000.

That was not the cost of the Olympics. The total cost of building and financing and administering the Olympics had another figure to represent it:

$2,000,000,000.

Bourassa obviously didn't want to get into the question of whether a man could or couldn't have a baby. His problem was more acute: how to get rid of a billion-dollar deficit. He came up with what looked to him like a model solution. The province of Quebec would crawl its way around the national and international financial community and beg to borrow 800 million dollars. Subtract that from the billion estimated as the Olympic deficit and that left a balance of 200 million dollars. Now, were 200 million dollars the total cost of the Games, Jean Drapeau could well use his favorite descriptive word about Olympic costs: "modest." Bourassa was a good sport: he would let Jean Drapeau pretend that the Games cost no more than 200 million dollars. In other words Bourassa took over 4/5ths of the Olympic "nut" and deeded the city of Montreal its modest share of 1/5th—a 4-1 ratio between a province and its wealthiest city seemed fair. Montreal had only to include 200 million dollars in its annual budget and work at absorbing it.

Jean Drapeau refused.

Jean Drapeau who had said that *no mayor is going to ruin his city in order to get the Olympics* was being asked by the realistic premier of his city's province to take over a share of the deficit he himself said could never happen, so Jean Drapeau said *non*. To put a deficit into the Montreal budget was to admit a deficit. Jean Drapeau said there was no deficit. Bourassa may have closed his books; Jean Drapeau had not closed *his*. All the returns weren't in yet. Lottery money was still there to illustrate the self-financing pledge. And Olympic facility rentals.

So Jean Drapeau refused: he refused provincially, he refused federally. Not Bourassa, not Prime Minister Trudeau was going to get him to break his promise to the people of Montreal that *in the long run* the Olympics wouldn't cost the city a cent.

If Mayor Abraham Beame of New York had told Governor Hugh Carey of New York State that New York's problems were temporary and that its deficits would *in time* be overcome by the principle of self-financing, chances are Beame would have been packed off to Bellevue Hospital for observation. Carey and Beame could at least agree on one thing: New York here and now had a deficit the city would have to face. Deficits are as palpable as black billiard balls. Either you have them or you don't.

Politically, Jean Drapeau could say *non*, but economically he was no more free to say *no* than Abe Beame. In almost every nation's chain of power, states and provinces stand higher than cities because states and provinces have access to federal money only they can channel to cities. The power to tax is sometimes ceded to a city, but the share of revenue a city gets is at the discretion of the state or province and, ultimately, of the federal government.

Premier Bourassa knows this. Prime Minister Trudeau knows this. Jean Drapeau knows this. But only Jean Drapeau, of the three, had anything to do with the day-to-day financing and building of the Olympics. Only Jean Drapeau lived with the Olympic deadline and with all the accidents and tricks of suppliers, manufacturers, workers. Only Jean Drapeau realized that everybody had only one message for him: "We must have more money, we must have more money." Jean Drapeau had been charmed into, bluffed into, argued into using the mode of construction that built the Olympic complex: to pay for a custom Olympic project he had first to pay for a custom plant that could be used totally only once—to build that custom Olympic project. As soon as the word got out that money was no object, a ripple went through the city of Montreal and its outer reaches. Drapeau had issued an invitation for every finagler to come drink at the public trough. Jean Drapeau's deadline date was no secret. The need to finish in time was a set-up: just 15 days after the July 17th deadline the Olympics would be over. No threat about holding back or holding out would work after August 1. The time to make Drapeau pay was *now*.

In the psychopathy that frequently accompanies great galas, public figures like Jean Drapeau divorce themselves from the consequences of a tomorrow. Even as the people at the Olympic Stadium were standing up to cheer and applaud Jean Drapeau for his gift to them, the clock was moving closer to the official end of Montreal's leap-year blast. Two days later, August 3, the banks would be open, the bourses would be open, the provincial offices in Quebec City would be open. The holiday was over. There was no ceremonial Olympic panache to cover over Premier Robert Bourassa's reading the big dollar-sign numbers.

The consequences of a six-year money binge ran into 10 figures. Premier Bourassa was stuck with a mittful of Jean Drapeau's markers and forced to make all of them good. The arrogant unreality of it all was staggering.

While the party was on, every wheeler-dealer wanted in. The Mafia wanted in. A refined form of blackmail sprang up. Everybody wanted to hold up the city bank. The Mayor was too busy to find reality in double-entry bookkeeping columns. His method was *pay now, look later*. And when Premier Bourassa said *now was later*, the Mayor came back with his old Expo trick of *not now*.

The horror stories began long before the Olympics. They will continue for years: how, for instance, the cost of renting a crane turned out to be many more times the cost of buying that crane. One could construct a model colloquy of how the city of Montreal was shafted by the Olympic project's gigantic cranes alone. Except that Drapeau referred all shafting instruments to Quebec City.

The ultimate scenario has already been drafted. It will go something like this:

> **Premier Bourassa:** When will Montreal take care of this Olympic item, M. Drapeau? The province is a little short of cash.
>
> **Mayor Drapeau:** Why do you not try a special hourly lottery?
>
> **Premier Bourassa:** The creditors have to be paid today, M. Mayor.
>
> **Mayor Drapeau:** You could rent the Olympic Stadium for a series of provincial money-raising athletic contests. Or use it for sunrise services.
>
> **Premier Bourassa:** You incurred the debt. You will pay.
>
> **Mayor Drapeau:** There is no debt, my friend, only a temporary shortage of cash.
>
> **Premier Bourassa:** There is a billion-dollar shortage of cash today.

> **Mayor Drapeau:** You lack faith in the province's future.
>
> **Premier Bourassa:** What Montreal has spent, Quebec is paying for.
>
> **Mayor Drapeau:** For this relief, much thanks.
>
> **Premier Bourassa:** The province has ways of making Montreal pay.
>
> **Mayor Drapeau:** I will resist such threats to my very last breath.
>
> **Premier Bourassa:** There are revenues we can withhold from Montreal.
>
> **Mayor Drapeau:** My people and I will not be brought to our knees. We will resist taxation without representation.
>
> **Premier Bourassa** *(weeping)*: You owe me—us—the province—200 million dollars. How can I make you pay?
>
> **Mayor Drapeau** *(sotto voce, after checking to see if anyone is listening)*: Hold a gun to my head somewhere public—on top of the Velodrome, how's that? Then everybody will know I tried to protect Montreal from an unreasonable debt, but had to give in to the province's superior fire power.

I can guarantee that the preceding dialogue is fictitious; I cannot guarantee that it isn't true.

The Olympics have been the Mayor's big show. Whether it was his last show is up to somebody politically powerful and good at in-fighting to demonstrate. Drapeau orchestrated disaster during his political career so he could ride in, a white knight on his credit-card charger, to rescue Montreal from boredom, and worse.

Not much attention has been paid to the mini-opening Drapeau staged Friday night, July 16, on the eve of the official ceremonies the Queen would preside over. It's a model of how he operates. He chose night, in contrast to all the other daytime

Olympic ceremonies (except the closing). He organized a dramatic, impressive, sentiment-ridden political-religious service around the Olympic torch being carried from Ottawa to Montreal. [The atmosphere was nothing like the angry bourgeois pots-and-pans-banging demonstrations organized by the Chilean friends-of-the-CIA to get rid of Salvatore Allende. This ritual was part of the Jean Drapeau-Good News Show.] If something, perchance, soured Jean Drapeau's opening day at the Olympic Stadium, he would already have had his hour of praise from the multitudes crowding alongside the roads between Ottawa and Montreal.

People lined up hours before the torchbearers came into sight, on the curbs and in the streets, children on their parents' shoulders, waving Quebec flags, Olympic flags, Olympic souvenirs, crests, banners. Moose horns blew, sirens, whistles. Kids shrieked from street to street like echoing bluejays. It was raining on the outskirts of Mount Royal, raining on the huge lighted cross in front of which Mayor Jean Drapeau had set up Montreal's first Olympic torch. Dark night surrounded everything: the stage was set for the laser-lit Canadian Olympic flame. When the CBC French network cameras played their lights on the podium there was the Mayor; there, like a captive guest, was Lord Killanin; there, like your sister's brother-in-law's brother, was COJO chief Roger Rousseau, not one of Jean Drapeau's favorite people.

This was no fête for tourists. This was Jean Drapeau bringing the Olympics right to his constituency, his middleclass people, to their streets and doorsteps. The coming Olympic torch would be like the effigy of a saint in a more somber religious procession. Everyone pressed forward, ignoring the rain, to be as close to the sacred flame as possible. Anybody who passed was cheered and applauded, joggers, bikeriders, cops in cars and motorcycles, tow trucks, ambulances. This was Jean Drapeau's neighborhood Mardi Gras: if the people of Mount Royal, or Verdun or La Salle or Lachine, wanted the more sensual street celebrations, they could head for the streets of Old Montreal where a wilder, less familial night party had been going on for some weeks now. Jean Drapeau tended to all tastes in his constituency.

For more explicit religion, Mayor Drapeau had two bishops on hand, one French, one English. Both would treat the Olympics as a form of Lent. Bishop Fallis, when it came his turn to speak, said:

"We now look to see the triumph of fraternity and brotherhood and excellence . . . and complete self-giving."

He wanted the people gathered under the Mount Royal cross to think of the Olympics as a Christian symbol. The Bishop cautioned that "the Olympics are not merely to entertain us." The Olympics had a lesson for the competition-watchers: "to do away with the slipshod." The Olympics, like the cross, "calls us to a new service to others."

Mayor Jean Drapeau, by the vigor of his nodding, seemed to agree.

But the bishops were only warm-ups to the real message, sent specially from the Vatican by the Pope (shown on French CBC television monitors) to the people of Mount Royal and other areas of Montreal.

For sports, Mayor Drapeau had lined up something Canada would prove to be quite short of in Montreal, gold medalists. He had Canada's "lucky" bobsled team that won a winter gold in 1964, the famous Vic Emery, along with Dr. John Emery, Peter Kirby, and Doug Anakin. The star of the nighttime procession, however, was Kathy Kreiner (whose gold medal in the winter downhill at Innsbruck would end up as Canada's only gold for Olympics '76); she came running through the streets, surrounded by troops and a full motorcycle escort, the Olympic torch held high. She was dressed in vestal virgin white T-shirt and white shorts. M. Drapeau received the torch from Miss Kreiner's hands, held it up to his people (with Kathy standing there beside him). Any camera aimed at Kathy Kreiner would get a piece of the Mayor.

Drapeau's orchestrations didn't cease. Now he handed the flame to Gerard Coté, the old distance runner who used to win the Boston Marathon year after year: jogging slightly uphill,

John Walker, New Zealand, gold medalist in the 1,500-metres, shown winning his heat with Canada's Dave Hill on the ground behind him. *(Canadian Press)*

Kathy McMillan, U.S.A., was the silver medalist in the women's long jump. (*Canadian Press*)

East Germany and Poland in the football (soccer) final, won by the East Germans, 3-1. *(Canadian Press)*

Greg Joy of Canada won the silver medal in the high jump. *(Canadian Press)*

Michel Vaillancourt, Canada, jumping for a silver medal in the individual Grand Prix equestrian event. *(The Toronto Star)*

Coté threaded his way through the crowd, peppily ran up the platform where the Olympic urn was set. He had to stand tiptoe to get his torch into the urn's open shell.

The rain fell harder. At first the flame wouldn't catch. Then it did. Coté stepped back, as if saluting. All up and down the hillside the crowd cheered and whistled and honked horns and banged those pots and pans some more.

*"Le grand jour est arrivé!"* Mayor Drapeau announced (sparing his fans a longer parody of the *Marseillaise*).

"Hip hip hooray," cried Lord Killanin, getting in a belated point for his side.

"We worked to illuminate the torch bright as the sun," said the Mayor. "The flame has reached the city of its destination."

Why the flame couldn't reach Montreal only once, at the appointed time, the next afternoon, in the presence of the Queen, the Mayor didn't explain: two official urns, one temporary at midfield, one permanent, stood unlit in the Olympic Stadium.

The opening-day torch ceremonies the Mayor would naturally have to share with the Queen. On Mount Royal he could easily upstage everyone, even the President of the International Olympic Committee, Lord Killanin. All through the night the Olympic flame and the illuminated cross on Mount Royal could project a double image of Drapeau's Vatican and Athenian connections. As he stood on the podium acknowledging the crowd's right to laud him, the Mayor smiled modestly. His spectacles reflecting the Olympic flame blazed with his triumph.

Down below, in the thoroughfares of the city, Drapeau was far from benign. A day earlier I had gone around Montreal with the "Save Montreal" people, in a bus booked to touch all of the city's blighted disaster areas. Arnold Bennett, a Montreal Citizens' Movement councilor, stood up from time to time to read out statistics or explain what had happened to a building or a district. The theme of Bennett's revelations was the same as Nick Auf der Maur's: that the Mayor operated secretly, arbitrarily, and that the Olympics were just the most horrendous Drapeau plan in a long line of similar prestidigitations.

On that same bus was a girl named Olga, a law student at McGill, who detailed a bill of particulars incriminating Drapeau and his buddies. She stood at the front of the bus, trying to speak without encountering the screech of electronic feedback. Olga had lots of statistics about the Olympics. She had lots of statistics on housing that had been wiped out in favor of parking lots. She and Bennett could quote specific figures dealing with Drapeau's dropping the tax evaluation of a certain business or building. Drapeau's best friends were, we were told, the local developers. Or anyone setting up a huge structure, private or public. Some of the familiar facts were recited again—that 780 houses were destroyed so that the CBC mausoleum could go up on Dorchester. That property Louis XIV had given to the church was now being sold to developers. That parking lots and extra traffic lanes were constantly going up in place of low-income housing. That the Autoroute had been built at a cost of 60 million dollars a mile. That the Canadian Pacific owned 22 acres off Dominion Square.

But the real purpose of the tour was to show "outsiders" how Jean Drapeau operated, particularly with regard to anybody or anything that stood between him and the Montreal image he wanted to project. The issue was the 386,000-dollar Corridart exhibit hung on hoardings that lined Sherbrooke Street between Atwater Avenue (the site of the Montreal Forum) and the Olympic Stadium. Corridart was an important addition to the purely sports nature of the usual Olympics. Montreal and the rest of Canada had decided to include a range of cultural and popular events and entertainments. Concerts, art exhibitions, poetry readings, dance recitals, rock groups, plays, opera, children's shows began early in July. An important part of the cultural display were the scaffoldings of photographs and art financed by the Quebec government under Cultural Affairs Minister Jean-Paul L'Allier. One of the features of those scaffoldings was a finger here and a finger there pointing right at a building that had gone up over a historical landmark, or a high rise that had wiped out some well-kept local neighborhood. Corridart was sponsored by COJO headed by Roger Rousseau, the man Drapeau openly snubbed.

Nick Auf der Maur showed me a letter he had received dated July 2 from a small developer protesting against "the finger pointing at our building." Undoubtedly that developer and others had recorded with Jean Drapeau their "unhappiness with the manner and choice of art" displayed in Corridart. Tuesday, July 13, four days before the Olympics opened, Mayor Drapeau and his executive committee met. That night, as darkness was falling, a huge crew of city public works demolition "experts" operating under Montreal police protection swooped down on Corridart. They left four-by-fours broken or scattered over the ground. The whole scene was reminiscent of the bully-boy bulldozing by Soviet police of outdoor abstract art displays in Moscow. When that happened, people from all over the world protested against the ugly assault against art, and the gratuitous police violence.

Protests were heard in Montreal. The Mayor suggested that Gerald Niding, chairman of the executive committee, should be the one to answer all inquiries about what happened and why. Mr Niding's press secretary responded to protests by issuing this statement:

"Various scaffolding and other odd structures . . . along Sherbrooke Street . . . contravened municipal laws governing the occupancy of the public domain and, moreover, . . . constituted a safety hazard. For those reasons, the city decided to have such structures removed without further delay."

Cultural Affairs Minister L'Allier "ordered" Corridart put back in place, but obviously a mayor who had said *no* to a premier's demand that he pick up 200 million dollars in his budget was unlikely to comply with the order of a mere cultural minister. L'Allier didn't even rate a Drapeau *no*. Mr. L'Allier had announced that the department of cultural affairs would "go to any length to force Drapeau to put everything back in place." Just as the department was threatening Drapeau with vengeful mystification, the Mayor and the Premier joined in a brotherly welcome of Her Majesty the Queen to Quebec.

Drapeau put nothing "back in place." His buddies the developers saw once again just where real power resided in Montreal. Jean Drapeau was obviously a mayor any realtor could do business with. Foreign investors, too, could do business with Jean Drapeau. He had vowed in West Germany in 1974 that Montreal would never impose special conditions on foreign investment. Swiss, German, Italian, as well as French money had been pouring into Montreal since then.

All this I heard from Olga, the McGill law student; though I checked out her material. The next time I saw Olga was opening day, wearing a brown peasant dress and white blouse, the uniform of a barmaid working the press centers at the Olympic Stadium!

"Olga," I said, "you?"

"The money's supposed to be good," she said, laughing. "I like the idea of living off Jean Drapeau."

[COJO had promised waitresses and barmaids two months of work, lavish tips from the big media spenders, a package guaranteeing a modest 2,000 dollars clear for each and every worker. Olga and her associates Roberta and Esther found that Europeans didn't tip much; that East Europeans hardly tipped at all—these were the press center's big spenders. The usual "tip" was a small pile of pennies foreign sportspeople considered a burden. Roberta and Olga soon realized they would be lucky to clear 200 dollars for the Olympic weeks. Soon girls were being laid off. Roberta quit first. Then Olga decided that only builders and developers could live in style off Jean Drapeau. She quit too. Esther told me she was hanging around because she had nothing better to do. On COJO promises she had burned her summer bridges.]

The monolithic style of Jean Drapeau is still intact. He is howled at, derided, threatened, but has never met serious defeat. In time, of course, the province of Quebec will get him to accept the 200-million-dollar deficit as Montreal's burden. He will take on that debt under protest and plead, perhaps, that a city has no power to equal that of a province. Drapeau will be the martyr, Quebec the bully. He will show the wounds of early 1976, when he was seemingly deposed by Victor Goldbloom and that same Bourassa. He will add the wounds of autumn, and swear to his dying day that the Montreal Olympics were self-financing, and never did have a deficit. For someone to blow a mean two billion dollars and cough up a lousy 200 million dollars is the kind of 10-cents-on-the-dollar settlement big spenders love.

Drapeau had his day, but Montreal will pick up the costs for decades. From everything I've been able to gather, it should have been possible to build a better stadium at perhaps half the cost. Making all possible allowances for inflation, managed shortages, squeeze plays by striking unions and graymailing suppliers, this project didn't have to reach even a billion dollars. Montreal's was perhaps the last Olympics of wild financial hysteria. When the shenanigans of the Olympic Village operation are added to the Olympic Stadium fiasco, Montreal appears as the New El Dorado, with endless supplies of gold to hand out to the arrogantly eager.

When I saw Roger Taillibert and we talked about his being a builder (in the medieval sense of the builders of Chartres, a subject he has written on), our meeting took place the morning that his fee for designing and supervising the construction of the Olympic Stadium, Swimming Pool, Velodrome, and various tunnels was estimated to be around 42 million dollars. Other estimates of Taillibert's fee ranged down from 30 million dollars, 24 million dollars, to 16 million dollars. The day Goldbloom took over, I was told Taillibert would be lucky coming out of the project with even two million dollars. I have not been able to get a hard figure on Taillibert's actual fee: his arrangement, as I have it from several sources, was to get a fixed percentage as architect, builder, and supervisor. The reason for the figures varying is that everyone assumes Taillibert's percentage was based on the original 250-million-dollar estimate that floated up to two billion.

Even at the lower figures, the Quebec institute of architects complained, Taillibert got more money than all the province's architects taken together earned in 1974. More than that: his Olympic complex, with only the Velodrome having a unique style, cost more than anything Gropius ever built, or Frank Lloyd Wright or Mies or Le Corbusier or those big American splurgers, Harrison & Abramowitz—making all allowances for inflation.

The two billion dollars was certainly spent, but the Olympic complex shows little evidence of costing that much. Munich's buildings for 1972 had more contemporary flair than the Stade Olympique. Expo had as much to show for a fraction of the Olympic money. The Olympic Village, which wasn't Drapeau's direct responsibility, is even less impressive architecturally.

All of Montreal's other sports facilities outside the Olympic complex picked up a fresh coat of paint here, a new sound system there, a few hundred extra seats, a new scoreboard—all courtesy of the Olympics. In time the Stadium tower will be finished, one supposes. Artificial turf has already been put in. In time that flimsy retractable roof diaphragm will be in place. Montreal's professional baseball team and football team will use the Stadium. (On September 25, 1976, the Montreal Alouettes played their first Canadian Football League Game in the new Stadium, before a full house. Many people who had not been able to get Olympic tickets wanted to see and be in the now-world-famous Stade Olympique.) Cycling will be a regular feature in the Velodrome. The Swimming Pool will accommodate international meets. Montreal will be a sports center, a convention center, and, if Drapeau hangs in, perhaps become Monte Carlo-on-the-St. Lawrence.

What I am saying does not detract from the athletes, from the drama, from the excitement of Canada's first Olympic Games. As a great event the Games, in spite of the African boycott, delivered everything the word *Olympics* promised. But this extravagantly irresponsible boondoggle remains an offense to taste, to measure, to economic justice, and to any concept of an amateur Olympics.

*158*

Toward the end of the Games I was asked on a television program whether I thought it was all worth it. I observed that the only ones who could answer that question were the people of Montreal. The doubleness of the 1976 Games will always be with us: as a happening, as an event, as memory, as nostalgia, as a high point in many a Canadian and American life, the Games come off triumphantly. Those great names, and the images they conjure up of extraordinary human athletic achievement, will reverberate through the rest of the century—Comaneci, Ender, Jenner, Alexeev, Naber, Montgomery, Stevenson, Spinks, Leonard, Andrianov, Kazankina, Szewinska, Juantorena, Cierpinski, Viren, Wilkins, Pace, Ryon, Joy, Saneev, the American men basketballers, the Soviet women basketballers, the East German footballers, the Polish men volleyballers, the Japanese women volleyballers, the West German, East German, British, Swedish and Danish yachtsmen.

Montreal for a fortnight was a succession of New Year's Eves, South American *carnivale*, days of misrule trying hard to equal the bull run at Pamplona, the Oktoberfest, the World Series, Super Bowl, World Cup soccer finals. A writer who said she really wasn't interested in sports told me she watched the Olympics because it seemed a kind of unifying experience—all those people all over the world homing in on this one grand event.

Again, in spite of committees and politicians and national chauvinism all over the globe, the athletes assumed their mythic roles in this long-run Olympic play, and simply tried to run faster, jump higher, throw farther, or reach the highest pitch of performing. Every new record set became the mark to be broken next.

In 1972 the East Germans were in Munich to learn. What they learned then and in the following three years was made apparent in Montreal. The U.S.S.R. in most sports had gone through this learning process earlier, and in 1976 could be considered as having arrived. At a very high level the Olympics can be a disinterested learning process for everyone, individual or country. One might even learn *only* to participate.

159

In the first heat of the men's 10,000-metres a runner from Haiti, Olmeus Charles, turned up, and became, after a lap or two, the comic hit of the Games. But there was more to him than met the eye: Charles was in the 10,000-metres without having registered a qualifying time—any country could enter one unclocked athlete in any event. All around Charles were strivers and strategists, the blood-washed or the blood-intact. At the gun they all took off in pursuit of a rabbity medal. Not Charles. Charles knew nothing about the 10,000-metres other than that 25 turns around a 400-metre track added up to the distance. Striding hard, elbowing by on corners, going into the lead or dropping back, the straining runners made one 400-metre lap after another. Not Charles. He fell into the unhurried jogging pace of an octogenarian trying to forfend a coronary. He not only kept hearing footsteps but felt the wind of a gaggle of runners whipping past him as he was lapped once, and again and again and again. The ambition-dogged Adidas-footed distance runners had collapsed at the finishing line, been revived, and dragged themselves off to await the final when Charles passed the lap-clock, all alone on the track, with six laps to go. Some up-and-doing businessmen booed and hollered at Charles to get off the track (there were two more heats to come), but the overwhelming response to his charming trot in front of 70,000 spectators was mock-cheering, great laughter, and delighted applause.

Charles was acting out the nonideological "Loneliness of the Long-Distance Runner," letting those upwardly mobile chaps pound their oxygenless way to advancement. In the stands were the business strivers, the political strivers, the careerists, those intent on making it. On the track Charles still had five laps to go. Then four. By this time all the strivers were frothing at the mouth. They wanted him dragged off the track so real athletes could reinherit the space. "Shoot him!" I heard someone shout as the stands convulsed with laughter. "Get him the hell out of there!" someone else hollered. Olmeus was evidently in the Haitian army. Someone had ordered him to run. The question of how fast had obviously never come up.

A pretty young woman in a safari hat, the lap-bell ringer, was the only track official paying serious attention to Charles. If he hadn't been out there, God knows what interesting things she might have been into by this time. The lap-clock read three, then two. Finally she stood up as if this were indeed the bell lap for John Walker and his personal ghost, Filbert Bayi. She flicked the clock till it read "1," then rang the bell as if unleashing the ride of Paul Revere. Anybody else might have been stampeded by all that fuss. Not Charles. He seemed oblivious of the fans rising to give him a mock standing ovation interspersed with shouts of "Sprint, sonny!" and "Try running backwards!" People who had gone out for a snack and taken their sweet time at it returned to find a cheering crowd saluting not Lasse Viren but Olmeus Charles, who like a good soldier crossed the finish line in a final gesture of duty.

Charles was exercising his and his country's Olympic option: to send an athlete to the opening and closing ceremonies fronted by the national flag and not burdened by something so onerous as winning. Call it blood packing, call it blood doping, even a transfusion of Lasse Viren's blood would little affect Olmeus Charles on his participatory mission. He, too, became one of the fabulous images of the Montreal Games under the caption of "Running is almost fun."

Charles described one extreme of Olympic participation; the great athletes like Jenner and Viren and Kazankina described the other. In between fell those hundreds, thousands of athletes who had as little hope of winning medals as Charles, but who rounded out national delegations, marching in the opening ceremonies, joying in the Olympic experience while filling a heat or being eliminated early. At the very top of every event were a few gifted people able to demonstrate that here and now they were the best in the world at this or that sport. But every country should know that it might pour all its national treasure into a sports program and still not produce a Bruce Jenner or a Kornelia Ender. It could take all its 10-year-old girls off its playgrounds, give them the intense Bela Caroly training treatment and never have one turn out a Nadia Comaneci. Money and planning and determination go only so far: will alone could never produce a Juantorena.

Sports and gala surroundings make the Olympics the world's spectacular of spectaculars. Montreal was no disappointment. The questions that arise aren't related to the Olympics as a triumphant demonstration of humankind's leap-year confrontation with space, time, gravity, and athletic history.

The doubleness that nags at these Games brings us back to Jean Drapeau and the people of Montreal. And the people of any city fortunate enough, or unfortunate enough, to be chosen as the site of a future Olympics. A city has to work hard for five or six years in order to prepare for what passes in the twinkling of an eye. That an Olympic city must be burdened with massive debt for generations to come makes the Games a rash indulgence. The splashy costs of Olympics '76 have consequences for the rich of Montreal, for the people in the middle, but greater consequences by far for Montreal's poor.

When a contractor cried, "We must have more money," Drapeau's men somehow found a way to provide it. Those who try to call to the Mayor and his executive committee for housing or shelter or food or medical care will hear only the sound of their voices. When the city finally inherits the wind of that six-year Olympic blow, the poor will assuredly feel the squeeze most sharply.

Drapeau has successfully erected his Olympic showpiece. His city can refer to 1976 as its Great Year. The people of Montreal, Quebec, Canada, and the world will hold encapsulated the exciting moments of this XXI Olympiad. Millions of people took the Games personally during the Olympic fortnight. They, like the people in the Stadium's temporary seats and standing-room sections, didn't want these Games ever to end. They wanted endless encores of Nadia Comaneci scoring her 10's and acknowledging the heard and unheard applause. Those who flew out of Montreal shortly after the closing ceremonies, or leaped into their automobiles and left the city behind, have only untroubled memories of a fabled time to remember. The morning after will always be Montreal's.

That's the doubleness: magnificent athletes, imperfect bureaucrats and politicians. Spectacular passing images, perpetual squalor. But for the overwhelming majority *in* Montreal as well as outside, the Games were an unqualified success. Everyone who experienced the Olympics in person or on television has absorbed the fabled athletes into a personal record of these and earlier Games. On that level Montreal's Stadium was every stadium in which the Olympic torch ever burned and the five-ring flag flew. In history, as nostalgia, in personal memory, all the stadiums converge, all the great athletes meet as contemporaries, everyone striving, nobody unvictorious. Everyman, Everywoman, his and her own Olympic Hall of Fame.

The Olympics are the ultimate dream of resolution. All the hypothetical questions are answered. Every Olympic sport has a beginning, a middle, and a medal-rewarding end. Nothing is left unsettled. There are the indelible facts—scores, times, heights, weights, distances. Even the manipulated sports such as diving end in the record books resolved and final.

Montreal, then, was not one but two places: the magic city where everything worked out beautifully and all the greats recorded their achievements on minds and electronic instruments: the modern city with all of the urban burdens and all of the urban blights surrounding its urban blessings. For 15 days the two cities were one, all of it magical. On the sixteenth day, with darkness fallen, the closing ceremonies began.

Some of the national delegations had left the city. Others were restricted to six athletes, no more. The new flagcarriers were those like Canada's Greg Joy, who had been chosen to lead his countrymen because of something achieved during the Games. There was no Queen Elizabeth to take a flag's salute. The ceremony was short, almost brisk. The smaller national delegations moved quickly into the Stadium and onto the grass. The music played about half as long as it had on opening day. For the kids in the crowd it was like camp closing. There were tears like the tears seen all over the Olympic Village.

Down came the Olympic flag, carried solemnly out of the Stadium. Maynard Ferguson spotlighted in white played a high piercing farewell on his solo trumpet. The Olympic flame went out. Up on the electronic scoreboard was a supposed live broadcast by satellite from Moscow. Somebody in faking a live broadcast had goofed. It was daylight on the scoreboard. Someone had forgotten that Moscow was seven hours ahead of Montreal. The music was faked, even the choirs singing in Montreal faked. There seemed to be an anticlimax in the closing ceremonies. Perhaps only the opening ceremonies could be the real thing.

But in the waning moments, when everyone held and waved green chemical candles in simulation of fireflies swarming, the realization that this was indeed the end struck. Tomorrow there was—nothing. The Swimming Pool would be dark. Repair work would have to begin on the leaky Velodrome roof. The turf that horses had kicked up all day would be once and for all stripped off. Green plastic "grass" would inherit the Stadium earth.

As the last athletic delegation left the Stadium, those who prefer their memories concrete tried to speed up the deturfing by ripping up chunks to carry off to memory lane. Banners and signs were grabbed at in snarly contests. Some souvenir freaks were trying to cut out pieces of tartan track. A few people tried to run full speed for the stretch of 100-metres. Others aimed long jumps and triple jumps over the plots of sand pits. A larger number dodged and danced through the crowd or simply stared up at the ring of roof glaring with lights. A couple of people inhaled the Olympic Stadium air in huge gulping draughts. The flashbulbs kept popping, but fewer. People in the temporary seats and standing room sections were singing *Auld Lang Syne*. It was their summer of New Year's Eves. Earlier they had shouted their thanks to the man who made it possible, Jean Drapeau. Now he and the hassles were forgotten. Memory's sieve would strain out all unpleasantries and make this first Canadian Olympics an unqualified triumph. Ten blocks from the Stadium a few unemployed teenagers were shooting pool in a crummy beer joint. They didn't see much of the Olympics on television. They didn't have money for tickets: one wag said, "I didn't even know who was playing."

For those leaving the Stadium this very last time, the fortnight was already packed in a memory jar purged of all political and economic complexities. A few children were fast asleep in a parent's arms. Taxi business was brisk. Teenagers were climbing light standards to bring down the Olympic signs and logos and carry away the silken windblown red banners. Souvenir shops were trying to flog their slowly dying five-ring T-shirts or those with the Montreal Olympic logo inscribed with a soon out-of-date 1976.

Mayor Jean Drapeau's car sped out of the underground parking pit—the only place in the Stadium that didn't leak when it rained. All those detractors of his grand civic achievements had heard what he heard, the people, his people, crying his name in gratitude for the major sporting experience of their lives he, the Mayor, had singlehandedly delivered:

DRA-PEAU

DRA-PEAU

DRA-PEAU

On Sherbrooke Street the Corridart scaffolds were gone. Other parts of the city looked like depressed sections of Brooklyn's Bedford-Stuyvesant. The Mayor wasn't going in that direction. He was in an Olympic chariot. The crowd had just crowned his brow with bays. This could not but be his finest hour. He had won. He was right. Hadn't the people said so?

*Final Results of All Olympic Medal Winners*

*Plus Results of Canadian and American Finalists*

New Olympic Record = (NOR)
New World Record = (NWR)

## Results Archery

*Joliette Archery Range*     *July 30*    *14:00*
**Women's final** (after 288 arrows)

| | | | |
|---|---|---|---|
| G | Luann Ryon | USA | 2499 NOR |
| S | Valentina Kovpan | USSR | 2460 |
| B | Zebiniso Rustamova | USSR | 2407 |
| | | | |
| 5 | Lucille Lemay | Can | 2401 |
| 7 | Linda Myers | USA | 2393 |
| 16 | Wanda Allan | Can | 2303 |

*Joliette Archery Range*     *July 30*    *14:00*
**Men's final** (after 288 arrows)

| | | | |
|---|---|---|---|
| G | Darrell Pace | USA | 2571 NOR |
| S | Hiroshi Michinaga | Jap | 2502 |
| B | Carlo Ferrari | Ita | 2495 |
| | | | |
| 4 | Richard McKinney | USA | 2471 |
| 7 | Dave Mann | Can | 2431 |
| 16 | Edward Gamble | Can | 2362 |

## Results  Athletics (Track and Field)

*Olympic Stadium      July 25    17:50*
**Women's 100-metres**   Olympic record = 11.0 / World record = 11.01

| G | Annegret Richter | WGer | 11.08 |
|---|---|---|---|
| S | Renate Stecher | EGer | 11.13 |
| B | Inge Helten | WGer | 11.17 |
| 5 | Evelyn Ashford | USA | 11.24 |
| 6 | Chandra Cheeseborough | USA | 11.31 |

*Olympic Stadium      July 28    18:10*
**Women's 200-m**   OR = 22.40 / WR = 22.21

| G | Baerbel Eckert | EGer | 22.37 NOR |
|---|---|---|---|
| S | Annegret Richter | WGer | 22.39 |
| B | Renate Stecher | EGer | 22.47 |

*Olympic Stadium      July 29    16:20*
**Women's 400-m**   OR = 50.48 / WR = 49.77

| G | Irena Szewinska | Pol | 49.29 NOR/NWR |
|---|---|---|---|
| S | Christina Brehmer | EGer | 50.51 |
| B | Ellen Streidt | EGer | 50.55 |
| 5 | Rosalyn Bryant | USA | 50.65 |
| 6 | Shelia Ingram | USA | 50.90 |
| 8 | Debra Sapenter | USA | 51.66 |

*Olympic Stadium*    *July 26*    *18:20*
**Women's 800-m**   OR = 1:56.6 / WR = 1:57.5

| G | Tatiana Kazankina | USSR | 1:54.94 NOR/NWR |
|---|---|---|---|
| S | Nikolina Chtereva | Bul | 1:55.42 |
| B | Elfi Zinn | EGer | 1:55.60 |

*Olympic Stadium*    *July 30*    *17:30*
**Women's 1500-m**   OR = 4:01.4 / WR = 4:01.4

| G | Tatiana Kazankina | USSR | 4:05.48 |
|---|---|---|---|
| S | Gunhild Hoffmeister | EGer | 4:06.02 |
| B | Ulrike Klapezynski | EGer | 4:06.09 |
| 8 | Janice Merrill | USA | 4:08.54 |

*Olympic Stadium*    *July 29*    *15:00*
**Women's 100-m hurdles**   OR = 12.59 / WR = 12.59

| G | Johanna Schaller | EGer | 12.77 |
|---|---|---|---|
| S | Tatiana Anisimova | USSR | 12.78 |
| B | Natalia Lebedeva | USSR | 12.80 |

**Women's 4x100-m relay   OR = 42.61 / WR = 42.51**

| G | Marlis Oelsner | EGer | 42.55 NOR |
|---|---|---|---|
|   | Renate Stecher | | |
|   | Carla Bodendorf | | |
|   | Baerbel Eckert | | |
| S | Elvira Possekel | WGer | 42.59 |
|   | Inge Helten | | |
|   | Annegret Richter | | |
|   | Annegret Kroniger | | |
| B | Tatyana Prorochenko | USSR | 43.09 |
|   | Liudmila Maslakova | | |
|   | Nadeshda Besfamilnaya | | |
|   | Vera Anisimova | | |
| 4 | Margaret Howe | Can | 43.17 |
|   | Patty Loverock | | |
|   | Joanne McTaggart | | |
|   | Marjorie Bailey | | |
| 7 | Martha Watson | USA | 43.35 |
|   | Evelyn Ashford | | |
|   | Debra Armstrong | | |
|   | Chandra Cheeseborough | | |

*Olympic Stadium      July 31      19:00*
**Women's 4x400 m relay   OR = 3:23.0 / WR = 3:23.0**

| | | | | |
|---|---|---|---|---|
| G | Doris Maletzki | EGer | 3:19.23 NOR/NWR | |
| | Brigitte Rohde | | | |
| | Ellen Streidt | | | |
| | Christina Brehmer | | | |
| S | Debra Sapenter | USA | 3:22.81 | |
| | Shelia Ingram | | | |
| | Pam Jiles | | | |
| | Rosalyn Bryant | | | |
| B | Inta Klimovocha | USSR | 3:24.24 | |
| | Lyudmila Aksenova | | | |
| | Natalia Sokolova | | | |
| | Nadezhda Ilyina | | | |
| 8 | Margaret Stride | Can | 3:28.91 | |
| | Joyce Yakubowich | | | |
| | Rachelle Campbell | | | |
| | Yvonne Saunders | | | |

*Olympic Stadium      July 28      14:00*
**Women's high jump   OR = 1.92 (6' 3⅝") WR = 1.95 (6' 4¾")**

| | | | | |
|---|---|---|---|---|
| G | Rosemarie Ackermann | EGer | 1.93 | (6' 4") NOR |
| S | Sara Simeoni | Ita | 1.91 | (6' 3¼") |
| B | Yordanka Blagoeva | Bul | 1.91 | (6' 3¼") |
| 5 | Joni Huntley | USA | 1.89 | (6' 2½") |
| 10 | Julie White | Can | 1.87 | (6' 1¾") |
| 18 | Paula Girven | USA | 1.84 | (6' ½") |
| 20 | Louise Walker | Can | 1.78 | (5' 10⅛") |

*Olympic Stadium*     *July 23*     *15:30*
**Women's long jump**   OR = 6.82 (22' 4½") WR = 6.99 (22' 11¼")

| | | | | |
|---|---|---|---|---|
| G | Angela Voigt | EGer | 6.72 | (22' ½") |
| S | Kathy McMillan | USA | 6.66 | (21' 10¼") |
| B | Lidiya Alfeeva | USSR | 6.60 | (21' 7¾") |
| | | | | |
| 11 | Diane Jones | Can | 6.13 | (20' 1¼") |

*Olympic Stadium*     *July 31*     *17:40*
**Women's shot put**   OR = 21.03 (69') WR = 21.60 (70' 8")

| | | | | |
|---|---|---|---|---|
| G | Ivanka Christova | Bul | 21.16 | (69' 5") NOR |
| S | Nadejda Chijova | USSR | 20.96 | (68' 9¼") |
| B | Helena Fibingerova | Cze | 20.67 | (67' 9¾") |
| | | | | |
| 12 | Maren Seidler | USA | 15.60 | (51' 2¼") |
| 13 | Lucette Moreau | Can | 15.48 | (50' 9½") |

*Olympic Stadium*     *July 29*     *15:00*
**Women's discus**   OR = 66.62 (218' 6¾") WR = 70.50 (231' 3½")

| | | | | |
|---|---|---|---|---|
| G | Evelin Schlaak | EGer | 69.00 | (226' 4½") NOR |
| S | Maria Vergova | Bul | 67.30 | (220' 9½") |
| B | Gabriele Hinzmann | EGer | 66.84 | (219' 3¼") |
| | | | | |
| 11 | Jane Haist | Can | 59.74 | (196') |
| 13 | Lucette Moreau | Can | 55.88 | (183' 4") |

Women's javelin   OR = 65.14 (213' 8½") WR = 67.22 (220' 6¼")

| | | | | |
|---|---|---|---|---|
| G | Ruth Fuchs | EGer | 65.94 | (216' 4") NOR |
| S | Marion Becker | WGer | 64.70 | (212' 3") |
| B | Kathryn Schmidt | USA | 63.96 | (209' 10") |
| 8 | Karin Smith | USA | 57.50 | (188' 7¾") |

*Olympic Stadium*     *July 26*     *10:00*
**Women's pentathlon**

| | | | 1 | 2 | 3 | 4 | 5 | |
|---|---|---|---|---|---|---|---|---|
| G | Siegrun Siegl | EGer | 13.31 | 12.92 | 1.74 | 6.49 | 23.09 | |
| | | | 957 | 775 | 974 | 1012 | 1027 | 4745 (points) |
| S | Christine Laser | EGer | 13.55 | 14.29 | 1.78 | 6.27 | 23.48 | |
| | | | 925 | 855 | 1012 | 965 | 988 | 4745 |
| B | Burglinde Pollak | EGer | 13.30 | 16.25 | 1.64 | 6.30 | 23.64 | |
| | | | 959 | 963 | 875 | 971 | 972 | 4740 |
| 6 | Diane Jones | Can | 13.79 | 14.58 | 1.80 | 6.29 | 25.33 | |
| | | | 893 | 871 | 1031 | 969 | 818 | 4582 |
| 7 | Jane Frederick | USA | 13.54 | 14.55 | 1.76 | 5.99 | 24.70 | |
| | | | 926 | 870 | 993 | 904 | 873 | 4566 |
| 13 | Gale Fitzgerald | USA | 14.16 | 12.51 | 1.68 | 5.89 | 24.73 | |
| | | | 846 | 750 | 915 | 882 | 870 | 4263 |
| 17 | Marilyn King | USA | 14.45 | 12.27 | 1.74 | 5.62 | 25.27 | |
| | | | 811 | 736 | 974 | 821 | 823 | 4165 |

(1 = 100-m hurdles; 2 = shot put; 3 = high jump; 4 = long jump; 5 = 200-m)

*Olympic Stadium*     *July 24*    *16:55*
**Men's 100-m**   OR = 9.90 / WR = 9.90

| G | Hasely Crawford | Tri | 10.06 |
|---|---|---|---|
| S | Donald Quarrie | Jam | 10.08 |
| B | Valery Borzov | USSR | 10.14 |
| | | | |
| 4 | Harvey Glance | USA | 10.19 |
| 6 | John Jones | USA | 10.27 |

*Olympic Stadium*     *July 26*    *16.50*
**Men's 200-m**   OR = 19.78 / WR = 19.78

| G | Donald Quarrie | Jam | 20.23 |
|---|---|---|---|
| S | Millard Hampton | USA | 20.29 |
| B | Dwayne Evans | USA | 20.43 |

*Olympic Stadium*     *July 29*    *16:00*
**Men's 400-m**   OR = 43.81 / WR = 43.81

| G | Alberto Juantorena | Cub | 44.26 |
|---|---|---|---|
| S | Fred Newhouse | USA | 44.40 |
| B | Herman Frazier | USA | 44.95 |
| | | | |
| 5 | Maxie Parks | USA | 45.24 |

*Olympic Stadium      July 25      17:15*
**Men's 800-m**   OR = 1:44.3 / WR = 1:43.7

| G | Alberto Juantorena | Cub | 1:43.50 NOR/NWR |
|---|---|---|---|
| S | Ivo Vandamme | Bel | 1:43.86 |
| B | Richard Wohlhuter | USA | 1:44.12 |

*Olympic Stadium      July 31      18:00*
**Men's 1500-m**   OR = 3:34.9 / WR = 3:32.2

| G | John Walker | NZ1 | 3:39.17 |
|---|---|---|---|
| S | Ivo Vandamme | Bel | 3:39.27 |
| B | Paul-H. Wellmann | WGer | 3:39.33 |
| 6 | Richard Wohlhuter | USA | 3:40.69 |

*Olympic Stadium      July 30      17:50*
**Men's 5000-m**   OR = 13:20.34 / WR = 13:13.0

| G | Lasse Viren | Fin | 13:24.76 |
|---|---|---|---|
| S | Dick Quax | NZ1 | 13:25.16 |
| B | Klaus Hildenbrand | WGer | 13:25.38 |
| 12 | Paul Geis | USA | 13:42.51 |

*175*

*Olympic Stadium*     *July 26*     *17:05*
Men's 10000-m   OR = 27:38.4 / WR = 27:30.8

| G | Lasse Viren | Fin | 27:40.38 |
| S | Carlos Sousa Lopes | Por | 27:45.17 |
| B | Brendan Foster | GBr | 27:54.92 |
| 13 | Garry Bjorklund | USA | 28:38.08 |

*Olympic Stadium*     *July 28*     *17:50*
Men's 110-m hurdles   OR = 13.24 / WR = 13.24

| G | Guy Drut | Fra | 13.30 |
| S | Alejandro Casanas | Cub | 13.33 |
| B | Willie Davenport | USA | 13.38 |
| 4 | Charles Foster | USA | 13.41 |
| 6 | James Owens | USA | 13.73 |

*Olympic Stadium*     *July 25*     *17:30*
Men's 400-m hurdles   OR = 47.82 / WR = 47.82

| G | Edwin Moses | USA | 47.64 NOR/NWR |
| S | Michael Shine | USA | 48.69 |
| B | Evgeniy Gavrilenko | USSR | 49.45 |
| 4 | Quentin Wheeler | USA | 49.86 |

*Olympic Stadium*     *July 28*     *18:25*
Men's 3000-m steeplechase   OR = 8:18.56 / WR = 8:09.8

| | | | |
|---|---|---|---|
| G | Anders Garderud | Swe | 8:08.02 NOR/NWR |
| S | Bronisla Malinowski | Pol | 8:09.11 |
| B | Frank Baumgartl | EGer | 8:10.36 |
| 10 | Henry Marsh | USA | 8:23.99 |

*Olympic Stadium*     *July 23*     *17:30*
Men's 20-km walk   best world performance = 1:24:45.0 /
best Olympic performance = 1:26:42.4

| | | | |
|---|---|---|---|
| G | Daniel Bautista | Mex | 1:24:40.6 |
| S | Hans Reimann | EGer | 1:25:13.8 |
| B | Peter Frenkel | EGer | 1:25:29.4 |
| 20 | Ronald Laird | USA | 1:33:27.6 |
| 22 | Larry Walker | USA | 1:34:19.4 |
| 23 | Marcel Jobin | Can | 1:34:33.4 |
| 29 | Clark Scully | USA | 1:36:37.4 |
| 33 | Pat Farrelly | Can | 1:41:36.2 |
| 35 | Alex Oakley | Can | 1:44:08.8 |

*Olympic Stadium*     *July 31*     *17:30*
**Marathon**

| | | | |
|---|---|---|---|
| G | Waldemar Cierpinski | EGer | 2:09:55.0 *best Olympic performa*, |
| S | Frank Shorter | USA | 2:10:45.8 |
| B | Karel Lismont | Bel | 2:11:12.6 |
| 4 | Donald Kardong | USA | 2:11:15.8 |
| 6 | Jerome Drayton | Can | 2:13:30.0 |
| 30 | Tom Howard | Can | 2:22:08.8 |
| 36 | Wayne Yetman | Can | 2:24:17.4 |
| 40 | William Rodgers | USA | 2:25:14.8 |

*Olympic Stadium*     *July 31*     *18:45*
**Men's 4x100-m relay**   OR = 38.19 / WR = 38.19

| | | | |
|---|---|---|---|
| G | Harvey Glance<br>John Jones<br>Millard Hampton<br>Steven Riddick | USA | 38.33 |
| S | Manfred Kokot<br>Jorg Pfeifer<br>K. Dieter Kurrat<br>Alexander Thieme | EGer | 38.66 |
| B | Alexander Aksinin<br>Nikolai Kolesnikov<br>Yuriy Silov<br>Valery Borzov | USSR | 38.78 |
| 8 | Hugh Spooner<br>Marvin Nash<br>Albin Dukowski<br>Hugh Fraser | Can | 39.47 |

*Olympic Stadium      July 31      19:20*
Men's 4x400-m relay   OR = 2:56.11 / WR = 2:56.1

| G | Herman Frazier<br>Benjamin Brown<br>Fred Newhouse<br>Maxie Parks | USA | 2:58.65 |
|---|---|---|---|
| S | Ryszard Podlas<br>Jan Werner<br>Zbigniew Jaremski<br>Jerzy Pietrzyk | Pol | 3:01.43 |
| B | Franz-P. Hofmeister<br>Lothar Krieg<br>Harald Schmid<br>Bernd Herrmann | WGer | 3:01.98 |
| 4 | Ian Seale<br>Don Domansky<br>Leighton Hope<br>Brian Saunders | Can | 3:02.64 |

*Olympic Stadium      July 31      16:30*
Men's high jump   OR = 2.24 (7' 4¼") WR = 2.30 (7' 6⅝")

| G | Jacek Wszola | Pol | 2.25 (7' 4⅝") NOR |
|---|---|---|---|
| S | Greg Joy | Can | 2.23 (7' 3¾") |
| B | Dwight Stones | USA | 2.21 (7' 3") |
| 11 | James Barrineau | USA | 2.14 (7' ¼") |
| 12 | Claude Ferragne | Can | 2.14 (7' ¼") |
| 13 | William Jankunis | USA | 2.10 (6' 10¾") |

*Olympic Stadium*     *July 29*    *15:00*
**Men's long jump**   OR = 8.90 (29′ 2½″) WR = 8.90 (29′ 2½″)

| G | Arnie Robinson | USA | 8.35 (27′ 4¾″) |
|---|---|---|---|
| S | Randy Williams | USA | 8.11 (26′ 7¼″) |
| B | Frank Wartenberg | EGer | 8.02 (26′ 3¾″) |

*Olympic Stadium*     *July 30*    *15:00*
**Men's triple jump**   OR = 17.39 (57′ ¾″) WR = 17.89 (58′ 8¼″)

| G | Viktor Saneev | USSR | 17.29 (56′ 8¾″) |
|---|---|---|---|
| S | James Butts | USA | 17.18 (56′ 4½″) |
| B | Joao C. De Oliviera | Bra | 16.90 (55′ 5½″) |
| 5 | Tommy Haynes | USA | 16.78 (55′ ¾″) |
| 12 | Rayfield Dupree | USA | 16.23 (53′ 3″) |

*Olympic Stadium*     *July 26*    *12:30*
**Men's pole vault**   OR = 5.50 (18′ ½″) WR = 5.65 (18′ 6½″)

| G | Tadeusz Slusarski | Pol | 5.50 equals Olympic record (1 |
|---|---|---|---|
| S | Antti Kalliomaki | Fin | 5.50 (18′ ½″) EOR |
| B | David Roberts | USA | 5.50 (18′ ½″) EOR |
| 6 | Earl Bell | USA | 5.45 (17′ 10½″) |
| 13 | Terry Porter | USA | 5.20 (17′ ¾″) |

*Olympic Stadium     July 24     15:00*
**Men's shot put**   OR = 21.32 (69' 11½") WR = 21.82 (71' 7¼")

| G | Udo Beyer | EGer | 21.05 (69' ¾") |
|---|---|---|---|
| S | Evgeni Mironov | USSR | 21.03 (69') |
| B | Alexander Barisnikov | USSR | 21.00 (68' 10¾") |
| | | | |
| 4 | Allan Feuerbach | USA | 20.55 (67' 5") |
| 7 | George Woods | USA | 20.26 (66' 5¾") |
| 9 | Peter Shmock | USA | 19.89 (65' 3") |

*Olympic Stadium     July 25     15:00*
**Men's discus**   OR = 68.28 (224') WR = 69.08 (226' 7½")

| G | Mac Wilkins | USA | 67.50 (221' 5½") |
|---|---|---|---|
| S | Wolfgang Schmidt | EGer | 66.22 (217' 3") |
| B | John Powell | USA | 65.70 (215' 6½") |
| | | | |
| 8 | L. Jay Silvester | USA | 61.98 (203' 4" |

*Olympic Stadium     July 26     14:30*
**Men's javelin**   OR = 90.48 (296' 10¼") WR = 94.08 (308' 8")

| G | Miklos Nemeth | Hun | 94.58 (310' 3½") NOR/NWR |
|---|---|---|---|
| S | Hannu Siitonen | Fin | 87.92 (288' 5¼") |
| B | Gheorghe Megelea | Rum | 87.16 (285' 11½") |
| | | | |
| 5 | Sam Colson | USA | 86.16 (282' 8") |
| 11 | Philip Olsen | Can | 77.70 (254' 11") |
| 15 | Anthony Hall | USA | 71.70 (235' 3") |

*Olympic Stadium*    *July 28*    *14:00*
Men's hammer throw    OR = 75.50 (247' 8⅝") WR = 79.30 (260' 2")

| G | Yuriy Sedyh | USSR | 77.52 (254' 4") NOR |
|---|---|---|---|
| S | Alexey Spiridonov | USSR | 76.08 (249' 7½") |
| B | Anatoliy Bondarchuk | USSR | 75.48 (247' 7½") |


*Olympic Stadium*    *July 30*    *10:00*
Men's decathlon

|   |   |   | 1 | 2 | 3 | 4 | 5 | 6 |
|---|---|---|---|---|---|---|---|---|
| G | Bruce Jenner | USA | 10.94 | 7.22 | 15.35 | 2.03 | 47.51 | 14.84 |
|   |   |   | 819 | 865 | 809 | 882 | 923 | 866 |
| S | Guido Kratschmer | WGer | 10.66 | 7.39 | 14.74 | 2.03 | 48.19 | 14.58 |
|   |   |   | 890 | 899 | 773 | 882 | 889 | 895 |
| B | Nikolay Avilov | USSR | 11.23 | 7.52 | 14.81 | 2.14 | 48.16 | 14.20 |
|   |   |   | 749 | 925 | 777 | 975 | 889 | 939 |
| 15 | Fred Samara | USA | 10.85 | 7.08 | 13.00 | 1.84 | 50.07 | 14.87 |
|   |   |   | 841 | 836 | 665 | 716 | 801 | 862 |
| 23 | Fred Dixon | USA | 10.94 | 6.91 | 14.44 | 2.03 | 48.38 | 18.11 |
|   |   |   | 819 | 802 | 755 | 882 | 880 | 574 |

|   |   |   | 7 | 8 | 9 | 10 |   |
|---|---|---|---|---|---|---|---|
| G | Bruce Jenner | USA | 50.04 | 4.80 | 68.52 | 4:12.61 |   |
|   |   |   | 873 | 1005 | 862 | 714 | 8618 NOR/NWR |
| S | Guido Kratschmer | WGer | 45.70 | 4.60 | 66.32 | 4:29.09 |   |
|   |   |   | 794 | 957 | 837 | 595 | 8411 |
| B | Nikolay Avilov | USSR | 45.60 | 4.45 | 62.28 | 4:26.26 |   |
|   |   |   | 792 | 920 | 789 | 614 | 8369 |
| 15 | Fred Samara | USA | 40.54 | 4.30 | 53.60 | 4:40.21 |   |
|   |   |   | 696 | 884 | 680 | 523 | 7504 |
| 23 | Fred Dixon | USA | 45.82 |   | 55.96 | 4:38.49 |   |
|   |   |   | 797 | 0 | 711 | 534 | 6754 |

*First Day:* 1 = 100-m; 2 = long jump; 3 = shot put; 4 = high jump; 5 = 400-m.
*Second Day:* 6 = 100-m hurdles; 7 = discus; 8 = pole vault; 9 = javelin;
                     10 = 1500-m

# Results Basketball

*Etienne Desmarteau*     *July 26*    *22:00*
**Women's championship pool**

| | | |
|---|---|---|
| G | USSR | 10 *(points)* |
| S | USA | 8 |
| B | Bul | 8 |

*Pool progress:*

|  | Bul | Can | Jap | Cze | USSR | USA |
|------|--------|--------|--------|--------|---------|---------|
| Bul  | x      | 85-62  | 66-63  | 67-66  | 68-91   | 79-95   |
| Can  | 62-85  | x      | 89-121 | 59-67  | 51-115  | 75-89   |
| Jap  | 63-66  | 121-89 | x      | 62-76  | 75-98   | 84-71   |
| Cze  | 66-67  | 67-59  | 76-62  | x      | 75-88   | 67-83   |
| USSR | 91-68  | 115-51 | 98-75  | 88-75  | x       | 112-77  |
| USA  | 95-79  | 89-75  | 71-84  | 83-67  | 77-112  | x       |

*Forum*     *July 27*    *22:30*
**Men's finals**

| | |
|---|---|
| G | USA |
| S | Yug |
| B | USSR |

*Finals:*

| | |
|---|---|
| Yug-USA | 74-95 |
| USSR-Can | 100-72 |
| Ita-Cze | 98-75 |
| Australia-Cub | 81-92 |
| PR-Mex | 89-84 |
| Jap-Egy | forfeit by Egy |

# Results Boxing

**Light flyweight 48-kg competition**   (105.6 lbs.)

| | | |
|---|---|---|
| G | Jorge Hernandez | Cub |
| S | Byong Uk Li | NKor |
| B | Chan-Hee Park | SKor |
| B | Payao Pooltarat | Thai |

*Eliminated earlier:*   Sidney McKnight    Can
                        Louis Curtis       USA

**Flyweight 51-kg competition**   (112.2 lbs.)

| | | |
|---|---|---|
| G | Leo Randolph | USA |
| S | Ramon Duvalon | Cub |
| B | David Torosyan | USSR |
| B | Leszek Blazynski | Pol |

*Eliminated earlier:*   Ian Clyde    Can

**Bantamweight 54-kg competition**   (118.8 lbs.)

| | | |
|---|---|---|
| G | Yong Jo Gu | NKor |
| S | Charles Mooney | USA |
| B | Patrick Cowdell | GBr |
| B | Chulsoon Hwang | SKor |

*Eliminated earlier:*   Chris Ius    Can

*Maurice Richard/Forum      July 31    18:00*
**Featherweight 57-kg competition**   (125.4 lbs.)

| | | |
|---|---|---|
| G | Angel Herrera | Cub |
| S | Richard Nowakowski | EGer |
| B | Leszek Kosedowski | Pol |
| B | Davey Armstrong | USA |

*Eliminated earlier:*  Camille Huard      Can


*Maurice Richard/Forum      July 31    18:00*
**Lightweight 60-kg competition**   (132 lbs.)

| | | |
|---|---|---|
| G | Howard Davis | USA |
| S | Simion Cutov | Rum |
| B | Vasily Solomin | USSR |
| B | Ace Rusevski | Yug |


*Maurice Richard/Forum      July 31    18:00*
**Light welterweight 63.5-kg competition**   (139.7 lbs.)

| | | |
|---|---|---|
| G | Ray Leonard | USA |
| S | Andres Aldama | Cub |
| B | Vladimir Kolev | Bul |
| B | Ulrich Beyer | EGer |

*Eliminated earlier:*  Chris Clarke      Can

*Maurice Richard/Forum*     *July 31     18:00*
**Welterweight 67-kg competition**   (147.4 lbs.)

G     Jochen Bachfeld          EGer
S     Pedro J. Gammarro        Ven
B     Reinhard Skricek         WGer
B     Carmen Rinke             Can

*Eliminated earlier:*   Clinton Jackson   USA


*Maurice Richard/Forum*     *July 31     18:00*
**Light Middleweight 71-kg competition**   (156.2 lbs.)

G     Jerzy Rybicki            Pol
S     Tadija Kacar             Yug
B     Victor Savchenko         USSR
B     Rolando Garbey           Cub

*Eliminated earlier:*   Charles Walker    USA
                        Michael Prevost   Can


*Maurice Richard/Forum*     *July 31     18:00*
**Middleweight 75-kg competition**   (165 lbs.)

G     Michael Spinks           USA
S     Rufat Riskiev            USSR
B     Alec Nastac              Rum
B     Luis Martinez            Cub

*Eliminated earlier:*   Bryan Gibson      Can

**Light heavyweight 81-kg competition**   (178.2 lbs.)

| | | |
|---|---|---|
| G | Leon Spinks | USA |
| S | Sixto Soria | Cub |
| B | Costica Dafinoiu | Rum |
| B | Ottomar Sachse | EGer |

*Eliminated earlier:*   Roger Fortin     Can

*Maurice Richard/Forum*     *July 31*    *18:00*
**Heavyweight 81+ kg competition**   (178.2+ lbs.)

| | | |
|---|---|---|
| G | Teofilo Stevenson | Cub |
| S | Mircea Simon | Rum |
| B | Johnny Tate | USA |
| B | Clarence Hill | Ber |

# Results Canoeing

**Women's kayak-1 500-m**

| G | Carola Zirzow | EGer | 2:01.05 |
|---|---|---|---|
| S | Tatiana Korshunova | USSR | 2:03.07 |
| B | Klara Rajnai | Hun | 2:05.01 |
| | | | |
| 7 | Julie Leach | USA | 2:06.92 |

**Women's kayak-2 500-m**

| G | Nina Gopova<br>Galina Kreft | USSR | 1:51.15 |
|---|---|---|---|
| S | Anna Pfeffer<br>Klara Rajnai | Hun | 1:51.69 |
| B | Barbel Koster<br>Carola Zirzow | EGer | 1:51.81 |
| 8 | Anne Dodge<br>Susan Holloway | Can | 1:56.75 |

**Men's kayak-1 500-m**

| G | Vasile Diba | Rum | 1:46.41 |
|---|---|---|---|
| S | Zoltan Sztanity | Hun | 1:46.95 |
| B | Rudiger Helm | EGer | 1:48.30 |

*Notre Dame Basin*     *July 30*     *17:30*
**Men's kayak-2 500-m**

| G | Joachim Mattern | EGer | 1:35.87 |
|---|-----------------|------|---------|
|   | Bernd Olbricht  |      |         |
| S | Sergey Nagorny  | USSR | 1:36.81 |
|   | Vladimir Romanovskiy | |         |
| B | Larion Serghei  | Rum  | 1:37.43 |
|   | Policarp Malihin |     |         |

*Notre Dame Basin*     *July 30*     *16:30*
**Men's Canadian-1 500-m**

| G | Aleksandr Rogov | USSR | 1:59.23 |
|---|-----------------|------|---------|
| S | John Wood       | Can  | 1:59.58 |
| B | Matija Ljubek   | Yug  | 1:59.60 |

*Notre Dame Basin*     *July 30*     *18:00*
**Men's Canadian-2 500-m**

| G | Sergej Petrenko | USSR | 1:45.81 |
|---|-----------------|------|---------|
|   | Aleksandr Vinogradov | |         |
| S | Jerzy Opara     | Pol  | 1:47.77 |
|   | Andrzej Gronowicz |    |         |
| B | Tamas Buday     | Hun  | 1:48.35 |
|   | Oszkar Frey     |      |         |
| 7 | Gregory Smith   | Can  | 1:50.74 |
|   | John Wood       |      |         |

*Notre Dame Basin*     *July 31*     *16:00*
**Men's kayak-1 1000-m**

| | | | |
|---|---|---|---|
| G | Rudiger Helm | EGer | 3:48.20 |
| S | Geza Csapo | Hun | 3:48.84 |
| B | Vasile Diba | Rum | 3:49.65 |


*Notre Dame Basin*     *July 31*     *17:00*
**Men's kayak-2 1000-m**

| | | | |
|---|---|---|---|
| G | Sergey Nagorny<br>Vladimir Romanovskiy | USSR | 3:29.01 |
| S | Joachim Mattern<br>Bernd Olbricht | EGer | 3:29.33 |
| B | Zoltan Bako<br>Istvan Szabo | Hun | 3:30.36 |
| 8 | Steve King<br>Denis Barre | Can | 3:34.46 |

*Notre Dame Basin*    *July 31*    *18:00*
**Men's kayak-4 1000-m**

| G | Sergey Chuhray<br>Aleksandr Degtiarev<br>Juriy Filatov<br>Vlademir Morozov | USSR | 3:08.69 |
| S | Jose E. Celorrio<br>Jose R. Diaz-Flor<br>Herminio Menendez<br>Luis R. Misione | Spa | 3:08.95 |
| B | Peter Bischof<br>Bernd Duvigneau<br>Rudiger Helm<br>Jurgen Lehnert | EGer | 3:10.76 |

*Notre Dame Basin*    *July 31*    *16:30*
**Men's Canadian-1 1000-m**

| G | Matija Ljubek | Yug | 4:09.51 |
| S | Vasiliy Urchenko | USSR | 4:12.57 |
| B | Tamas Wichmann | Hun | 4:14.11 |
| 9 | John Edwards | Can | 4:30.55 |

*Notre Dame Basin*    *July 31*    *17:30*
**Men's Canadian-2 1000-m**

| G | Sergej Petrenko<br>Aleksandr Vinogradov | USSR | 3:52.76 |
| S | Gheorghe Danielov<br>Gheorghe Simionov | Rum | 3:54.28 |
| B | Tamas Buday<br>Oszkar Frey | Hun | 3:55.66 |

*191*

# Results Cycling

**1000-m time trial**

| G | Klaus-Jurgen Grunke | EGer | 1:05.927 |
|---|---|---|---|
| S | Michel Vaarten | Bel | 1:07.516 |
| B | Niels Fredborg | Den | 1:07.617 |

| 13 | Jocelyn Lovell | Can | 1:08.852 |
|---|---|---|---|
| 15 | Robert Vehe | USA | 1:09.057 |

*Olympic Velodrome*   *July 24*   *15:15*
**Sprint final**

| G | Anton Tkac | Cze |
|---|---|---|
| S | Daniel Morelon | Fra |
| B | Hans-Jurgen Geschke | EGer |

*Olympic Velodrome*   *July 22*   *17:00*
**4000-m individual pursuit**

| G | Gregor Braun | WGer | 4:47.61 |
|---|---|---|---|
| S | Herman Ponsteen | Hol | 4:49.72 |
| B | Thomas Huschke | EGer | 4:52.71 |

*Olympic Velodrome*     *July 24     16:30*
**4000-m team pursuit**

| G | Gregor Braun | WGer | 4:21.06 |
|---|---|---|---|
| | Hans Lutz | | |
| | Guenther Schumacher | | |
| | Peter Vonhof | | |
| S | Vladimir Osokin | USSR | 4:27.15 |
| | Alexandr Perov | | |
| | Vitaly Petrakov | | |
| | Victor Sokolov | | |
| B | Ian Banbury | GBr | 4:22.41 |
| | Michael Bennett | | |
| | Robin Croker | | |
| | Ian Hallam | | |

*Mount Royal Course*     *July 26     10:00*
**Individual road race**

| G | Bernt Johansson | Swe | 4:46:52.0 |
|---|---|---|---|
| S | Giuseppe Martinelli | Ita | 4:47:23.0 |
| B | Mieczysl Nowicki | Pol | 4:47:23.0 |
| 6 | George Mount | USA | 4:47:23.0 |
| 24 | Pierre Harvey | Can | 4:50:07.0 |
| 42 | John Howard | USA | 4:57:41.0 |
| 54 | Gilles Durand | Can | 5:55:58.0 |
| 56 | David Boll | USA | 6:31:56.0 |

*193*

**100-km team time trial**

| | | | |
|---|---|---|---|
| G | Anatoly Chukanov<br>Valery Chaplygin<br>Vladimir Kaminsky<br>Aavo Pikkuus | USSR | 2:08:53.0 |
| S | Tadeusz Mytnik<br>Mieczysl Nowicki<br>Stanisla Szozda<br>Ryszard Szurkowski | Pol | 2:09.13.0 |
| B | Verner Blaudzun<br>Gert Frank<br>Jorgen E. Hansen<br>Jorn Lund | Den | 2:12:20.0 |
| 16 | Marc Blouin<br>Brian Chewter<br>Tom Morris<br>Serge Proulx | Can | 2:17:15.0 |
| 19 | John Howard<br>Wayne Stetina<br>Marc Thompson<br>Alan Kingsbery | USA | 2:18:53.0 |

# Results  Equestrian Sports

*Bromont       July 30      14:00*
**Individual Grand Prix dressage**

|   |   | *horse* |   |   |
|---|---|---|---|---|
| G  | Christine Stueckelberger | Granat     | Swi  | 1486.0 |
| S  | Harry Boldt              | Woycek     | WGer | 1435.0 |
| B  | Dr. Reiner Klimke        | Mehmed     | WGer | 1395.0 |
|    |                          |            |      |        |
| 5  | Dorothy Morkis           | Monaco     | USA  | 1249.0 |
| 7  | Chris Boylen             | Gaspano    | Can  | 1217.0 |
| 10 | Hilda Gurney             | Keen       | USA  | 1167.0 |
| 11 | Lorraine Stubbs          | True North | Can  | 1153.0 |

*Bromont       July 29      14:00*
**Team Grand Prix dressage**

| G | Harry Boldt              | Woycek      | WGer | 1863.0 |        |
|---|-------------------------|-------------|------|--------|--------|
|   | Dr. Reiner Klimke       | Mehmed      |      | 1751.0 |        |
|   | Gabriela Grillo         | Ultimo      |      | 1541.0 | 5155.0 |
| S | Christine Stueckelberger| Granat      | Swi  | 1869.0 |        |
|   | Ulrich Lehmann          | Widin       |      | 1425.0 |        |
|   | Doris Ramseier          | Roch        |      | 1390.0 | 4684.0 |
| B | Hilda Gurney            | Keen        | USA  | 1607.0 |        |
|   | Dorothy Morkis          | Monaco      |      | 1559.0 |        |
|   | Edith Master            | Dahlwitz    |      | 1481.0 | 4647.0 |
| 5 | Chris Boylen            | Gaspano     | Can  | 1590.0 |        |
|   | Lorraine Stubbs         | True North  |      | 1549.0 |        |
|   | Barbara Stracey         | Jungherr II |      | 1399.0 | 4538.0 |

**Individual jumping three-day event**

| | | | dressage | endur | faults | time faults | jumps | total |
|---|---|---|---|---|---|---|---|---|
| G | Edmund Coffin *Bally-Cor* | USA | 64.59 | 50.4 | 0 | .00 | .00 | 114.99 |
| S | John Plumb *Better & Better* | USA | 66.25 | 49.6 | 10 | .00 | 10.00 | 125.85 |
| B | Karl Schultz *Madrigal* | WGer | 46.25 | 63.2 | 20 | .00 | 20.00 | 129.45 |
| 10 | Bruce Davidson *Irish Cap* | USA | 54.16 | 136.0 | 10 | .00 | 10.00 | 200.16 |
| 11 | Juliet Graham *Sumatra* | Can | 110.84 | 81.6 | 10 | .25 | 10.25 | 202.69 |
| 21 | Mary Tauskey *Marcus-Aurelius* | USA | 97.09 | 162.4 | 10 | .00 | 10.00 | 269.49 |
| 23 | Cathy Wedge *City Fella* | Can | 99.16 | 187.6 | 0 | .00 | .00 | 286.76 |
| 26 | Robin Hahn *L'Esprit* | Can | 94.16 | 215.2 | 10 | .00 | 10.00 | 319.36 |

**Team three-day event**

| | | | dressage | endur | jumps | total | team total |
|---|---|---|---|---|---|---|---|
| G | Edmund Coffin *Bally-Cor* | USA | 64.59 | 50.4 | .00 | 114.99 | |
| | John Plumb *Better & Better* | | 66.25 | 49.6 | 10.00 | 125.85 | |
| | Bruce Davidson *Irish Cap* | | 54.16 | 136.0 | 10.00 | 200.16 | |
| | Mary Tauskey *Marcus-Aurelius* | | 97.09 | 162.4 | 10.00 | 269.49* | 441.00 |
| S | Karl Schultz *Madrigal* | WGer | 46.25 | 63.2 | 20.00 | 129.45 | |
| | Herbert Bloecker *Albrant* | | 108.75 | 94.4 | 10.00 | 213.15 | |
| | Helmut Rethemeier *Pauline* | | 70.00 | 152.0 | 20.00 | 242.00 | |
| | Otto Ammermann *Volturno* | | 58.75 | eliminated | | | 584.60 |
| B | Wayne Roycroft *Laurenson* | Australia | 80.84 | 97.2 | .00 | 178.04 | |
| | Mervyn Bennett *Regal Reign* | | 120.84 | 85.2 | .00 | 206.04 | |
| | William Roycroft *Version* | | 86.66 | 128.8 | .00 | 215.46 | |
| | Denis Pigott *Hillstead* | | 92.91 | 153.6 | .00 | 246.51* | 599.54 |
| 6 | Juliet Graham *Sumatra* | Can | 110.84 | 81.6 | 10.25 | 202.69 | |
| | Cathy Wedge *City Fella* | | 99.16 | 187.6 | .00 | 286.76 | |
| | Robin Hahn *L'Esprit* | | 94.16 | 215.2 | 10.00 | 319.36 | |
| | James Day *Viceroy* | | 60.00 | 220.4 | retired | | 808.81 |

Bromont     *July 27     14:30*
## Individual Grand Prix jumping

|   |   |   | total rnd 1 | faults | time | time faults | total rnd 2 | final total |
|---|---|---|---|---|---|---|---|---|
| G | Alwin Schockemoehle *Warwick Rex* | WGer | .00 | 0 | 1:34.0 | .00 | .00 | .00 |
|   | *Michel Vaillancourt *Branch County* | Can | 4.00 | 8 | 1:34.6 | .00 | 8.00 | 12.00 |
|   | *Debbie Johnsey *Moxy* | GBr | 4.00 | 8 | 1:30.7 | .00 | 8.00 | 12.00 |
|   | *François Mathy *Gai Luron* | Bel | 8.00 | 4 | 1:38.3 | .00 | 4.00 | 12.00 |
| 5 | Frank Chapot *Viscount* | USA | 4.00 | 12 | 1:27.8 | .00 | 12.00 | 16.00 |
| 15 | James Elder *Raffles II* | Can | 8.00 | 20 | 1:28.4 | .00 | 20.00 | 28.00 |
| 15 | James Day *Sympatico* | Can | 8.00 | 20 | 1:35.6 | .00 | 20.00 | 28.00 |

(*ties for 2nd competed in jump-off to decide silver and bronze medals)

Bromont     *July 27     16:30*
## Jump-off

|   |   |   | faults | time | time faults | total |
|---|---|---|---|---|---|---|
| S | Michel Vaillancourt *Branch County* | Can | 4 | 49.8 | .00 | 4.00 |
| B | François Mathy *Gai Luron* | Bel | 8 | 53.9 | .00 | 8.00 |

# Results Fencing

**Ladies foil**

| | | |
|---|---|---|
| G | Ildiko Schwarczenberger | Hun |
| S | Brigitte Dumont | Fra |
| B | Maria Consolata Collino | Ita |

*University of Montreal*      *July 28     18:00/16:00*
**Ladies foil—team**

| | | |
|---|---|---|
| G | Elena Belova | USSR |
| | Olga Kniazeva | |
| | Valentina Sidorova | |
| | Nailia Guiliazova | |
| S | Brigitte Latrille | Fra |
| | Brigitte Dumont | |
| | Christi Muzio | |
| | Veroniq Trinquet | |
| B | Karin Rutz | WGer |
| | Cornelia Hanisch | |
| | Ute Kircheis | |
| | Brigitte Oertel | |

*University of Montreal*      *July 21     18:00*
**Men's foil**

| | | |
|---|---|---|
| G | Bernard Talvard | Fra |
| S | Alexandr Romankov | USSR |
| B | Gregory Benko | Australia |

*199*

*University of Montreal*     *July 22    18:00*
**Men's saber**

| | | |
|---|---|---|
| G | Viktor Krovopouskov | USSR |
| S | Vladimir Nazlymov | USSR |
| B | Viktor Sidiak | USSR |


*University of Montreal*     *July 23    18:00*
**Men's épée**

| | | |
|---|---|---|
| G | Gyozo Kulcsar | Hun |
| S | Alexander Pusch | Ger |
| B | Jerzy Janikowski | Pol |


*University of Montreal*     *July 25    18:00/14:00*
**Men's foil—team**

| | | |
|---|---|---|
| G | Matthias Behr | WGer |
| | Thomas Bach | |
| | Harald Hein | |
| | Klaus Reichert | |
| S | Fabio Dal Zotto | Ita |
| | Carlo Montano | |
| | Stefano Simoncelli | |
| | Giovan Battista Coletti | |
| B | Vassili Stankovich | USSR |
| | Alexandr Romankov | |
| | Vladimir Denisov | |
| | Sabirjan Rouziev | |

*University of Montreal*    *July 27*    *18:00/15:00*
**Men's saber—team**

G    Viktor Krovopouskov         USSR
     Edouard Vinokurov
     Viktor Sidiak
     Vladimir Nazlymov

S    Mario A. Montano            Ita
     Michele Maffei
     Angelo Arcidiacono
     Tommaso Montano

B    Peter Marot                 Hun
     Tamas Kovacs
     Imre Gedovari
     Ferenc Hammang


*University of Montreal*    *July 29*    *18:00/14:00*
**Men's épée—team**

G    Alexander Pusch             WGer
     Jurgen dr. Hehn
     Reinhold Behr
     Volker Fischer

S    Carl Von Essen              Swe
     Hans Jocobson
     Rolf Edling
     Leif Hogstrom

B    François Suchanecki         Swi
     Michel Poffet
     Daniel Giger
     Christian Kauter

# Results Field Hockey

**Final standing matches**

| G | NZl |
|---|-----|
| S | Australia |
| B | Pak |

| | |
|---|---|
| NZl—Aus | 1-0 |
| Hol—Pak | 2-3 |
| WGer—Spa | 9-1 |
| Ind—Mal | 2-0 |
| Can—Bel | 2-3 |

# Results Football

*Olympic Stadium*     *July 31*     *21:30*
**Final match**   (EGer - 3; Pol - 1)

G    EGer
S    Pol
B    USSR

| *EGerman team* | *Polish team* |
| --- | --- |
| Jurgen Croy | Jan Tomaszewski |
| Gerd Weber | Antoni Szymanowski |
| H. Jurgen Dorner | Jerzy Gorgon |
| Konrad Weise | Wojciech Rudy |
| Lothar Kurbjuweit | Wladysla Zmuda |
| Reinhard Lauck | Zygmunt Maszozyk |
| Gerd Heidler | Grzegorz Lato |
| Reinhard Hafner | Henryk Kasperczak |
| H. Jurgen Riediger | Kazimier Deyna |
| Bernd Bransch | Andrzej Szarmach |
| Martin Hoffmann | Kazimier Kmiecik |
| Gerd Kische | Piotr Mowlik |
| Wolfram Lowe | Henryk Wawrowski |
| Hartmut Schade | Henryk Wieczorek |
| Dieter Riedel | Leskaw Cmikiewicz |
| Ullrich Grapenthin | Jan Beniger |
| Wilfried Grobner | Roman Ogaza |

# Results Gymnastics

**Women's team competition**

|   |      | *horse vault* | *uneven bars* | *bal. beam* | *floor ex.* | *compul.* | *option.* | *total* |
|---|------|-------|--------|-------|-------|-----------|----------|---------|
| G | USSR | 48.70 | 48.85  | 47.95 | 48.70 | 194.20    |          |         |
|   |      | 49.00 | 49.00  | 48.95 | 49.20 |           | 196.15   | 390.35  |
| S | Rum  | 47.95 | 49.15  | 48.05 | 47.55 | 192.70    |          |         |
|   |      | 48.05 | 49.35  | 48.80 | 48.25 |           | 194.45   | 387.15  |
| B | EGer | 47.95 | 48.70  | 47.10 | 47.85 | 191.60    |          |         |
|   |      | 48.75 | 49.10  | 47.30 | 48.35 |           | 193.50   | 385.10  |
|   |      |       |        |       |       |           |          |         |
| 6 | USA  | 47.15 | 47.60  | 46.05 | 46.85 | 187.65    |          |         |
|   |      | 46.85 | 48.10  | 44.60 | 47.85 |           | 187.40   | 375.05  |
| 9 | Can  | 45.90 | 45.75  | 44.70 | 46.10 | 182.45    |          |         |
|   |      | 46.80 | 47.75  | 45.30 | 47.35 |           | 187.20   | 369.65  |

**Women's individual all-around competition**

|    |                     |      | *vault* | *un. bars* | *beam* | *floor* | *total** |
|----|---------------------|------|---------|------------|--------|---------|----------|
| G  | Nadia Comaneci      | Rum  | 9.85    | 10.00      | 10.00  | 9.90    | 79.275   |
| S  | Nelli Kim           | USSR | 10.00   | 9.90       | 9.70   | 9.95    | 78.675   |
| B  | Ludmila Tourischeva | USSR | 9.95    | 9.80       | 9.85   | 9.90    | 78.625   |
|    |                     |      |         |            |        |         |          |
| 14 | Kimberly Chace      | USA  | 9.50    | 9.70       | 9.45   | 9.50    | 75.875   |
| 18 | Debra Willcox       | USA  | 9.60    | 9.45       | 9.25   | 9.50    | 75.325   |
| 18 | Leslie Wolfsberger  | USA  | 9.40    | 9.60       | 9.45   | 9.55    | 75.325   |
| 27 | Karen Kelsall       | Can  | 9.00    | 9.60       | 9.25   | 9.60    | 74.625   |
| 29 | Patti Rope          | Can  | 9.35    | 9.55       | 9.15   | 9.50    | 74.500   |
| 33 | Nancy McDonnell     | Can  | 9.35    | 9.50       | 8.75   | 9.50    | 74.050   |

*(includes final and prelim.)*

*Forum      July 22    19:30*
**Women's finals on horse vault**

|   |                      |      | compul. | option. | prelim. | final | total  |
|---|----------------------|------|---------|---------|---------|-------|--------|
| G | Nelli Kim            | USSR | 9.80    | 9.90    | 9.850   | 9.95  | 19.800 |
| S | Ludmila Tourischeva  | USSR | 9.80    | 9.80    | 9.800   | 9.85  | 19.650 |
| B | Carola Dombeck       | EGer | 9.60    | 9.90    | 9.750   | 9.90  | 19.650 |


*Forum      July 22    19:30*
**Women's finals on uneven bars**

|   |                    |     | compul. | option. | prelim. | final | total  |
|---|--------------------|-----|---------|---------|---------|-------|--------|
| G | Nadia Comaneci     | Rum | 10.00   | 10.00   | 10.000  | 10.00 | 20.000 |
| S | Teodora Ungureanu  | Rum | 9.90    | 9.90    | 9.900   | 9.90  | 19.800 |
| B | Marta Egervari     | Hun | 9.85    | 9.90    | 9.875   | 9.90  | 19.775 |


*Forum      July 22    19:30*
**Women's finals on balance beam**

|   |                    |      | compul. | option. | prelim. | final | total  |
|---|--------------------|------|---------|---------|---------|-------|--------|
| G | Nadia Comaneci     | Rum  | 9.90    | 10.00   | 9.950   | 10.00 | 19.950 |
| S | Olga Korbut        | USSR | 9.80    | 9.85    | 9.825   | 9.90  | 19.725 |
| B | Teodora Ungureanu  | Rum  | 9.75    | 9.85    | 9.800   | 9.90  | 19.700 |


*Forum      July 22    19:30*
**Women's finals in floor exercise**

|   |                     |      | compul. | option. | prelim. | final | total  |
|---|---------------------|------|---------|---------|---------|-------|--------|
| G | Nelli Kim           | USSR | 9.80    | 9.90    | 9.850   | 10.00 | 19.850 |
| S | Ludmila Tourischeva | USSR | 9.90    | 9.95    | 9.925   | 9.90  | 19.825 |
| B | Nadia Comaneci      | Rum  | 9.75    | 9.85    | 9.800   | 9.95  | 19.750 |

*Forum       July 20    20:45*
Men's team competition

| | | floor | side horse | rings | vault | par. bars | hor. bars | comp. | option. | total |
|---|---|---|---|---|---|---|---|---|---|---|
| G | Jap | 47.20 | 47.70 | 47.20 | 47.80 | 48.15 | 48.25 | 286.30 | | |
| | | 47.95 | 48.70 | 48.65 | 47.85 | 48.30 | 49.10 | | 290.55 | 576.85 |
| S | USSR | 47.80 | 48.00 | 48.00 | 47.60 | 47.70 | 47.70 | 286.80 | | |
| | | 48.80 | 47.90 | 49.35 | 47.60 | 47.60 | 48.40 | | 289.65 | 576.45 |
| B | EGer | 46.50 | 47.20 | 46.55 | 46.85 | 47.00 | 47.15 | 281.25 | | |
| | | 47.25 | 47.40 | 47.80 | 46.85 | 46.65 | 47.45 | | 283.40 | 564.65 |
| | | | | | | | | | | |
| 7 | USA | 45.20 | 45.35 | 45.80 | 45.90 | 46.65 | 46.70 | 275.60 | | |
| | | 46.70 | 47.20 | 46.60 | 46.45 | 46.00 | 47.55 | | 280.50 | 556.10 |

*Forum       July 21    20:00*
Men's individual all-around competition

| | | | floor | s.hor | rings | vault | par. b | hor. b | total* |
|---|---|---|---|---|---|---|---|---|---|
| G | Nikolai Andrianov | USSR | 9.80 | 9.70 | 9.75 | 9.80 | 9.65 | 9.70 | 116.650 |
| S | Sawao Kato | Jap | 9.60 | 9.60 | 9.45 | 9.55 | 9.70 | 9.80 | 115.650 |
| B | Mitsuo Tsukahara | Jap | 9.50 | 9.60 | 9.40 | 9.80 | 9.70 | 9.70 | 115.575 |
| | | | | | | | | | |
| 12 | Wayne Young | USA | 9.55 | 9.55 | 9.60 | 9.55 | 9.45 | 9.55 | 113.025 |
| 15 | Peter Kormann | USA | 9.65 | 9.30 | 9.50 | 9.60 | 9.45 | 9.60 | 112.475 |
| 21 | Kurt Thomas | USA | 9.20 | 9.30 | 9.40 | 9.10 | 9.05 | 9.60 | 111.175 |
| 22 | Philip Delesalle | Can | 9.30 | 9.65 | 9.35 | 9.50 | 9.30 | 9.15 | 110.750 |
| 24 | Keith Carter | Can | 9.15 | 9.30 | 9.30 | 9.35 | 9.25 | 9.30 | 110.300 |
| 35 | Pierre Leclerc | Can | 1.00 | 0.00 | 0.00 | 0.00 | 9.05 | 9.35 | 73.750 |

*(includes final & prelim.)*

**Men's finals in floor exercise**

|   |                    |      | *compul.* | *option.* | *prelim.* | *final* | *total* |
|---|--------------------|------|-----------|-----------|-----------|---------|---------|
| G | Nikolai Andrianov  | USSR | 9.45      | 9.85      | 9.650     | 9.80    | 19.450  |
| S | Vladimir Marchenko | USSR | 9.55      | 9.80      | 9.675     | 9.75    | 19.425  |
| B | Peter Kormann      | USA  | 9.30      | 9.70      | 9.500     | 9.80    | 19.300  |

**Men's finals on side horse**

|   |                   |      |      |      |       |      |        |
|---|-------------------|------|------|------|-------|------|--------|
| G | Zoltan Magyar     | Hun  | 9.75 | 9.85 | 9.800 | 9.90 | 19.700 |
| S | Eizo Kemmotsu     | Jap  | 9.70 | 9.85 | 9.775 | 9.80 | 19.575 |
| B | Nikolai Andrianov | USSR | 9.70 | 9.75 | 9.725 | 9.80 | 19.525 |

**Men's finals on rings**

|   |                   |      |      |      |       |      |        |
|---|-------------------|------|------|------|-------|------|--------|
| G | Nikolai Andrianov | USSR | 9.80 | 9.90 | 9.850 | 9.80 | 19.650 |
| S | Alexandr Ditiatin | USSR | 9.60 | 9.90 | 9.750 | 9.80 | 19.550 |
| B | Danut Grecu       | Rum  | 9.65 | 9.85 | 9.750 | 9.75 | 19.500 |

**Men's finals on horse vault**

|   |                   |      |      |      |       |       |        |
|---|-------------------|------|------|------|-------|-------|--------|
| G | Nikolai Andrianov | USSR | 9.65 | 9.70 | 9.675 | 9.775 | 19.450 |
| S | Mitsuo Tsukahara  | Jap  | 9.50 | 9.80 | 9.650 | 9.725 | 19.375 |
| B | Hiroshi Kajiyama  | Jap  | 9.65 | 9.70 | 9.675 | 9.600 | 19.275 |

*Forum    July 23    19:30*
**Men's finals on parallel bars**

| | | | compul. | option. | prelim. | final | total |
|---|---|---|---|---|---|---|---|
| G | Sawao Kato | Jap | 9.75 | 9.80 | 9.775 | 9.90 | 19.675 |
| S | Nikolai Andrianov | USSR | 9.80 | 9.70 | 9.750 | 9.75 | 19.500 |
| B | Mitsuo Tsukahara | Jap | 9.70 | 9.65 | 9.675 | 9.80 | 19.475 |

*Forum    July 23    19:30*
**Men's finals on horizontal bar**

| G | Mitsuo Tsukahara | Jap | 9.75 | 9.90 | 9.825 | 9.85 | 19.675 |
|---|---|---|---|---|---|---|---|
| S | Eizo Kemmotsu | Jap | 9.65 | 9.85 | 9.750 | 9.75 | 19.500 |
| B | Eberhard Gienger | WGer | 9.65 | 9.70 | 9.675 | 9.80 | 19.475 |

# Results  Handball

*Claude Robillard Arena*      *July 28*    *15:40*
**Women's finals**

| G | USSR | 10 *(points)* |
|---|------|------|
| S | EGer | 7 |
| B | Hun | 7 |

*Tournament progress:*

|      | EGer | USSR | Hun | Rum | Jap | Can |
|------|------|------|-----|-----|-----|-----|
| EGer | x | 11-14 | 7-7 | 18-12 | 24-10 | 29-4 |
| USSR | 14-11 | x | 12-9 | 14-8 | 31-9 | 21-3 |
| Hun | 7-7 | 9-12 | x | 20-15 | 25-18 | 24-3 |
| Rum | 12-18 | 8-14 | 15-20 | x | 21-20 | 17-11 |
| Jap | 10-24 | 9-31 | 18-25 | 20-21 | x | 15-14 |
| Can | 4-29 | 3-21 | 3-24 | 11-17 | 14-15 | x |

*Claude Robillard Arena*      *July 28*    *20:10*
**Men's finals**

| G | USSR |
|---|------|
| S | Rum |
| B | Pol |

| USSR-Rum | 19-15 |
|----------|-------|
| WGer-Pol | 18-21 |
| Yug-Hun | 21-19 |
| Den-Cze | 21-25 |
| Jap-USA | 27-20 |

# Results Judo

*Olympic Velodrome*    *July 30    14:00*
**Lightweight 63-kg competition (138.6 lbs.)**

| G | Hector Rodriguez | Cub |
|---|---|---|
| S | Eunkyung Chang | SKor |
| B | Felice Mariani | Ita |
| B | Jozsef Tuncsik | Hun |

*Eliminated earlier:*    Brad W. Farrow    Can
Joseph Bost    USA


*Olympic Velodrome*    *July 29    14:00*
**Light middleweight 70-kg competition (154 lbs.)**

| G | Vladimir Nevzorov | USSR |
|---|---|---|
| S | Koji Kuramoto | Jap |
| B | Patrick Vial | Fra |
| B | Changsun Lee | SKor |

*Eliminated earlier:*    Patrick Burris    USA
Wayne Erdman    Can


*Olympic Velodrome*    *July 28    14:00*
**Middleweight 80-kg competition (176 lbs.)**

| G | Isamu Sonoda | Jap |
|---|---|---|
| S | Valery Dvoinikov | USSR |
| B | Slavko Obadov | Yug |
| B | Fred Marhenke | WGer |

*Eliminated earlier:*    Rainer Fischer    Can

*Olympic Velodrome*      *July 27*    *14:00*
**Light heavyweight 93-kg competition (204.6 lbs.)**

| | | |
|---|---|---|
| G | Kazuhiro Ninomiya | Jap |
| S | Ramaz Harshiladze | USSR |
| B | David Starbrook | GBr |
| B | Juerg Roethlisberger | Swi |

*Eliminated earlier:*   Joe Meli          Can
                        Tommy Martin      USA

*Olympic Velodrome*      *July 26*    *14:00*
**Heavyweight 93+-kg competition (204.6+ lbs.)**

| | | |
|---|---|---|
| G | Sergei Novikov | USSR |
| S | Gunther Neureuther | WGer |
| B | Keith Remfry | GBr |
| B | Allen Coage | USA |

*Olympic Velodrome*      *July 31*    *14:00*
**Judo—open category**

| | | |
|---|---|---|
| G | Haruki Uemura | Jap |
| S | Keith Remfry | GBr |
| B | Shota Chochishvili | USSR |
| B | Jorge Portelli | Arg |

*Eliminated earlier:*   James Wooley      USA
                        Tom Greenway      Can

# Results Modern Pentathlon

*Modern Pentathlon*    *July 22    19:20*
**Individual competition**

|   |                     |      | riding | fencing | shoot. | swim. | run. | total |
|---|---------------------|------|--------|---------|--------|-------|------|-------|
| G | Janusz Pyciak-Peciak | Pol  | 1066   | 928     | 1044   | 1164  | 1318 | 5520  |
| S | Pavel Lednev        | USSR | 1032   | 1096    | 1022   | 1092  | 1243 | 5485  |
| B | Jan Bartu           | Cze  | 1100   | 976     | 1044   | 1184  | 1162 | 5466  |
| 6 | John Fitzgerald     | USA  | 1036   | 952     | 1000   | 1232  | 1066 | 5286  |
| 16 | Michael Burley     | USA  | 1068   | 760     | 692    | 1212  | 1327 | 5059  |
| 26 | Robert Nieman      | USA  | 1036   | 784     | 604    | 1324  | 1153 | 4901  |
| 43 | John D. Hawes      | Can  | 1068   | 856     | 230    | 1272  | 1108 | 4534  |
| 45 | George Skene       | Can  | 1100   | 520     | 274    | 1176  | 1102 | 4172  |
| 46 | Jack Alexander     | Can  | 478    | 472     | 692    | 1268  | 1213 | 4123  |

*Modern Pentathlon*    *July 22    19:20*
**Team competition**

|   |                      |      | riding | fenc. | shoot. | swim. | run. | total | team total |
|---|----------------------|------|--------|-------|--------|-------|------|-------|------------|
| G | Adrian Parker        | GBr  | 1100   | 752   | 868    | 1240  | 1378 | 5338  |            |
|   | Robert Nightingale   |      | 1012   | 814   | 934    | 1172  | 1309 | 5241  |            |
|   | Jeremy Fox           |      | 1100   | 690   | 846    | 1080  | 1264 | 4980  | 15559      |
| S | Jan Bartu            | Cze  | 1100   | 969   | 1044   | 1184  | 1162 | 5459  |            |
|   | Bohumil Starnovsky   |      | 1068   | 876   | 868    | 1144  | 1144 | 5100  |            |
|   | Jiri Adam            |      | 794    | 938   | 1088   | 1072  | 1000 | 4892  | 15451      |
| B | Tamas Kancsal        | Hun  | 866    | 990   | 956    | 1164  | 1219 | 5195  |            |
|   | Tibor Maracsko       |      | 972    | 845   | 890    | 1204  | 1228 | 5139  |            |
|   | Szvetiszlav Sasics   |      | 934    | 938   | 912    | 1160  | 1117 | 5061  | 15395      |
| 5 | John Fitzgerald      | USA  | 1036   | 969   | 1000   | 1232  | 1066 | 5303  |            |
|   | Michael Burley       |      | 1068   | 752   | 692    | 1212  | 1327 | 5051  |            |
|   | Robert Nieman        |      | 1036   | 814   | 604    | 1324  | 1153 | 4931  | 15285      |
| 13 | John D. Hawes       | Can  | 1068   | 845   | 230    | 1272  | 1108 | 4523  |            |
|   | George Skene         |      | 1100   | 504   | 274    | 1176  | 1102 | 4156  |            |
|   | Jack Alexander       |      | 478    | 442   | 692    | 1268  | 1213 | 4093  | 12772      |

# Results Rowing

*Notre Dame Basin*     *July 24*    *11:55*
**Women's single scull 1000-m**

| | | | |
|---|---|---|---|
| G | Christine Scheiblich | EGer | 4:05.56 |
| S | Joan Lind | USA | 4:06.21 |
| B | Elena Antonova | USSR | 4:10.24 |

*Notre Dame Basin*     *July 24*    *10:45*
**Women's double sculls 1000-m**

| | | | |
|---|---|---|---|
| G | Svetla Otzetova<br>Zdravka Yordanova | Bul | 3:44.36 |
| S | Sabine Jahn<br>Petra Boesler | EGer | 3:47.86 |
| B | Leonora Kaminskaite<br>Genovate Ramoshkene | USSR | 3:49.93 |
| 5 | Jan Palchikoff<br>Diane Braceland | USA | 3:58.25 |
| 6 | Cheryl Howard<br>Bev Cameron | Can | 4:06.23 |

*Notre Dame Basin*      *July 24*      *11:20*
**Women's pair without coxswain 1000-m**

| G | Siika Kelbetcheva<br>Stoyanka Grouitcheva | Bul | 4:01.22 |
|---|---|---|---|
| S | Angelika Noack<br>Sabine Dahne | EGer | 4:01.64 |
| B | Edith Eckbauer<br>Thea Einoeder | WGer | 4:02.35 |
| 5 | Tricia Smith<br>Elisabeth Craig | Can | 4:08.09 |

*Notre Dame Basin*      *July 24*      *12:30*
**Women's four sculls-coxswain 1000-m**

| G | Anke Borchmann<br>Jutta Lau<br>Viola Poley<br>Roswietha Zobelt<br>Liane Weigelt | EGer | 3:29.99 |
|---|---|---|---|
| S | Anna Kondrachina<br>Mira Bryunina<br>Larisa Alexandrova<br>Galina Ermolaeva<br>Nadezhda Chernysheva | USSR | 3:32.49 |
| B | Ioana Tudoran<br>Maria Micsa<br>Felicia Afrasiloaia<br>Elisabe Lazar<br>Elena Giurca | Rum | 3:32.76 |

*Notre Dame Basin*     *July 24*     *10:10*
**Women's four with coxswain 1000-m**

| G | Karin Metze | EGer | 3:45.08 |
| | Bianka Schwede | | |
| | Gabriele Lohs | | |
| | Andrea Kurth | | |
| | Sabine Hess | | |
| | | | |
| S | Ginka Gurova | Bul | 3:48.24 |
| | Liliana Vasseva | | |
| | Reni Yordanova | | |
| | Mariika Modeva | | |
| | Kapka Gueorguieva | | |
| | | | |
| B | Nadezhda Sevostyanova | USSR | 3:49.38 |
| | Lyudmila Krokhina | | |
| | Galina Mishenina | | |
| | Anna Pasokha | | |
| | Lidiya Krylova | | |
| | | | |
| 6 | Pamela Behrens | USA | 3:56.50 |
| | Catherin Menges | | |
| | Nancy Storrs | | |
| | Julia Geer | | |
| | Mary Kellogg | | |

*Notre Dame Basin      July 24     13:05*
**Women's eight with coxswain 1000-m**

| | | | |
|---|---|---|---|
| G | Viola Goretzki | EGer | 3:33.32 |
| | Christiane Knetsch | | |
| | Ilona Richter | | |
| | Brigitte Ahrenholz | | |
| | Monika Kallies | | |
| | Henrietta Ebert | | |
| | Helma Lehmann | | |
| | Irina Muller | | |
| | Marina Wilke | | |
| | | | |
| S | Lyubov Talalaeva | USSR | 3:36.17 |
| | Nadezda Roshchina | | |
| | Klavdiya Kozenkova | | |
| | Elena Zubko | | |
| | Olga Kolkova | | |
| | Nelli Tarakanova | | |
| | Nadezhda Rozgon | | |
| | Olga Guzenko | | |
| | Olga Pugovskaya | | |
| | | | |
| B | Jacqueli Zoch | USA | 3:38.68 |
| | Anita DeFrantz | | |
| | Carie Graves | | |
| | Marion Greig | | |
| | Anne Warner | | |
| | Peggy McCarthy | | |
| | Carol Brown | | |
| | Gail Ricketson | | |
| | Lynn Silliman | | |
| | | | |
| 4 | Carol Eastmore | Can | 3:39.52 |
| | Rhonda Ross | | |
| | Nancy Higgins | | |
| | Mazina Delure | | |
| | Susan Antoft | | |
| | Wendy Pullan | | |
| | Christine Neuland | | |
| | Gail Cort | | |
| | Illona Smith | | |

*216*

*Notre Dame Basin*     *July 25*    *11:55*
**Men's single scull 2000-m**

| | | | |
|---|---|---|---|
| G | Pertti Karppinen | Fin | 7:29.03 |
| S | Peter-M. Kolbe | WGer | 7:31.67 |
| B | Joachim Dreifke | EGer | 7:38.03 |

*Notre Dame Basin*     *July 25*    *10:45*
**Men's double sculls 2000-m**

| | | | |
|---|---|---|---|
| G | Frank Hansen<br>Alf Hansen | Nor | 7:13.20 |
| S | Chris Baillieu<br>Michael Hart | GBr | 7:15.26 |
| B | H. Ulrich Schmied<br>Jurgen Bertow | EGer | 7:17.45 |

*Notre Dame Basin*     *July 25*    *11:20*
**Men's pair without coxswain 2000-m**

| | | | |
|---|---|---|---|
| G | Jorg Landvoigt<br>Bernd Landvoigt | EGer | 7:23.31 |
| S | Calvin Coffey<br>Michael Staines | USA | 7:26.73 |
| B | Peter Van Roye<br>Thomas Strauss | WGer | 7:30.03 |

*Notre Dame Basin*      *July 25*      *12:30*
**Men's pair with coxswain 2000-m**

| G | Harald Jahrling<br>Friedrich Ulrich<br>Georg Spohr | EGer | 7:58.99 |
|---|---|---|---|
| S | Dmitri Bekhterev<br>Yuri Shurkalov<br>Yuri Lorentson | USSR | 8:02.82 |
| B | Oldrich Svojanovsky<br>Pavel Svojanovsky<br>Ludvik Vebr | Cze | 8:03.28 |

*Notre Dame Basin*      *July 25*      *13:40*
**Men's four sculls 2000-m**

| G | Wolfgang Guldenpfennig<br>Rudiger Reiche<br>K. Heinz Bussert<br>Michael Wolfgramm | EGer | 6:18.65 |
|---|---|---|---|
| S | Yevgeny Duleev<br>Yuri Yakimov<br>Aivar Lazdenieks<br>Vitautas Butkus | USSR | 6:19.89 |
| B | Jaroslav Helebrand<br>Vaclav Vochoska<br>Zdenek Pecka<br>Vladek Lacina | Cze | 6:21.77 |
| 6 | Peter Cortes<br>Kenneth Foote<br>Neil Halleen<br>John Van Blom | USA | 6:34.33 |

*Notre Dame Basin*     *July 25*     *10:10*
**Men's four with coxswain 2000-m**

| | | | |
|---|---|---|---|
| G | Vladimir Eshinov | USSR | 6:40.22 |
| | Nikolai Ivanov | | |
| | Mikhail Kuznetsov | | |
| | Alexandr Klepikov | | |
| | Alexandr Lukianov | | |
| | | | |
| S | Andreas Schulz | EGer | 6:42.70 |
| | Rudiger Kunze | | |
| | Walter Diessner | | |
| | Ullrich Diessner | | |
| | Johannes Thomas | | |
| | | | |
| B | Johann Faerber | WGer | 6:46.96 |
| | Ralph Kubail | | |
| | Siegfried Fricke | | |
| | Peter Niehusen | | |
| | Hartmut Wenzel | | |

**Men's four without coxswain 2000-m**

G      Siegfried Brietzke            EGer          6:37.42
       Andreas Decker
       Stefan Semmler
       Wolfgang Mager

S      Ole Nafstad                   Nor           6:41.22
       Arne Bergodd
       Finn Tveter
       Rolf Andreassen

B      Raul Arnemann                 USSR          6:42.52
       Nikolai Kuznetsov
       Valeri Dolinin
       Anushavan Gasan-Dzhalalov

5      Brian Dick                    Can           6:46.11
       Philip Monckton
       Andrew Van Ruyven
       Ian Gordon

*Notre Dame Basin*     *July 25*    *14:15*
**Men's eight with coxswain 2000-m**

G    Bernd Baumgart          EGer     5:58.29
     Gottfried Dohn
     Werner Klatt
     H. Joachim Luck
     Dieter Wendisch
     Roland Kostulski
     Ulrich Karnatz
     K. Heins Prudohl
     K. Heinz Danielowski

S    Richard Lester           GBr     6:00.82
     John Yallop
     Timothy Crooks
     Hugh Matheson
     David Maxwell
     James Clark
     Fred Smallbone
     Leonard Robertson
     Patric Sweeney

B    Ivan Sutherland         NZl     6:03.51
     Trevor Coker
     Peter Dignan
     Lindsay Wilson
     Athol Earl
     Dave Rodger
     Alex McLean
     Tony Hurt
     Simon Dickie

# Results Shooting

*L'Acadie Range     July 18     09:00*
**Free pistol   OR = 567 / WR = 572**

| G  | Uwe Potteck        | EGer    | 573 NOR/NWR |
|----|--------------------|---------|-------------|
| S  | Harald Vollmar     | EGer    | 567         |
| B  | Rudolf Dollinger   | Austria | 562         |
|    |                    |         |             |
| 10 | Hershel Anderson   | USA     | 556         |
| 23 | Thomas Guinn       | Can     | 548         |
| 24 | Jules Sobrian      | Can     | 547         |
| 37 | Richard Crawford   | USA     | 534         |

*L'Acadie Range     July 19     09:30*
**Small-bore rifle prone position   OR = 599 / WR = 599**

| G  | Karlheinz Smieszek   | WGer  | 599 |
|----|----------------------|-------|-----|
| S  | Ulrich Lind          | WGer  | 597 |
| B  | Gennady Lushchikov   | USSR  | 595 |
|    |                      |       |     |
| 6  | Arne Sorensen        | Can   | 593 |
| 20 | David Ross           | USA   | 590 |
| 28 | Hans Adloch          | Can   | 589 |
| 31 | Victor Auer          | USA   | 588 |

*L'Acadie Range*     *July 21*     *09:30*
**Small-bore rifle three positions**   OR = 1167 / WR = 1167

| | | | |
|---|---|---|---|
| G | Lanny Bassham | USA | 1162 |
| G(S) | Margaret Murdock | USA | 1162 |
| B | Werner Seibold | WGer | 1160 |
| | | | |
| 14 | Hans Adloch | Can | 1144 |
| 16 | Kurt Mitchell | Can | 1143 |

*L'Acadie Range*     *July 23*     *09:30*
**Rapid-fire pistol**   OR = 597 / WR = 598

| | | | |
|---|---|---|---|
| G | Norbert Klaar | EGer | 597 NOR |
| S | Jurgen Wiefel | EGer | 596 |
| B | Roberto Ferraris | Ita | 595 |
| | | | |
| 20 | William McMillan | USA | 586 |
| 31 | Jules Sobrian | Can | 583 |
| 36 | Thomas Treinen | USA | 576 |
| 38 | Steven Kelly | Can | 570 |

*L'Acadie Range*     *July 20*     *09:30*
**Olympic trap shooting**   OR = 199 / WR = 199

| | | | |
|---|---|---|---|
| G | Donald Haldeman | USA | 190 |
| S | Armando Silva Marques | Por | 189 |
| B | Ubaldesc Baldi | Ita | 189 |
| | | | |
| 7 | John Primrose | Can | 183 |
| 11 | Charvin Dixon | USA | 181 |
| 25 | Susan Nattrass | Can | 173 |

*L'Acadie Range        July 24     09:00*
**Skeet shooting**   OR = 198 / WR = 200

| G  | Josef Panacek         | Cze  | 198 |
| S  | Eric Swinkels         | Hol  | 198 |
| B  | Wieslaw Gawlikowski   | Pol  | 196 |
|    |                       |      |     |
| 14 | John Satterwhite      | USA  | 192 |
| 35 | Harry Willsie         | Can  | 188 |
| 44 | Bradley Simmons       | USA  | 186 |
| 56 | Paul Laporte          | Can  | 176 |


*L'Acadie Range        July 23     09:30*
**Running-game target**   OR = 579 / WR = 579

| G  | Alexandr Gazov        | USSR | 579 NOR/NWR |
| S  | Alexandr Kedyarov     | USSR | 576 |
| B  | Jerzy Greszkiewicz    | Pol  | 571 |
|    |                       |      |     |
| 8  | Louis Theimer         | USA  | 564 |
| 14 | Martin Edmondson      | USA  | 558 |
| 25 | Daniel Nadeau         | Can  | 526 |

# Results Swimming

**Women's 100-m freestyle**  OR = 55.81 / WR = 55.73

| | | | |
|---|---|---|---|
| G | Kornelia Ender | EGer | 55.65 NOR/NWR |
| S | Petra Priemer | EGer | 56.49 |
| B | Enith Brigitha | Hol | 56.65 |
| | | | |
| 4 | Kim Peyton | USA | 56.81 |
| 5 | Shirley Babashoff | USA | 56.95 |
| 7 | Jill Sterkel | USA | 57.06 |

*Olympic Pool*    *July 22*    *19:45*
**Women's 200-m freestyle**  OR = 2:01.54 / WR = 1:59.78

| | | | |
|---|---|---|---|
| G | Kornelia Ender | EGer | 1:59.26 NOR/NWR |
| S | Shirley Babashoff | USA | 2:01.22 |
| B | Enith Brigitha | Hol | 2:01.40 |
| | | | |
| 5 | Gail Amundrud | Can | 2:03.32 |
| 6 | Jennifer Hooker | USA | 2:04.20 |

*Olympic Pool*    *July 20*    *19:45*
**Women's 400-m freestyle**  OR = 4:15.71 / WR = 4:11.69

| | | | |
|---|---|---|---|
| G | Petra Thumer | EGer | 4:09.89 NOR/NWR |
| S | Shirley Babashoff | USA | 4:10.46 |
| B | Shannon Smith | Can | 4:14.60 |
| | | | |
| 5 | Kathy Heddy | USA | 4:15.50 |
| 6 | Brenda Borgh | USA | 4:17.43 |

*Olympic Pool*     *July 25*     *19:00*
**Women's 800-m freestyle**   OR = 8:46.58 / WR = 8:39.63

| G | Petra Thumer | EGer | 8:37.14 NOR/NWR |
|---|---|---|---|
| S | Shirley Babashoff | USA | 8:37.59 |
| B | Wendy Weinberg | USA | 8:42.60 |
| | | | |
| 5 | Nicole Kramer | USA | 8:47.33 |
| 6 | Shannon Smith | Can | 8:48.15 |


*Olympic Pool*     *July 21*     *19:30*
**Women's 100-m backstroke**   OR = 1:02.39 / WR = 1:01.51

| G | Ulrike Richter | EGer | 1:01.83 NOR/NWR |
|---|---|---|---|
| S | Birgit Treiber | EGer | 1:03.41 |
| B | Nancy Garapick | Can | 1:03.71 |
| | | | |
| 4 | Wendy Hogg | Can | 1:03.93 |
| 5 | Cheryl Gibson | Can | 1:05.16 |


*Olympic Pool*     *July 25*     *20:00*
**Women's 200-m backstroke**   OR = 2:16.49 / WR = 2:12.47

| G | Ulrike Richter | EGer | 2:13.43 NOR |
|---|---|---|---|
| S | Birgit Treiber | EGer | 2:14.97 |
| B | Nancy Garapick | Can | 2:15.60 |
| | | | |
| 5 | Melissa Belote | USA | 2:17.27 |
| 8 | Wendy Hogg | Can | 2:17.95 |

*Olympic Pool     July 24     19:15*
**Women's 100-m breaststroke**   OR = 1:10.86 / WR = 1:10.86

| | | | |
|---|---|---|---|
| G | Hannelore Anke | EGer | 1:11.16 |
| S | Liubov Rusanova | USSR | 1:13.04 |
| B | Marina Koshevaia | USSR | 1:13.30 |

*Olympic Pool     July 21     19:45*
**Women's 200-m breaststroke**   OR = 2:35.14 / WR = 2:34.99

| | | | |
|---|---|---|---|
| G | Marina Koshevaia | USSR | 2:33.35 NOR/NWR |
| S | Marina Iurchenia | USSR | 2:36.08 |
| B | Liubov Rusanova | USSR | 2:36.22 |

*Olympic Pool     July 22     19:30*
**Women's 100-m butterfly**   OR = 1:01.03 / WR = 1:00.13

| | | | |
|---|---|---|---|
| G | Kornelia Ender | EGer | 1:00.13 EWR |
| S | Andrea Pollack | EGer | 1:00.98 |
| B | Wendy Boglioli | USA | 1:01.17 |
| 4 | Camille Wright | USA | 1:01.41 |
| 6 | Wendy Quirk | Can | 1:01.75 |
| 7 | Lelei Fonoimoana | USA | 1:01.95 |

*Olympic Pool     July 19     20:45*
**Women's 200-m butterfly**   OR = 2:11.56 / WR = 2:11.22

| | | | |
|---|---|---|---|
| G | Andrea Pollack | EGer | 2:11.41 NOR |
| S | Ulrike Tauber | EGer | 2:12.50 |
| B | Rosemarie Gabriel | EGer | 2:12.86 |
| 4 | Karen Thornton | USA | 2:12.90 |
| 5 | Wendy Quirk | Can | 2:13.68 |
| 6 | Cheryl Gibson | Can | 2:13.91 |

*Olympic Pool     July 24     20:00*
**Women's 400-m individual medley**   OR = 4:51.24 / WR = 4:48.79

| | | | |
|---|---|---|---|
| G | Ulrike Tauber | EGer | 4:42.77 NOR/NWR |
| S | Cheryl Gibson | Can | 4:48.10 |
| B | Becky Smith | Can | 4:50.48 |
| 6 | Donnalee Wennerstrom | USA | 4:55.34 |
| 7 | Joann Baker | Can | 5:00.19 |

*Olympic Pool*     *July 25*     *20:45*
**Women's 4 x 100 m freestyle relay**   OR = 3:48.95 / WR = 3:48.80

| | | | |
|---|---|---|---|
| G | Kim Peyton | USA | 3:44.82 NOR/NWR |
| | Wendy Boglioli | | |
| | Jill Sterkel | | |
| | Shirley Babashoff | | |
| S | Kornelia Ender | EGer | 3:45.50 |
| | Petra Priemer | | |
| | Andrea Pollack | | |
| | Claudia Hempel | | |
| B | Gail Amundrud | Can | 3:48.81 |
| | Barbara Clark | | |
| | Becky Smith | | |
| | Anne Jardin | | |

*Olympic Pool*     *July 18*     *19:45*
**Women's 4 x 100 m medley relay**   OR = 4:13.98 / WR = 4:13.41

| | | | |
|---|---|---|---|
| G | Ulrike Richter | EGer | 4:07.95 NOR/NWR |
| | Hannelore Anke | | |
| | Andrea Pollack | | |
| | Kornelia Ender | | |
| S | Linda Jezek | USA | 4:14.55 |
| | Lauri Siering | | |
| | Camille Wright | | |
| | Shirley Babashoff | | |
| B | Wendy Hogg | Can | 4:15.22 |
| | Robin Corsiglia | | |
| | Susan Sloan | | |
| | Anne Jardin | | |

*Olympic Pool*  *July 20*  *21:00*
**Women's springboard diving**

| G | Jennifer Chandler | USA | 506.19 |
|---|---|---|---|
| S | Christa Kohler | EGer | 469.41 |
| B | Cynthia McIngvale | USA | 466.83 |
| 8 | Barbara Nejman | USA | 365.07 |

*Olympic Pool*  *July 25*  *21:45*
**Women's platform diving**

| G | Elena Vaytsekhovskaia | USSR | 406.59 |
|---|---|---|---|
| S | Ulrika Knape | Swe | 402.60 |
| B | Deborah Wilson | USA | 401.07 |
| 5 | Cindy Shatto | Can | 389.58 |
| 6 | Teri York | Can | 378.39 |
| 7 | Melissa Briley | USA | 376.86 |

*Olympic Pool*  *July 25*  *20:15*
**Men's 100-m freestyle**  OR = 50.39 / WR = 50.39

| G | Jim Montgomery | USA | 49.99 NOR/NWR |
|---|---|---|---|
| S | Jack Babashoff | USA | 50.81 |
| B | Peter Nocke | WGer | 51.31 |
| 6 | Joe Bottom | USA | 51.79 |

*Olympic Pool*     *July 19     20:00*
**Men's 200-m freestyle**   OR = 1:50.93 / WR = 1:50.32

| | | | |
|---|---|---|---|
| G | Bruce Furniss | USA | 1:50.29 NOR/NWR |
| S | John Naber | USA | 1:50.50 |
| B | Jim Montgomery | USA | 1:50.58 |

*Olympic Pool*     *July 22     19:15*
**Men's 400-m freestyle**   OR = 3:55.24 / WR = 3:53.08

| | | | |
|---|---|---|---|
| G | Brian Goodell | USA | 3:51.93/NOR/NWR |
| S | Tim Shaw | USA | 3:52.54 |
| B | Vladimir Raskatov | USSR | 3:55.76 |
| 8 | Stephen Badger | Can | 4:02.83 |

*Olympic Pool*     *July 20     19:30*
**Men's 1500-m freestyle**   OR = 15:20.74 / WR = 15:06.66

| | | | |
|---|---|---|---|
| G | Brian Goodell | USA | 15:02.40 NOR/NWR |
| S | Bobby Hackett | USA | 15:03.91 |
| B | Stephen Holland | Austra. | 15:04.66 |
| 7 | Paul Hartloff | USA | 15:32.08 |

*Olympic Pool*      *July 19*     *19:30*
**Men's 100-m backstroke**    OR = 56.19 / WR = 56.19

| | | | |
|---|---|---|---|
| G | John Naber | USA | 55.49 NOR/NWR |
| S | Peter Rocca | USA | 56.34 |
| B | Roland Matthes | EGer | 57.22 |
| 6 | Bob Jackson | USA | 57.69 |

*Olympic Pool*      *July 24*     *20:30*
**Men's 200-m backstroke**    OR = 2:02.01 / WR = 2:00.64

| | | | |
|---|---|---|---|
| G | John Naber | USA | 1:59.19 NOR/NWR |
| S | Peter Rocca | USA | 2:00.55 |
| B | Dan Harrigan | USA | 2:01.35 |

*Olympic Pool*      *July 20*     *20:00*
**Men's 100-m breaststroke**    OR = 1:03.62 / WR = 1:03.62

| | | | |
|---|---|---|---|
| G | John Hencken | USA | 1:03.11 NOR/NWR |
| S | David Wilkie | GBr | 1:03.43 |
| B | Arvidas Iuozaytis | USSR | 1:04.23 |
| 4 | Graham Smith | Can | 1:04.26 |
| 8 | Chris Woo | USA | 1:05.13 |

*Olympic Pool     July 24     19:30*
**Men's 200-m breaststroke**   OR = 2:18.29 / WR = 2:18.21

| G | David Wilkie | GBr | 2:15.11 NOR/NWR |
|---|---|---|---|
| S | John Hencken | USA | 2:17.26 |
| B | Rick Colella | USA | 2:19.20 |
| 4 | Graham Smith | Can | 2:19.42 |
| 5 | Charles Keating | USA | 2:20.79 |


*Olympic Pool     July 21     19:15*
**Men's 100-m butterfly**   OR = 54.27 / WR = 54.27

| G | Matt Vogel | USA | 54.35 |
|---|---|---|---|
| S | Joe Bottom | USA | 54.50 |
| B | Gary Hall | USA | 54.65 |
| 6 | Clay Evans | Can | 55.81 |


*Olympic Pool     July 18     19:30*
**Men's 200-m butterfly**   OR = 2:00.24 / WR = 1:59.63

| G | Mike Bruner | USA | 1:59.23 NOR/NWR |
|---|---|---|---|
| S | Steven Gregg | USA | 1:59.54 |
| B | Bill Forrester | USA | 1:59.96 |

*Olympic Pool*　　*July 25*　　*19:30*
**Men's 400-m individual medley**   OR = 4:27.15 / WR = 4:26.00

| G | Rod Strachan | USA | 4:23.68 NOR/NWR |
|---|---|---|---|
| S | Tim McKee | USA | 4:24.62 |
| B | Andrey Smirnov | USSR | 4:26.90 |
| | | | |
| 5 | Graham Smith | Can | 4:28.64 |
| 6 | Steve Furniss | USA | 4:29.23 |
| 7 | Andy Ritchie | Can | 4:29.87 |


*Olympic Pool*　　*July 21*　　*20:00*
**Men's 4 x 200 m freestyle relay**   OR = 7:30.33 / WR = 7:30.33

| G | Mike Bruner<br>Bruce Furniss<br>John Naber<br>Jim Montgomery | USA | 7:23.22 NOR/NWR |
|---|---|---|---|
| S | Vladimir Raskatov<br>Andrey Bogdanov<br>Sergey Kopliakov<br>Andrey Krylov | USSR | 7:27.97 |
| B | Alan McClatchey<br>David Dunne<br>Gordon Downie<br>Brian Brinkley | GBr | 7:32.11 |

*Olympic Pool*     *July 22*     *20:00*
**Men's 4 x 100 m medley relay**   OR = 3:47.28 / WR = 3:47.28

| | | | |
|---|---|---|---|
| G | John Naber | USA | 3:42.22 NOR/NWR |
| | John Hencken | | |
| | Matt Vogel | | |
| | Jim Montgomery | | |
| S | Stephen Pickell | Can | 3:45.94 |
| | Graham Smith | | |
| | Clay Evans | | |
| | Gary MacDonald | | |
| B | Klaus Steinbach | WGer | 3:47.29 |
| | Walter Kusch | | |
| | Michael Kraus | | |
| | Peter Nocke | | |

*Olympic Pool*     *July 22*     *21:00*
**Men's springboard diving**

| | | | |
|---|---|---|---|
| G | Philip Boggs | USA | 619.05 |
| S | Franco Cagnotto | Ita | 570.48 |
| B | Aleksandr Kosenkov | USSR | 567.24 |
| 5 | Robert Cragg | USA | 548.19 |
| 6 | Gregory Louganis | USA | 528.96 |

*Olympic Pool*     *July 27*    20:00
**Men's platform diving**

| G | Klaus Dibiasi | Ita | 600.51 |
|---|---|---|---|
| S | Gregory Louganis | USA | 576.99 |
| B | Vladimir Aleynik | USSR | 548.61 |
| | | | |
| 4 | Kent Vosler | USA | 544.14 |
| 5 | Patrick Moore | USA | 538.17 |


*Olympic Pool*     *July 27*    18:00
**Water polo final round**

| G | Hun | 9 *(points)* |
|---|---|---|
| S | Ita | 6 |
| B | Hol | 6 |

*Round progress:*

|      | Hol | Ita | WGer | Hun | Rum | Yug |
|------|-----|-----|------|-----|-----|-----|
| Hol  | x   | 3-3 | 3-2  | 3-5 | 4-4 | 5-3 |
| Ita  | 3-3 | x   | 4-3  | 5-6 | 4-4 | 5-4 |
| WGer | 2-3 | 3-4 | x    | 3-5 | 3-5 | 4-4 |
| Hun  | 5-3 | 6-5 | 5-3  | x   | 9-8 | 5-5 |
| Rum  | 4-4 | 4-4 | 5-3  | 8-9 | x   | 5-5 |
| Yug  | 3-5 | 4-5 | 4-4  | 5-5 | 5-5 | x   |

# Results Volleyball

*Paul Sauvé Centre*   *July 30*   *16:00*
**Women's finals**

| G | Jap |
| S | USSR |
| B | SKor |

| Jap-USSR | 3-0 |
| SKor-Hun | 3-1 |
| EGer-Cub | 0-3 |
| Can-Peru | 1-3 |

*Paul Sauvé Centre*   *July 30*   *23:59*
**Men's finals**

| G | Pol |
| S | USSR |
| B | Cub |

| USSR-Pol | 2-3 |
| Cub-Jap | 3-0 |
| Cze-SKor | 3-1 |
| Bra-Ita | 3-0 |

# Results Weightlifting

*St. Michel Arena*     *July 18     14:30*
52-kg (114.4 lbs.) snatch and clean jerk   WR = 242.5 (533.50 lbs.)

|   |   |   | athlete's weight | snatch | clean jerk | total |
|---|---|---|---|---|---|---|
| G | Alexandr Voronin | USSR | 51.85 (114.07) | 105.0 | 137.5 | 242.5 (533.50) NOR |
| S | Gyorgy Koszegi | Hun | 51.80 (113.96) | 107.5 | 130.0 | 237.5 (522.50) |
| B | Mohammad Nassiri | Iran | 51.75 (113.85) | 100.0 | 135.0 | 235.0 (517) |

*St. Michel Arena*     *July 19     19:00*
56-kg (123.2 lbs.) snatch and clean jerk   WR = 260.0 (572 lbs.)

|   |   |   |   |   |   |   |
|---|---|---|---|---|---|---|
| G | Norair Nurikyan | Bul | 55.70 (122.54) | 117.5 | 145.0 | 262.5 (577.5) NOR |
| S | Grzegorz Cziura | Pol | 55.85 (122.87) | 115.0 | 137.5 | 252.5 (555.5) |
| B | Kenkichi Ando | Jap | 55.85 (122.87) | 107.5 | 142.5 | 250.0 (550) |

*St. Michel Arena*     *July 20     19:00*
60-kg (132 lbs.) snatch and clean jerk   WR = 287.5 (632.5 lbs.)

|   |   |   |   |   |   |   |
|---|---|---|---|---|---|---|
| G | Nikolai Kolesnikov | USSR | 59.25 (130.35) | 125.0 | 160.0 | 285.0 (627) NOR |
| S | Georgi Todorov | Bul | 58.85 (129.47) | 122.5 | 157.5 | 280.0 (616) |
| B | Kazumasa Hirai | Jap | 59.75 (131.45) | 125.0 | 150.0 | 275.0 (605) |

*St. Michel Arena*     *July 21     19:00*
67.5-kg (148.5 lbs.) snatch and clean jerk   WR = 312.5 ( 687.5 lbs.)

|   |   |   |   |   |   |   |
|---|---|---|---|---|---|---|
| G | Zbigniew Kaczmarek* | Pol | 67.10 (147.62) | 135.0 | 172.5 | 307.5 (676.5) NOR |
| S | Piotr Korol | USSR | 66.95 (147.29) | 135.0 | 170.0 | 305.0 (671) |
| B | Daniel Senet | Fra | 67.00 (147.4) | 135.0 | 165.0 | 300.0 (660) |
| 12 | Dan Cantore | USA | 67.15 (147.73) | 120.0 | 152.0 | 272.5 (599.5) |

*238*

*St. Michel Arena*     *July 22     19:00*
**75-kg (165 lbs.) snatch and clean jerk**   WR = 345.0 (759 lbs.)

|   |   |   | athlete's weight | snatch | clean jerk | total |
|---|---|---|---|---|---|---|
| G | Yordan Mitkov | Bul | 74.70 (164.34) | 145.0 | 190.0 | 335.0 (737) NOR |
| S | Vartan Militosyan | USSR | 74.80 (164.56) | 145.0 | 185.0 | 330.0 (726) |
| B | Peter Wenzel | EGer | 74.75 (164.45) | 145.0 | 182.5 | 327.5 (720.5) |
| 11 | Frederick Lowe | USA | 74.80 (164.56) | 135.0 | 170.0 | 305.0 (671) |

*St. Michel Arena*     *July 24     19:00*
**82.5-kg (181.5 lbs.) snatch and clean jerk**   WR = 372.5 (819.5 lbs.)

|   |   |   |   |   |   |   |
|---|---|---|---|---|---|---|
| G | Valeri Shary | USSR | 81.70 (179.74) | 162.5 | 202.5 | 365.0 (803) NOR |
| S | Blagoi Blagoev* | Bul | 81.75 (179.85) | 162.5 | 200.0 | 362.5 (797.5) |
| B | Trendafil Stoichev | Bul | 81.90 (180.18) | 162.5 | 197.5 | 360.0 (792) |
| 11 | Samuel Bigler | USA | 82.15 (180.73) | 130.0 | 177.5 | 307.5 (676.5) |

*St. Michel Arena*     *July 25     19:00*
**90-kg (198 lbs.) snatch and clean jerk**   WR = 400.0 (880 lbs.)

|   |   |   |   |   |   |   |
|---|---|---|---|---|---|---|
| G | David Rigert | USSR | 89.35 (196.57) | 170.0 | 212.5 | 382.5 (841.5) NOR |
| S | Lee James | USA | 88.50 (194.7) | 165.0 | 197.5 | 362.5 (797.5) |
| B | Atanas Shopov | Bul | 89.70 (197.34) | 155.0 | 205.0 | 360.0 (792) |
| 4 | Philip Grippaldi | USA | 88.80 (195.36) | 150.0 | 205.0 | 355.0 (781) |

*St. Michel Arena*   *July 26   19:00*
**110-kg (242 lbs.) snatch and clean jerk**   WR = 417.5 (918.5 lbs.)

|   |   |   | athlete's weight | snatch | clean jerk | total |
|---|---|---|---|---|---|---|
| G | Valentin Khristov* | Bul | 109.45 (240.79) | 175.0 | 225.0 | 400.0 (880) NOR |
| S | Yuri Zaitsev | USSR | 107.95 (237.49) | 165.0 | 220.0 | 385.0 (847) |
| B | Krastio Semerdjiev | Bul | 109.15 (240.13) | 170.0 | 215.0 | 385.0 (847) |
| 10 | Russ Prior | Can | 109.65 (241.23) | 167.5 | 195.0 | 362.5 (797.5) |
| 13 | Gary Drinnon | USA | 109.80 (241.56) | 152.5 | 200.0 | 352.5 (775.5) |
| 17 | Bob Santavy | Can | 100.40 (220.88) | 147.5 | 190.0 | 337.5 (742.5) |

*St. Michel Arena*   *July 27   19:00*
**110+-kg (242+ lbs.) snatch and clean jerk**   WR = 442.5 (973.5 lbs.)

|   |   |   |   |   |   |   |
|---|---|---|---|---|---|---|
| G | Vasilyi Alexeev | USSR | 156.80 (344.96) | 185.0 | 255.0 | 440.0 (968) NOR |
| S | Gerd Bonk | EGer | 151.30 (332.86) | 170.0 | 235.0 | 405.0 (891) |
| B | Helmut Losch | EGer | 110.65 (243.43) | 165.0 | 222.5 | 387.5 (852.5) |
| 5 | Bruce Wilhelm | USA | 147.30 (324.06) | 172.5 | 215.0 | 387.5 (852.5) |
| 9 | Sam Walker | USA | 115.15 (253.33) | 142.5 | 182.5 | 325.0 (715) |

*Disqualified because of positive steroid tests.

# Results  Wrestling

*Maisonneuve Centre*  *July 31*  *20:05*
**Freestyle 48-kg competition (105.6 lbs.)**

| G | Khassan Issaev | Bul |
|---|---|---|
| S | Roman Dnitriev | USSR |
| B | Akira Kudo | Jap |

*Maisonneuve Centre*  *July 31*  *20:11*
**Freestyle 52-kg competition (114.4 lbs.)**

| G | Yuji Takada | Jap |
|---|---|---|
| S | Alexandr Ivanov | USSR |
| B | Hae-Sup Jeon | SKor |

*Maisonneuve Centre*  *July 31*  *20:30*
**Freestyle 57-kg competition (125.4 lbs.)**

| G | Vladimir Umin | USSR |
|---|---|---|
| S | Hans-Dieter Bruchert | EGer |
| B | Masao Arai | Jap |

*Maisonneuve Centre*  *July 31*  *21:00*
**Freestyle 62-kg competition (136.4 lbs.)**

| G | Jung-Mo Yang | SKor |
|---|---|---|
| S | Zeveg Oidov | Mong |
| B | Gene Davis | USA |

*Maisonneuve Centre*     *July 31*    *21:35*
**Freestyle 68-kg competition (149.6 lbs.)**

| | | |
|---|---|---|
| G | Pavel Pinigin | USSR |
| S | Lloyd Keaser | USA |
| B | Yasaburo Sugawara | Jap |

*Maisonneuve Centre*     *July 31*    *21:50*
**Freestyle 74-kg competition (162.8 lbs.)**

| | | |
|---|---|---|
| G | Jiichiro Date | Jap |
| S | Mansour Barzegar | Iran |
| B | Stanley Dziedzic | USA |

*Maisonneuve Centre*     *July 31*    *15:46*
**Freestyle 82-kg competition (180.4 lbs.)**

| | | |
|---|---|---|
| G | John Peterson | USA |
| S | Viktor Novojilov | USSR |
| B | Adolf Seger | WGer |

*Maisonneuve Centre*     *July 31*    *22:08*
**Freestyle 90-kg competition (198 lbs.)**

| | | |
|---|---|---|
| G | Levan Tediashvili | USSR |
| S | Benjamin Peterson | USA |
| B | Stelica Morcov | Rum |
| 5 | Terry Paice | Can |

*242*

*Maisonneuve Centre*     *July 31     16:52*
**Freestyle 100-kg competition (220 lbs.)**

| G | Ivan Yarygin | USSR |
|---|---|---|
| S | Russell Hellickson | USA |
| B | Dimo Kostov | Bul |


*Maisonneuve Centre*     *July 31     12:40*
**Freestyle 100+-kg competition (220+ lbs.)**

| G | Soslan Andiev | USSR |
|---|---|---|
| S | Jozsef Balla | Hun |
| B | Ladislau Simon | Rum |


*Maisonneuve Centre*     *July 24     19:37*
**Greco-Roman style 48-kg competition (105.6 lbs.)**

| G | Alexey Shumakov | USSR |
|---|---|---|
| S | Gheorghe Berceanu | Rum |
| B | Stefan Anghelov | Bul |
| 6 | Mitchell Kawasaki | Can |


*Maisonneuve Centre*     *July 24     19:55*
**Greco-Roman style 52-kg competition (114.4 lbs.)**

| G | Vitaly Konstantinov | USSR |
|---|---|---|
| S | Nicu Ginga | Rum |
| B | Koichiro Hirayama | Jap |

*243*

*Maisonneuve Centre*     *July 24     20:35*
**Greco-Roman style 57-kg competition (125.4 lbs.)**

| G | Pertti Ukkola | Fin |
|---|---|---|
| S | Ivan Frgic | Yug |
| B | Farhat Mustafin | USSR |

*Maisonneuve Centre*     *July 24     12:50*
**Greco-Roman style 62-kg competition (136.4 lbs.)**

| G | Kazimier Lipien | Pol |
|---|---|---|
| S | Nelson Davidian | USSR |
| B | Laszlo Reczi | Hun |

*Maisonneuve Centre*     *July 24     12:20*
**Greco-Roman style 68-kg competition (149.6 lbs.)**

| G | Suren Nalbandyan | USSR |
|---|---|---|
| S | Stefan Rusu | Rum |
| B | Heinz-Helmut Wehling | EGer |

*Maisonneuve Centre*     *July 24     21:15*
**Greco-Roman style 74-kg competition (162.8 lbs.)**

| G | Anatolyi Bykov | USSR |
|---|---|---|
| S | Vitezslav Macha | Cze |
| B | Karlheinz Helbing | WGer |

*Maisonneuve Centre*     *July 24     20:15*
**Greco-Roman style 82-kg competition** (180.4 lbs.)

| | | |
|---|---|---|
| G | Momir Petkovic | Yug |
| S | Vladimir Cheboksarov | USSR |
| B | Ivan Kolev | Bul |


*Maisonneuve Centre*     *July 24     21:40*
**Greco-Roman style 90-kg competition** (198 lbs.)

| | | |
|---|---|---|
| G | Valery Rezantsev | USSR |
| S | Stoyan Ivanov | Bul |
| B | Czeslaw Kwiecinski | Pol |
| 7 | James Johnson | USA |


*Maisonneuve Centre*     *July 24     21:55*
**Greco-Roman style 100-kg competition** (220 lbs.)

| | | |
|---|---|---|
| G | Nikolai Bolboshin | USSR |
| S | Kamen Goranov | Bul |
| B | Andrzej Skrzylewski | Pol |
| 4 | Brad Rheinganz | USA |


*Maisonneuve Centre*     *July 24     22:15*
**Greco-Roman style 100+-kg competition** (220+ lbs.)

| | | |
|---|---|---|
| G | Alexandr Kolchinski | USSR |
| S | Alexandr Tomov | Bul |
| B | Roman Codreanu | Rum |
| 5 | William Lee | USA |

# Results Yachting

**Soling class**

| | | | *total points* | *net points* |
|---|---|---|---|---|
| G | Poul R.H. Jensen<br>Vald Bandolowski<br>Erik Hansen | Den | 65.70 | 46.70 |
| S | John Kolius<br>Walter Glasgow<br>Richard Hoepfner | USA | 64.40 | 47.40 |
| B | Dieter Below<br>Michael Zachries<br>Olaf Engelhardt | EGer | 60.40 | 47.40 |
| 8 | Glen Dexter<br>Sandy Macmillan<br>Andreas Josenhans | Can | 87.70 | 68.70 |

**Flying Dutchman class**

| | | | *total points* | *net points* |
|---|---|---|---|---|
| G | Joerg Diesch<br>Eckart Diesch | WGer | 56.70 | 34.70 |
| S | Rodney Pattisson<br>Julian Brooke Houghton | GBr | 75.70 | 51.70 |
| B | Reinaldo Conrad<br>Peter Ficker | Bra | 76.10 | 52.10 |
| 4 | Hans Fogh<br>Evert Bastet | Can | 76.10 | 57.10 |
| 6 | Norman Freeman<br>John Mathias | USA | 84.70 | 65.70 |

*Kingston, Ontario*     *July 27*     *13:10*
**Finn class**

|   |                  |           | *total points* | *net points* |
|---|------------------|-----------|----------------|--------------|
| G | Jochen Shumann   | EGer      | 53.40          | 35.40        |
| S | Andrei Balashov  | USSR      | 67.70          | 39.70        |
| B | John Bertrand    | Australia | 74.40          | 46.40        |
|   |                  |           |                |              |
| 8 | Sanford Riley    | Can       | 120.00         | 83.00        |
| 11| Peter Commette   | USA       | 115.70         | 95.70        |

*Kingston, Ontario*     *July 27*     *13:20*
**Tempest class**

|   |                                            |      |        |        |
|---|--------------------------------------------|------|--------|--------|
| G | John Albrechtson<br>Ingvar Hansson         | Swe  | 27.00  | 14.00  |
| S | Valentin Mankin<br>Vladislav Akimenko      | USSR | 40.40  | 30.40  |
| B | Dennis Conner<br>Conn Findlay              | USA  | 47.70  | 32.70  |
| 7 | Allan Leibel<br>Lorne Leibel               | Can  | 89.10  | 65.10  |

*Kingston, Ontario*　　　*July 27*　　*13:00*
**Class 470**

| | | | *total points* | *net points* |
|---|---|---|---|---|
| G | Frank Huebner<br>Harro Bode | WGer | 71.40 | 42.40 |
| S | Antonio Gorostegui<br>Pedro Millet | Spa | 63.70 | 49.70 |
| B | Ian Brown<br>Ian Ruff | Australia | 80.00 | 57.00 |
| 9 | Robert Whitehurst<br>David Whitehurst | USA | 123.00 | 89.00 |
| 16 | Colin Park<br>Jay Cross | Can | 143.70 | 109.70 |

*Kingston, Ontario*　　　*July 28*　　*13:00*
**Tornado class**

| | | | | |
|---|---|---|---|---|
| G | Reginald White<br>John Osborn | GBr | 38.00 | 18.00 |
| S | David McFaull<br>Michael Rothwell | USA | 52.00 | 36.00 |
| B | Jorg Spengler<br>Jorg Schmall | WGer | 54.70 | 37.70 |
| 7 | Larry Woods<br>Michael de la Roche | Can | 86.70 | 69.70 |

*248*